The Future of Management

The Future of Management

Entrepreneurship, Change and Flexibility

Scientific editors
Piotr Buła · Bogdan Nogalski

Jagiellonian University Press

Scientific editors
Prof. Piotr Buła, Ph.D.
Department of International Management, Cracow University of Economics
Department of Business Management, University of Johannesburg

Prof. Bogdan Nogalski, Ph.D.
WSB University in Gdańsk
Committee on Organizational and Management Sciences of the Polish Academy of Sciences

Scientific reviewer
Prof. Szymon Cyfert, Ph.D.
Department of Organization and Management Theory, Poznań University of Economics and Business

Publication coordination
Piotr Sedlak, Ph.D.
Department of International Management, Cracow University of Economics

Cover design
Sebastian Wojnowski

Publication financed by Cracow University of Economics

ISBN 978-83-233-4845-0
ISBN 978-83-233-7124-3 (e-book)

www.wuj.pl

Jagiellonian University Press
Editorial Offices: Michałowskiego 9/2, 31-126 Kraków
Phone: +48 12 663 23 80, Fax: +48 12 663 23 83
Distribution: Phone: +48 12 631 01 97, Fax: +48 12 631 01 98
Cell Phone: +48 506 006 674, e-mail: sprzedaz@wuj.pl
Bank: PEKAO SA, IBAN PL 80 1240 4722 1111 0000 4856 3325

Contents

Preface

It would be typical to start such a book with a phrase: "change is immanent aspect of the future." However, we would like to point out a different aspect. What does a change require? Both actually making it happen and also adapting to a new reality. What does it require from managers? This book demonstrates how change influences many areas of management. We believe that the world is standing on the very edge of the fastest industrial revolution ever. A revolution which will rapidly increase the efficiency of many production processes. Some say that the development of AI will solve most of our problems. In our opinion the need for the activity of human beings will be even bigger.

With this book we try to provide the reader with information about miscellaneous parts of life and the social-economical environment. For this purpose, we have invited authors representing the leading scientific research centers in Poland but also specialists from foreign universities. We believe that everyone can find some valuable knowledge from his or her field of interest here. The book can be read as a whole, but it can also be done selectively to become acquainted with separate chapters depending on the reader's needs. Time is precious today more than ever.

Piotr Buła
Bogdan Nogalski

Contemporary Dilemmas of Management Sciences

Prof. Stanisław Sudoł, Ph.D.   https://orcid.org/0000-0002-0743-3541

High School of Management, Warsaw

Abstract

As we lack one, uniform understanding of the concept of management, the author gathers different definitions available in literature. The text describes potential boundaries in which management can be described both when it comes to its subject and function. This article is also a search for the place of management among other sciences. Important part of the text is devoted to a discussion on whether we can talk about the management paradigm.

Keywords: boundaries of management, management as a science, management paradigm, functions of management

1. How do we understand management?

It can be considered a strange situation that Poland does not yet have a uniform understanding of the concept of management. It is used in very different semantic contexts. Tadeusz Oleksyn[1] said that everything is managed today. Most often, it is the company that is managed, but also the state, the national economy, diversity, conflict, time, own health and own career, uncertainty, environment, future, politics, fear, time, etc. Hence, this word is absolutely ambiguous. Bolesław R. Kuc[2] said that there are as many management concepts as there were authors writing on this subject in 100 years. Łukasz Sułkowski adds the following to this strange situation: "Today, the term management is abused in relation to all social processes, e.g. conflict management or organisational culture management, and even in relation to

---

[1] T. Oleksyn, *Granice zarządzania* [in:] *Współczesne paradygmaty nauk o zarządzaniu*, ed. by W. Kowalczewski, Difin, Warszawa 2008, p. 54.

[2] B. R. Kuc, *Aksjologia organizacji i zarządzania. Na krawędzi kryzysu wartości*, Ementon, Warszawa 2015, p. 115.

abstract entities, managed by chaos."[3] This "allism" of the word management could be somehow tolerated if it only applied to colloquial language. Unfortunately, the ambiguous understanding of the word has been granted the right of citizenship also in science, including management sciences.[4] It suffices to open any book or article in a management journal to find out. This situation applies not only to Poland, as evidenced by, for example, the following statement in a German academic textbook from 1990: "Neither the scope of management science is clearly outlined, nor the concept of management itself has yet been uniformly defined."[5]

One should definitely strive to develop and widely adopt a proper understanding of all basic management concepts, starting from the very concept of management. People who doubt the sense of specifying concepts and terms can be told that every young science begins its existence by specifying the basic concepts it uses. Without this, the biblical Tower of Babel will be posing a risk for science. Despite the fact that we will use the same words, but endowing them with different content, we will not understand each other.

Management is one of the types of broadly understood leading, next to administration, command and governance. Individual forms/types of management vary in objects of interest and research and to some extent in the methods used. They also have counterparts in separate scientific disciplines: management science, administration science, defense science and political science. Not all authors distinguish between these synonymous categories.

The concept of management can be defined differently, depending on what is most important in management; the definition may not be too long, however, in meeting—in my opinion—the following conditions.

1. Management is a professional action / process / managerial collective effort of people, undertaken by the management body/authority on the basis of superior rights in relation to employees.
2. Management is a process taking place in an organisation/institution regardless of its ownership, legal form, size, spatial structure and type of activity, which has a common goal(s).
3. The managed organisation has the necessary human, tangible and intangible resources, which are used to achieve the goals of the organisation, the initial goal of which is to ensure the organisation's survival in a changing environment.

---

[3] Ł. Sułkowski, *Epistemologia w naukach o zarządzaniu*, PWE, Warszawa 2005, p. 54.

[4] In 1989, the Silesian Branch of TNOiK organised a conference in Szczyrk entitled *Discussion on the identity of organisation and management sciences* and conducted a survey among the lecturers on the topic of "organisation and management." The materials prepared for this conference and the opinions resulting from the survey displayed a very wide diversity of understanding of management sciences.

[5] H. Steinmann, G. Schreyogg, *Grundlagen der Unternehmensfuhrung Konzepte, Funktionen, Praxisfalle*, Verlag D. Gabler, Wiesbaden 1990.

4. The organisation's management body, by performing managerial functions—planning, organising, motivating, controlling—has an impact on its functioning and development.

When the above four conditions do not apply, the word management should be replaced by other words, e.g. instead of "uncertainty management," we should omit the word "management" and talk about "conditions of uncertainty", instead of "managing the environment," which we usually have limited influence on, we should say "influencing the environment." Instead of "managing the future," on which our influence is minimal or even zero ("how can you manage something that does not yet exist"),[6] it is appropriate to talk about predicting or forecasting the future, or making decisions about the future. It is nonsense to speak of managing yourself, your health or your own career. It is common to consider management as a system in which subsystems are identified that relate to specific areas / issues / its activities.

2. Management as a practical activity, science and art

Management practice has been around for thousands of years, since people began to undertake complex team activities, e.g. organising the hunt for big animals by the Primitive man. It can be safely said that without planning, organising and controlling, and yet these three functions, plus motivating, are still considered to be the basic canons of management, the seven wonders of the ancient world, giant Egyptian pyramids, the great Chinese wall, amazing Mayan and Aztec buildings and soaring medieval cathedrals would not be erected. Huge masses of people and serious material resources participated in their implementation.

While management practice has been around for many generations, management sciences are very young, not only in relation to exact and natural sciences, but also to many social sciences. In general, it is not disputed that their beginning dates back to the first years of the 20th century. Acceleration of the development of management science is visible in the 30s, after the end of World War II, especially since the 60s. Management has now become one of the most important factors in economic and social development. In the business spheres of the United States, even the saying has been coined that "Management is the greatest innovation of the 20th century."

Today, management is a very complex and difficult activity. Tadeusz Gospodarek[7] reasonably writes that "The complexity of management issues is an objective fact,

---

[6]   E. Bendyk, *Powrót do przyszłości*, "Polityka" 2013, 1.

[7]   T. Gospodarek, *Aspekty złożoności i filozofii nauki w zarządzaniu*, Wydawnictwo Wałbrzyskiej Wyższej Szkoły Zarządzania i Przedsiębiorczości, Wałbrzych 2012, p. 62.

impossible to eliminate," and Bogdan Wawrzyniak[8] goes even further saying that
". . . the world of organisations is increasingly difficult to understand, even for experienced politicians or experts." And another statement by Krzysztof Obłój[9] on this
topic: "Organisations are creatures so complex that only in special cases the theory
can describe, explain and predict their functioning well . . ." In this situation, people
are particularly desirable in organisations, especially managers who are able to fulfil
their management perfectly, which we define as the **art of management**. The mastery
of such people results from education, experience gained, but also from possessed
talents and character traits.

3. Subject and limits of management sciences

To date, the subject and scope of management sciences, which would be universally
or almost universally accepted, have not been defined either in Poland, or in other
countries. However, ambiguities, and even more so confusion over what belongs to
management sciences, what the scope of their problem is and what the boundaries
in relation to other sciences are, is not conducive to their development, inhibits this
development, lowering the rank of these sciences.

The subject of management sciences is the creation, functioning, transformation
and development as well as relations with the environment of economic organisations,
public administration organisations, public utility organisations and various other
non-profit social organisations. These sciences are to contribute to their rationalisation,
efficiency and effectiveness.

Each science must have its limits that would distinguish it from other sciences. The
problem of distinction, i.e. delimitation/demarcation of borders of many sciences, including management sciences, is not simple. It is generally accepted that the factors
that distinguish individual sciences are:

    a) the subject of their interests and research, i.e. the scope of reality covered by
       a given science,

    b) research consideration, i.e. the point of view from which the subject of the study
       is analysed and exposed,

    c) research methods used in a given science.

In the past, the diversity of research methods was emphasised as a key factor separating
science. Currently, this factor is rarely raised, because nowadays something normal,
even standard, is the flow of research methods between sciences, and at times, very
distant from each other. It is understandable that in the first period of development of

---

[8]   B. Wawrzyniak, *Odnawianie przedsiębiorstwa. Na spotkanie XXI wieku*, Poltext, Warszawa 1999, p. 17.
[9]   K. Obłój, *Zarządzanie. Ujęcie praktyczne*, PWE, Warszawa 1986, p. 38.

a given science, i.e. at the stage of its youth, probably every scientific discipline adopts research methods from older, already formed disciplines, absorbing them in themselves. Over time, the young discipline develops its own original methods of scientific cognition. As a result, research methods distinguish between scientific disciplines less and less. This also applies to management sciences. To this it must be added that currently, the classification of sciences is not as important as it used to be. "Currently, classifications of sciences were created during historical development and that this process is still ongoing."[10] Witold Morawski states that a more important issue than setting boundaries between disciplines of science is cooperation between scientists representing them.[11]

Solving complex management problems often requires highlighting them from many sides, not just from the stance of management sciences. In solving numerous management problems, we use the achievements of sciences and research methods developed in other scientific disciplines: statistics, mathematics, technology, sociology, law and other sciences. For this reason, we quite often meet with the definition of management sciences as interdisciplinary science (they are said to be interdisciplinary or to have interdisciplinary character). This definition is not good. The boundaries of scientific disciplines are mixed here with the cooperation of researchers from various fields in solving management problems. Medicine uses multiple achievements in biological, technical and many other sciences, and yet it is not said that medicine is an interdisciplinary science.

Leszek Krzyżanowski[12] appropriately wrote that it is **not sciences but the problems studied by these teachings that are interdisciplinary**. I fully share this view and the statement of Kazimierz Kuciński,[13] that "interdisciplinarity should consist in creating research teams composed of representatives of various disciplines of science and reaching for the achievements of these disciplines, not on attempts to practice them." The interdisciplinary nature of management research in which representatives of other management disciplines participate, may penetrate the examined problem deeper and more comprehensively, which is extremely valuable in a situation where management problems are becoming more and more complex. Incorporating researchers from other scientific disciplines rather than management sciences into research on management and creating interdisciplinary research programmes in which representatives of various scientific disciplines participate is simply indispensable.

In my opinion, there are not sufficient arguments for management sciences to enter macroeconomic or macro-social areas, except for the functioning of specific institutions related to these areas.

---

[10]   M. Heller, *Filozofia nauki,* Copernicus Center Press, Kraków 2016, p. 28.
[11]   W. Morawski, *Socjologia ekonomiczna*, Wydawnictwo Naukowe PWN, Warszawa 2001, p. 15.
[12]   L. Krzyżanowski, *Podstawy nauki zarządzania*, PWN, Warszawa 1985, pp. 57–58.
[13]   K. Kuciński, *Ekonomia jako nauka wątpliwa i niewątpliwa*, "Kwartalnik Nauk o Przedsiębiorstwie" 2009, 3, 12, p. 43.

Considering the issue of borders in 2018, I would like to come back to the discussion in the Polish scientific community, created around the Scientific Society for Organisation and Management and the Department of Labour of the Polish Academy of Sciences in the sixties. During these years, 13 discussion meetings were held under the direction of Professor Jerzy Kurnal. At the last meeting of this cycle in 1970, the "general theory of organisation" (the equivalent of today's management sciences) was discussed. In the discussion, the view that this boundary should apply to organisations on a micro scale clearly prevailed, although the statement by Professor Jan Zieleniewski was characteristic:

> . . . common to both of us: Associate Professor Koźmiński and me that the moment is coming to the point where the theory of organisation cannot be limited to only micro-organisational issues. In my opinion, this belief did not come true. At the end of the remarks on the boundaries of management sciences, it must be stated that at the present stage of their development these boundaries cannot always be clearly and precisely defined, however, the statement of Ł. Sułkowski that "management sciences have, **by definition**, [bold—S.S.] blurred borders . . .[14]

These statements can be considered a bit exaggerated. This blurriness currently results, to some extent, from not always sufficiently defined management sciences and from the fact that they interact in solving their problems with other scientific disciplines.

4. Design and a cognitive function of management sciences?

Due to the relationship between sciences and practical human activity, they are divided into basic/theoretical and applied/practical sciences, although today this distinction is not as sharp as it used to be. The former tend to become acquainted with the natural or social world without usually asking themselves what their results can be directly used by man in changing/improving/bettering natural, technical or social conditions of his life. This does not mean that the results of basic research will be useless. Quite the opposite—the results of applied sciences are based on their results and most often they constitute the starting point of great progress, and even a breakthrough/revolution in a given field. Applied sciences aim to be useful to people by using their results to improve people's lives and the natural or social environment in which they live. They suggest rules of conduct in specific human activities.

The main function of management sciences as applied sciences is the application function, i.e. the formulation of suggestions, indications and projects[15] on how to

---

[14]   Ł. Sułkowski, *Epistemologia w naukach...*, p. 86.
[15]   Tadeusz Kotarbiński said that "practical science is such a science which mainly focuses on designing"; T. Kotarbiński, *Elementy teorii poznania i metodologii nauk*, Ossolineum, Wrocław 1961, pp. 447–448.

improve management processes. Therefore, the question may arise whether they can also perform a cognitive function. There were statements that negated this possibility. One of the Polish professors represents a definitely negative position in this respect, stating: "The methodological mistake in management sciences is the search for cognitive results. There are no laws governing reality in management sciences, because reality remains to be constructed. There are methods for strategic construction of reality." I assess this stance as completely irrelevant. I do not share the position of Kazimierz Zimniewicz,[16] who expressed doubts about the scientific nature of management sciences due to the fact that there is no simple relationship between causes and effects of events in management, that there are a multitude of causes and effects that are difficult to associate with. I must emphasise that a similar situation occurs in other social sciences and not just there. On this basis, the scientificity of all these sciences could be questioned. The difficult problem of binding the relationship between causes requires the use of appropriate methods, e.g. econometric.

Denying the possibility of performing cognitive functions by management science is unjustified. Łukasz Sułkowski's stance is unequivocal in this respect: "Management has cognitive and practical aspects." They seek to solve the specific practical needs of different organisations, but they can also analyse theoretical problems. To be able to propose rational management solutions, these sciences must describe existing management processes, distinguish between their various types, and learn about the factors that shape them and the power to influence them. Management is a part of social reality and reflects many factors in which there are certain regularities that can and must be studied before undertaking project work, as a result of which proposals for management practice will be formulated. There is a full analogy to the situation in other social sciences: sociology, social psychology and political science and others.

Recognising management sciences as applied science does not mean that they do not carry out theoretical studies within them. Specific management test results that are not useful for practice at a given time, but which may be the foundation for management changes at a later time, and often to a high degree.

5. Theorems and paradigms of management sciences

Each scientific discipline is an internally ordered, logical and coherent set of scientific statements and truths as well as theories that explain—might be better said: they attempt to explain—some part of the world. This collection includes both theorems, theories and paradigms, which are the foundations of a given scientific discipline, but there is also room for theorems and scientific truths of lesser importance. This collection

---

[16]   K. Zimniewicz, *Linearność a holizm w nauce o zarządzaniu* [in:] *Nauki o zarządzaniu wobec nieprzewidywalności i złożoności zmian*, ed. by J. Rokita, Górnośląska Wyższa Szkoła Handlowa, Katowice 2011.

is subject to constant verification based on the results of scientific research. Science is, figuratively speaking, a building to which—on the one hand—new bricks are constantly added, and on the other hand—rotten bricks are rejected, verified negatively by newer studies. The development of science occurs through the accumulation of knowledge, its constant growth, but also by way of a scientific revolution, when existing theories are negated and replaced with new ones. These are often epoch-making phrases in the scientific knowledge of the world.

Both academics who formulate theories in management sciences as well as practitioners who are their recipients should be aware of the characteristic features of management sciences assertions. These features are similar to those of other social sciences. They are as follows:

1. **The claims of management science for all organisations are of a very general nature**, and thus have little relevance to management practice. And this generality is due to the wide diversity of organisations in many respects. Much less general, more specific may only be the principles and statements about specific groups of organisations.

2. **The degree of certainty and accuracy in management science theorems**—similarly to other social sciences—**is lower than in exact and natural sciences.** Peter F. Drucker[17] clearly stated that ". . . management can never be an exact science." This is due not only to the fact that they are young, but by their nature. Aristotle is already credited with saying that "precision is not to be sought for alike in all discussions." In the preface to his own book, Władysław Tatarkiewicz[18] writes that, striving for it to be of a scientific nature, he tried to make it contain statements that were as certain as possible, clear, strictly formulated, but stating that happiness cannot be spoken of so surely, clearly and precisely as in mathematics or physics. Łukasz Sułkowski also writes about the uncertainty of management knowledge.[19]

3. In contrast to the natural sciences, in which quantifiable problems prevail, **in research of management** and other social sciences **quantitativeness of processes is very limited.** These studies must mainly take into account qualitative factors resulting from the fact that management processes deal with the attitudes of people who are guided not only by rationality, but also by subjective views and emotions that are hardly subject to measurements. The theorems of sciences discussed herein can be verified only on the basis of experiments repeated by various people and institutions only to a very limited extent.

4. The claims of management sciences have **a limited range of validity in space**. Organisations that are objects of research in management are very diverse today in many respects related to different natural conditions, the level of civilisation

---

[17]   P. F. Drucker, *Praktyka zarządzania*, transl. T. Basiuk, Z. Broniarek, MT Biznes, Warszawa 2017, p. 10.
[18]   W. Tatarkiewicz, *O szczęściu*, PWN, Warszawa 1962, p. 10.
[19]   Ł. Sułkowski, *Epistemologia w naukach...*, p. 7.

development and the cultural context of countries and regions. Thus, the scope of management used is limited depending on the country and region. The mechanical transfer of management claims from country to country, from region to region, from organisation to organisation involves the risk of these statements being false.

5. **Management science's predictions about future management changes are limited.** This is due to the very high variability of the factors of the organisation's national environment as well as the international environment and changes in the organisations themselves. The results of forecasting the future by management sciences can only be approximate, determined by the theory of probability.

6. **The sustainability of management science assertions is limited.** They change under the influence of changes in the environment of the organisation, development of science, changes in technology, in economic and social life, as well as in the organisations themselves. The theorems after some time may no longer fit into the new reality, become outdated, false, which means that instead of helping management practice, they can harm it. Some representatives of management sciences like Gary G. Hamel,[20] W. Grudzewski, I. Hejduk[21] express the view that current management sciences are already obsolete.

The above review of the characteristics of theorems leads to the conclusion that **theorems of management sciences lack universality,** like other social sciences. Łukasz Sułkowski[22] writes that at the present stage of development of management sciences they should become rid of universalistic ambitions.

Among scientists, in the context of scientific statements, the term **paradigm** is significant, and even fundamental, introduced by Georg Ch. Lichtenberg to general philosophy, and to the philosophy of science by Thomas S. Kuhn in the book *The Structure of Scientific Revolution* in 1963, returning with its interpretation in 1977 in the publication *The Essential Tension: Selected Studies in Scientific Tradition and Change*, giving it additional exposure therein. The concept of paradigm has a high rank in world science, although in science its very concept is, even by methodologists, understood and defined very differently.[23]

In this study, I understand the word paradigm as a scientific category, as a key scientific statement/belief, which has been proven by scientific methods and which

[20]   G. G. Hamel, *The Way, What and How of Management Innovation*, "Harvard Business Review" 2006, 84.

[21]   W. Grudzewski. I. Hejduk, *Przedsiębiorstwo przyszłości. Zmiana paradygmatów zarządzania*, "Master of Business Administration" 2011, 1.

[22]   Ł. Sułkowski, *O potrzebie rozwoju epistemologii zarządzania* [in:] *Krytycznie i twórczo o zarządza Wybrane zagadnienia*, academic supervision by W. Kieżun, Oficyna Wolters Kluwer Business, Warszawa 2011, p. 146.

[23]   We find such statements, among others in the following publications: K. Jodkowski, *Wspólnota uczonych. Paradygmaty i rewolucje naukowe*, UMCS, Lublin 1990, p. 10; D. Jamali, *Changing Management Paradigms Implementations for Educational Insitutions*, "Journal of Management Development" 2005, 24, 2.

has been recognised by the public (community) scholars for a long time, or at least, a significant part of it. It is the foundation of a given scientific discipline. On its basis other, more detailed scientific statements are built. They may concern large areas of science or only specific disciplines, and even sub-disciplines.

It is often asked whether management sciences have a generally accepted scientific paradigm, or several paradigms that would determine the dominant research approach in the discipline. It is said that a characteristic of management sciences is that they do not yet have the accepted scientific paradigm or a number of paradigms that would define the dominant approach in the discipline and which would merge its currents, fields and schools. This worries many researchers and is a source of doubt or scepticism about the future of management sciences.

I believe that Piotr Płoszajski[24] and Łukasz Sułkowski rightly state[25] that management sciences are in a pre-paradigmatic stage of development. P. Płoszajski refers to this stage as empirical and collective, in contrast to the theoretical and explanatory stage, when management sciences are already developed, having then argued theories. It seems right to say that "History of science indicates that every scientific discipline must begin with the formulation of simple laws, which are later generalised to cover cases that are really interesting."[26]

There are also views that in management sciences such paradigms already exist, but are evolving rapidly according to frequent changes in the business environment and in the organisations themselves.[27]

Formulating scientific truths and paradigms in social sciences, including management sciences, is difficult "because of—as John G. Kemeny writes[28]—the traditional soft focus, ambiguity and emotional colouring of the study, and because of the complexity inherent in human beings." Establishing paradigms in management sciences is additionally difficult due to the large variety of theories in their scope and theories that are formulated without a comparative analysis between successive theories, are not a coherent whole, which disintegrates these sciences. Another factor that is unfavourable for establishing paradigms in management sciences is their low spatial and temporal universality.

The following criteria should be taken into account when selecting theorems for the management sciences paradigms:

---

[24] P. Płoszajski, *Między refleksją a działaniem. Dylematy praktycznej teorii zarządzania*, Ossolineum, Wrocław 1985, p. 33.
[25] Ł. Sułkowski, *Epistemologia w naukach...*, pp. 52–54.
[26] J. G. Kemeny, *Nauka w oczach filozofa*, transl. S. Amsterdamski, PWN, Warszawa 1967, p. 248.
[27] T. Klarke, S. Clegg, *Changing Paradigms. The Transformation of Management Knowledge for the 21st Century*, Harper Cillins Business, London 1998, chapter 1; W. M. M. Grudzewski, K. Hejduk, A. Sankowska, M. Wańtuchowicz, *Sustainability w biznesie, czyli przedsiębiorstwo przyszłości. Zmiana paradygmatów i koncepcji zarządzania*, Poltex, Warszawa 2010, pp. 19 ff.
[28] J. G. Kemeny, *Nauka...*, p. 252; J. Lichtarski, *Praktyczny wymiar nauk o zarządzaniu*, PWE, Warszawa 2015, pp. 40–41.

a) compliance of the claims with reality in organisations,

b) materiality/importance for the functioning and development of the organisation,

c) such a degree of generality that allows them to refer to a large group of organisations,

d) taking into account achievements in Polish and foreign management sciences.

One can appreciate the situation that management sciences, despite their youth, have already developed on the basis of research of many important principles and generalisations of a rather detailed nature, without claiming high-scale generalisations. They have a character of **microparadigms**. Here are some examples:

- Each organisation operates under the influence of the environment and problems related to its functioning must be considered taking into account its relationship with the economic, social, political and cultural environment.
- Each organisation can be considered as a system, so introducing changes in the organisation requires taking into account the links between the components of its system.
- The basis for the survival and development of the organisation in conditions of turbulence of the environment is—while maintaining or changing its core values—its flexible adaptation to changes.
- The organisation should adhere to the principle of locating decisions on development and strategic matters at the highest management levels, and operational type decisions at its lower levels.

6. Place of management sciences in the classification of sciences

Management sciences occur in Poland as a discipline in two areas, namely in the field of economic sciences—next to economics, financial science, labour and social policy and commodity science—and in the field of humanities among a multitude of disciplines: history, archaeology, bibliology, philosophy, pedagogy, psychology, sociology, religious studies, and other. It is bizarre that one scientific discipline should be in two fields of science. It cannot be accepted that management can be based only on economic criteria or only on humanistic criteria. Economic and humanistic criteria must be included in all management. I am convinced that **management sciences should be considered as an independent field of science.** It is obvious that these sciences are strongly associated with economic sciences, but they also have significant connections with other sciences. In management issues, it is often necessary to refer to many other sciences: psychology, sociology, computer science, statistics, mathematics, techniques, law, ethics, medicine, political sciences and cultural phenomena. I shall refer here to Tadeusz Oleksyn, analogous to my view: "Management deserves full autonomy . . . There are no reasons to situate management in economics or to tie it only to the economy. Management is everywhere—also in administration, culture, healthcare, judiciary and science."

In Western countries, management studies occur alongside "economic sciences" and "management sciences" or "business administration." In Poland, the separate occurrence of economics and management was officially adopted in the years 1974–1975. In the German-speaking countries, in which the two sciences are also separated, they appear under the names *Volkswirtschaftslehre* and *Betriebswrtschaftslehre*.

The occurrence of management sciences in two fields of science is a very difficult reason for rational definition of their boundaries as a scientific discipline. Jan Lichtarski strongly emphasises that the lack of a clear identity of management sciences and the lack of universally accepted methodological foundations of this scientific discipline is a source of many ambiguities, misunderstandings and even conflicts in universities in the course of doctoral dissertations in the field of management. In my opinion, the decision regarding recognition of management sciences in legal acts as an independent field is an important matter having a significant impact on their development.

7. Pros and cons of sub-disciplines in management sciences

The current state of management sciences and their future development in Poland justify the establishment of subdisciplines within them, as is the case in other sciences. I am in favour of forming several subdisciplines in management sciences in Poland, such as in English management sciences and in German *Betriebswirtschaftslehre*.[29] The emergence of subdisciplines is nowadays a characteristic feature of the development of many sciences.

A clear formation in sub-discipline management sciences and their adoption in the scientific community would give the following benefits:

a) recognition of a certain autonomy of sub-disciplines, and thus raising their rank, which will be an incentive for academics to devote themselves to the issues of the selected sub-discipline,

b) enriching the problems and research methods, and thus the possibility of deepening the scientific penetration of complex problems and their greater scientific value and practical utility,

c) creation of more integrated scientific communities, i.e. more than those willing to cooperate today.[30]

---

[29] The name *Betriebswirtschaftslehre* was formed in Germany at the turn of the 19th and 20th centuries under the influence of eminent authorities: H. Nicklisch, E. Schmalenbach, K. Mellerowicz, and E. Gutenberg and traditionally persist to this day, adopting the sense of management science, although recently it has been increasingly replaced with the word "Management."

[30] In the German language area (Germany, Austria, Switzerland) *Verband der Hochschullehrer fur Betriebswirtschaft* is active, with a large tradition dating back to the first years after World War I, associating professors in management with the participation of professors from many not only German-speaking countries. Once a year, the association organises a conference for all members. Within its framework there are several sections that also organise conferences (seminars) for section members.

The most general division of management sciences that has already taken place in many highly developed countries, especially English-speaking ones, and which is also taking shape in Poland, is the division into **management in business units**, often referred to as **business management** and **management in public**—non-business entities/public management.[31]

It should be taken into account that over time, the number of sub-disciplines in management sciences will increase. It can be said that a number of sub-disciplines are underway: "marketing," "quality management" or "management of production processes" (the emergence of this sub-discipline is particularly evident in polytechnics), "work resource management" and "project management." "Strategic management" can probably already be considered a fully formed and mature subdiscipline of management sciences. It was already formulated in the 1970s. This also applies to "project management."

Recently, the tendency to establish many—up to 21—subdisciplines has emerged among young Polish academics in the field of management sciences.[32] I do not support this proposition. A large number of sub-disciplines would lead to a narrow consideration of management problems, to a substantive narrowing of their view. This can lead to disintegration of management sciences. Jerzy Trzcieniecki warned against this.[33] Different terminologies and different specific research methods of sub-disciplines may lead in this direction.

An excessive number of sub-disciplines in management sciences would also have a negative impact on the level of education of students. This would mean that the issues of management would be presented to them by several people as if in pieces, and not in complex form. Only when all management problems are considered in their entirety can their complexity be shown. For these reasons, moderation should be exercised when establishing the number of sub-disciplines.

The ways to counteract the danger of disintegration in management sciences are as follows: a) restraint in determining the number of sub-disciplines, b) establishing research specialisations as part of the sub-disciplines, c) lively cooperation of research

---

[31] Definitely support for the formation of the "public management" subdiscipline is in the study: S. Sudoł, B. Kożuch, *Rozszerzyć nauki o zarządzaniu jako ich subdyscyplinę* [in:] *Osiągnięcia i perspektywy nauk o zarządzaniu*, ed. by S. Lachiewicz, B. Nogalski, Wolters Kluwer Polska, Warszawa 2010, pp. 382–401.

[32] S. Cyfert, W. Dyduch, D. Latosek-Jurczyk, J. Niemczyk, A. Sopińska, *Subdyscypliny w naukach o zarządzaniu. Logika wyodrębnienia modelu, identyfikacja modelu koncepcyjnego oraz zawartość tematyczna*, "Organizacja i Kierowanie" 2014. Sułkowski even writes that "in the area of interest of this science [management science—S. S.] we will find from a dozen to several dozen subdisciplines...."; *Podstawy metodologii badań w naukach o zarządzaniu*, ed. by W. Czakon, Wydawnictwo Nieoczywiste, Warszawa 2016, p. 18.

[33] J. Trzcieniecki, *Wykład doktoranta. Nauka organizacji i zarządzania – garść refleksji*, "Organizacja i Kierowanie" 2005, p. 4: "... management science is changing into a set of numerous specific provisions with limited applicability, it breaks down into fragments of an increasing degree of specialisation and complexity, it grows into textbooks constituting a list of increasingly detailed practical directives."

workers from individual disciplines and research specialisations, d) not neglecting theoretical studies in management. The above routes will also protect management sciences from their degradation as sciences.

8. Challenges facing management sciences

Young sciences in the world and in Poland display a number of weaknesses. Through the efforts of science workers and with the support of management practice representatives, they should be removed. In a nutshell, with reference to the problems analysed above, they can be presented with several challenges.

1. Bringing management understanding in the scientific community as well as equal understanding of other basic concepts in management sciences. A diverse understanding of these concepts reduces the credibility of science and adversely affects their development, and is a growing obstacle to communication among science workers and practitioners.

2. There is an urgent need to constantly raise standards (rigors) scientific in relation to management sciences, in the field of research methods, knowledge gathering and academic teaching. It is necessary to verify through competent empirical research a number of scientific statements and theories formulated so far in the management sciences. We should all contribute to raising the standards of our discipline to increase its credibility and authority, so that no one can say that we are unserious science. In this regard, I would primarily see the role of the younger generation of researchers.

3. Constantly adapting these teachings to the changing reality in many areas: in science, in the economic, social and cultural situation. The delay in this adaptation leads to outdated theorems and theories of management sciences. At present, at the beginning of the 21st century, this adaptation must be particularly efficient, as we have entered the age of multilateral and even rapid change.

4. Undertaking by scientists, in cooperation with managers, of a serious effort to systematise the existing achievements of management sciences in the form of formulating several general management theories, which will involve more detailed management theories and concepts is an extremely difficult task, but necessary for their further development.

5. Constant conducting of theoretical studies and empirical research on new concepts and management methods adapted to the changing world and operating conditions of various organisations.

6. Maintaining and expanding constant creative contact and cooperation between Polish institutions and persons practicing management sciences with research centres and persons abroad, in particular in countries with a high level of development, to enrich Polish science with achievements from these countries.

7. Management science should be given the status of an independent field of science.
8. A difficult discussion should be started in the entire Polish scientific community in the field of management sciences regarding the definition of several sub-disciplines in management sciences.

Bibliography

Bendyk E., *Powrót do przyszłości*, "Polityka" 2013, 1.

Cyfert S., Dyduch W., Latosek-Jurczyk D., Niemczyk J., Sopińska A., *Subdyscypliny w naukach o zarządzaniu. Logika wyodrębnienia modelu, identyfikacja modelu koncepcyjnego oraz zawartość tematyczna*, "Organizacja i Kierowanie" 2014.

Drucker P. F., *Praktyka zarządzania*, transl. T. Basiuk, Z. Broniarek, MT Biznes, Warszawa 2017.

Gospodarek T., *Aspekty złożoności i filozofii nauki w zarządzaniu*, Wydawnictwo Wałbrzyskiej Wyższej Szkoły Zarządzania i Przedsiębiorczości, Wałbrzych 2012.

Grudzewski W., Hejduk I., *Przedsiębiorstwo przyszłości. Zmiana paradygmatów zarządzania*, "Master of Business Administration" 2011, 1.

Grudzewski W., Hejduk I., Sankowska A., Wańtuchowicz M., *Sustainability w biznesie, czyli przedsiębiorstwo przyszłości. Zmiana paradygmatów i koncepcji zarządzania*, Poltex, Warszawa 2010.

Hamel G. G., *The Way, What and How of Management Innovation*, "Harvard Business Review" 2006, 84.

Heller M., *Filozofia nauki*, Copernicus Center Press, Kraków 2016.

Jamali D., *Changing Management Paradigms Implementations for Educational Insitutions*, "Journal of Management Development" 2005, 24, 2.

Jodkowski K., *Wspólnota uczonych. Paradygmaty i rewolucje naukowe*, UMCS, Lublin 1990.

Kemeny J. G., *Nauka w oczach filozofa*, transl. S. Amsterdamski, PWN, Warszawa 1967.

Klarke T., Clegg S., *Changing Paradigms. The Transformation of Management Knowledge for the 21st Century*, Harper Cillins Business, London 1998.

Kotarbiński T., *Elementy teorii poznania i metodologii nauk*, Ossolineum, Wrocław 1961.

Krzyżanowski L., *Podstawy nauki zarządzania*, PWN, Warszawa 1985.

Kuc B. R., *Aksjologia organizacji i zarządzania. Na krawędzi kryzysu wartości*, Ementon, Warszawa 2015.

Kuciński K., *Ekonomia jako nauka wątpliwa i niewątpliwa*, "Kwartalnik Nauk o Przedsiębiorstwie" 2009, 3, 12.

Lichtarski J., *Praktyczny wymiar nauk o zarządzaniu*, PWE, Warszawa 2015.

Morawski M., *Socjologia ekonomiczna*, Wydawnictwo Naukowe PWN, Warszawa 2001.

Obłój K., *Zarządzanie. Ujęcie praktyczne*, PWE, Warszawa 1986.

Oleksyn T., *Granice zarządzania* [in:] *Współczesne paradygmaty nauk o zarządzaniu*, ed. by W. Kowalczewski, Difin, Warszawa 2008.

Płoszajski P., *Między refleksją a działaniem. Dylematy praktycznej teorii zarządzania*, Ossolineum, Wrocław 1985.

Podstawy metodologii badań w naukach o zarządzaniu, ed. by W. Czakon, Wydawnictwo Nieoczywiste, Warszawa 2016.

Steinmann H., Schreyogg G., *Grundlagen der Unternehmensfuhrung Konzepte, Funktionen, Praxisfalle*, Verlag D. Gabler, Wiesbaden 1990.

Sudoł S., Kożuch B., *Rozszerzyć nauki o zarządzaniu jako ich subdyscyplinę* [in:] *Osiągnięcia i perspektywy nauk o zarządzaniu*, ed. by S. Lachiewicz, B. Nogalski, Wolters Kluwer Polska, Warszawa 2010.

Sułkowski Ł., *Epistemologia w naukach o zarządzaniu*, PWE, Warszawa 2005.

Sułkowski Ł., *O potrzebie rozwoju epistemologii zarządzania* [in:] *Krytycznie i twórczo o zarządza
Wybrane zagadnienia*, academic supervision by W. Kieżun, Oficyna Wolters Kluwer Business,
Warszawa 2011.

Tatarkiewicz W., *O szczęściu*, PWN, Warszawa 1962.

Trzcieniecki J., *Wykład doktoranta. Nauka organizacji i zarządzania – garść refleksji*, "Organizacja i Kierowanie" 2005.

Wawrzyniak B., *Odnawianie przedsiębiorstwa. Na spotkanie XXI wieku*, Poltext, Warszawa 1999.

Zimniewicz K., *Linearność a holizm w nauce o zarządzaniu* [in:] *Nauki o zarządzaniu wobec nieprzewidywalności i złożoności zmian*, ed. by J. Rokita, Górnośląska Wyższa Szkoła Handlowa,
Katowice 2011.

Organisational Change: Continuous Threat or a Chance for a Better Tomorrow Despite a Worse Today?

Prof. Adela Barabasz, Ph.D. https://orcid.org/0000-0002-2926-3029
Wrocław University of Economics

Abstract

The main goal of this article is to present the views of representatives of the managerial staff of Polish enterprises concerning the essence of organisational change, mainly taking into account the conditions that determine success in the process of its implementation. The presented empirical studies are of qualitative nature and are a part of a bigger whole. Conclusions are drawn on the basis of semi-structured interviews with managers of enterprises that have implemented intense organisational change projects over the recent years. The presented results concern the views of key managers on the managerial and psychosocial conditions of the changes implemented in the studied enterprises. The empirical part presents the views of twenty-two managers, identified as key for the transformation process. The managers talked about their attitudes to change, the essence of organisational change in their companies, the causes of resistance to change and the actions aimed at overcoming the resistance. The article is a voice in the discussion on factors that determine the success of change implementation, mainly from the perspective of management practice.

Keywords: organisational change, management, resistance to change, commitment in the change process

Introduction

We recognise that change provides both challenges and opportunities for individuals, groups, and organisations. The complexity and pace of change occurring in the external environment of an organisation require undertaking continuous follow-ups or anticipative actions. Enterprises that wish to develop and be successful strive to undertake actions to optimise their functioning. To achieve success, they try to take into account the dynamics of the processes that occur in their environment, especially those that are the most significant from the perspective of implementation of busi-ness goals. As a result, organisation members keep facing the challenge of adjusting their individual needs and preferences to the expectations of the organisation, they keep participating in the process of organisational change, of both evolutionary and revolutionary nature. In these circumstances, implementation of employees' individ-ual goals in conjunction with the goals and vision of the enterprise requires efficient management; not only from the point of view of implementation of strategic goals but also taking into account the satisfaction of all organisation members.

Meanwhile, M. Meaney and C. Pung[1] report that two-thirds of interviewed managers concede that their companies failed to cross the assumed "change threshold," especially in the area of organisational behaviour. G. Probst and S. Raisch[2] go as far as to claim that implementation of change sometimes leads to serious crises in the organisation, caused mainly by ineptitude of the managerial staff. Their representatives, despite re-ferring to specific theoretical concepts or models of change, in practice face enormous difficulties in terms of effective use of the theoretical assumptions they know, which need to be translated into specific conditions of functioning of enterprises.

Theoretical background

Despite all the authors of the books, papers, and reports, despite a large number of discussions between scholars and managers, and despite best endeavours, too many organisational change efforts still fail. In practice, leaders develop clear, excellent strategies about how to redesign and restructure their companies. They create change programs and hope that their visions will be shared by the followers. In the end they mainly have to "extinguish fires" and overcome crises. This is because people generally do not want changes, employees are often afraid of them, and even more often, having bad experiences from previous organisational changes, they do not want to engage in further, new ones. However, as is claimed by J. Kotter, all change processes go through a series of phases, and each of these stages requires appropriate actions on the part of managerial staff, responsible for the success of changes.[3]

Referring to the conception of phases of response to change, we know that employ-ees and organisations move through the phases of denial, resistance, exploration, and finally, commitment, when the change occurs.[4] Transition from one phase to another does not happen either at one moment, or in an unambiguous manner for all parties

[1]   M. Meaney, C. Pung, *McKinsey Global Results: Creating Organizational Transformations*, "McKinsey Quarterly" 2008, August.
[2]   G. Probst, S. Raisch, *Organizational Crisis: The Logic of Failure*, "Academy of Management Review" 2005, 19, pp. 90–105.
[3]   J. P. Kotter, *Leading Change*, Harvard Business School Press, Boston 1996.
[4]   E. Kübler-Ross, *Rozmowy o śmierci i umieraniu*, transl. I. Doleżal-Nowicka, PAX, Warszawa 1979.

involved in the change process. We can see, in practice, that managers usually expect employees to move very quickly from one stage to the next; especially from the denial phase to the commitment and they fail to recognise that each individual will go through all of the phases at a different pace. Of course, this is not the only reason difficulties in efficient management of organisational change, however, it is extremely important from the psychological perspective.

M. Stanleigh points to the following activities of managers that can cause a crisis in change management:

- failure to engage all employees;
- managing change only at the executive level;
- telling people who have to change that we are in a crisis;
- sending staff on a change program and expecting change to occur;
- not honouring the past,
- and not giving the staff time to vent first and then to change.[5]

According to the assumptions on which the so called triad model of change[6] is based, organisational change is a multi-stage process that should arouse a kind of power and motivation needed to overcome all the sources of resistance, apathy, dislike.[7] It requires high-quality leadership ensured by managers who should demonstrate their commitment to implementation of the change program each day. The studies presented below are based on that triad model of change, according to which there are two planes of change implementation—managerial and psychological, and the actions undertaken within each of them can be expressed through the questions: where to? who? what?

The first—managerial—plane, referring to the response to the three questions above, determines three actions indispensable for change implementation. They comprise determination of the direction of change, attracting people for change and planned transformation of the organisation.

The triad model assumes that the process of specifying and verifying the goal and direction of change is continuous, yet it takes place at an ever higher level of detail. Therefore, within the triad of change, it is necessary to keep providing answers to the questions: where to? who? and what?

What is an important factor for success of change is, however, adjustment of the method of operation to the specific requirements of a given organisation. This means the occurrence of disruptions to the previously established order of actions. What

---

[5]   M. Stanleigh, *Effecting Successful Change Management Initiative*, "Industrial and Commercial Training" 2008, 40, 1, pp. 34–37.

[6]   A. Barabasz, G. Bełz, *Management Triumvirate in Processes of Corporate Renewal* [in:] *Transformations and Dynamics in Management Concepts and Cases of Corporate Renewal*, ed. by J. Skalik, G. Bełz, Wrocław 2010, pp. 13–27.

[7]   A. Barabasz, G. Bełz, *Psychodynamiczna perspektywa zarządzania rozwojem przedsiębiorstw*, Wydawnictwo Uniwersytetu Ekonomicznego we Wrocławiu, Wrocław 2017.

a condition contributes to success is thus gradual ordering of the change process in a way to ensure quickness, effects, and permanence of the implemented change, despite the occurring disruptions.

Although the triad model goes beyond the area of individual and group mental phenomena related to the transformation processes, this does not mean that it overlooks them. For it focuses on them on a parallel plane. It concentrates on psychological factors regarding individuals and groups, such as cognitive processes, emotions and behaviour. The second plane enables conceptualisation of the change process by referring to psychodynamic concepts. The major function implemented on this plane is lowering the level of anxiety in the organisation, and at the same time acting in favour of accepting responsibility for the decisions made and the actions implemented. It is beyond doubt that involvement and participation of organisation members in change preparation and implementation are the preconditions for successful implementation of change programs.

The behavioural element of the attitudes to change is relatively the easiest to describe, as it can be examined directly. But to understand the behaviour of organisation members it is necessary to take into account the emotions, the needs and beliefs of the employees. In order to do that, it is necessary to communicate, which is the necessary condition for cooperation between people and the functioning of an organisation. The best planned communication process will not bring the expected results, if in their work employees experience such behaviours of their superiors that are contrary to or inconsistent with the models declared by the official (formal) corporate communication. In this context, the managerial staff plays a key role in communications related to planned changes. Acceptance of behaviour of managers that is contrary to the declared model undermines the credibility of managers, and thus, destroys employees' readiness to become involved in the vision of change proposed by the superiors.

Methodology

The goal of these case studies was to examine a broad context in which the change and company development processes take place, taking into account their key goals, obtained results, as well as their psychological context. From a broader perspective, the studies focused on the determination of the key variables for the conceptions that describe the development potential of the companies, incorporating the psychodynamic mechanisms that determine the behaviour of managers.

The presented results were obtained in the course of larger studies implemented within a greater research project (financed by the NCN, NN 115 440040). They represent the statements of managers of two enterprises, selected during web research, and referred to as Company A and Company B. Both companies have implemented intense change projects in the recent years, which determined the choice of these companies for detailed studies, focusing on the behaviour of the managerial staff in the conditions of intense organisational change.

Company A is a Polish enterprise which employs more than fifteen hundred employees, so it belongs to the category of large enterprises. It is also confirmed by the scale of turnover. Company A functions within the structure of a capital group, and its branches and subsidiaries are located both in Poland and in several other European countries. Because of the specificity of the sector and the business environment, it may be assumed that it operates in a particularly unstable, dynamically changing environment. During the period of intensive transformation, different kinds of problems emerged there, usually accompanying all undertakings to transform the status quo.[8] Problems included, among other things, lack of successes in the implementation of a new type of project, large international projects; difficulties in providing customers with comprehensive, broad offer that would meet their expectations despite the existing capacity, lack of efficient central organisational units coordinating the key functional areas of the newly created capital group.

Company B is a business unit of an international corporation in the Utilities industry. The enterprise, which employs around one thousand employees, should be categorised as a large one, which is confirmed by the scale of turnover. Company B is composed of several facilities in Poland and connected to other corporate units, complexes of which are located both in the country and abroad.

In relation to changes on the markets where the corporation, of which Company B forms a part, operates, broad restructuring actions were undertaken, aimed at adjusting the organisational model to the one of a growing corporation and obtaining synergistic effects, despite very different specificity of the local markets, on which the company operates. Restructuring actions have been continued for a few years now. They result both from transforming markets, and looking for new organisational models determined at the level of the whole corporation. The scope of that transformation covers mechanisms of integration, coordination and searching for organisational synergy.

Because of the specificity of the sector and the environment in which Company B operates, it can be assumed that, unlike Company A, it operates in a stable environment, in which its position is not threatened in medium term. By adopting model solutions and concepts created at the level of the whole corporation, Company B developed, among others, a new organisational model, one of the most important elements of which became the improvement of coordination of key functions through their centralisation at the company level. The case described is connected to the presence of some transformational problems. In connection to the plans, specific problems emerged there, concerning among others the prolongation of the change period, within

---

[8]   Detailed results of the research are described in book by A. Barabasz and G. Bełz (ibidem).

which subsequent ideas of organisational solutions were implemented; this led to turnover at specific positions, changes in scopes of responsibility, and assignment to organisational units, concerning a large number of employees, especially engineering staff. While centrally coordinated units were being created, relations of cooperation at the level of facilities, which are directly responsible for generation of value, were weakened. In addition, newly established centrally coordinated organisational units comprise employees with little experience in the scope of inter-facility cooperation at the corporation scale, to which Company B belongs.

The study covered managers of organisational units of the headquarters and managers of companies that belong to the capital group. An individual, semi-structured interview was carried out with each of the selected managers. Each conversation was recorded and their duration ranged between 45 and 90 minutes. Qualitative approach to interpretation of results was adopted in the research.

Questions focused on issues directly connected to the implementation of the change process; they concerned the role of the identified managers in the change management process, the weaknesses and strengths of the analysed enterprises in the context of the implemented organisational change, as well as the beliefs of the previously selected managers concerning the causes of resistance to change and actions that neutralise that resistance. The process of the identification of key managers was based on web research.[9]

Organisational change in the eyes of managers: Study results

Managers in both examined companies talk about change as a dynamic, natural, constantly present phenomenon. What attracts attention is the fact that the managers from Company B tend to talk about the negative consequences of the change process more often than the managers from Company A (insecurity, frustration due to lack of impact on its nature, course and scope). The difference can be explained by a different nature of the operations in both companies, in terms of their key operations, the forms of ownership and the organisational structures of both enterprises. However, it cannot be unambiguously stated whether such factors could have influenced the perceived differences according to the managers of the examined companies.

---

9   Ibidem.

Table 1. The essence of change according to the managers of Companies A and B

Company A	Company B
Change is a natural, dynamic phenomenon; it is a continuous process in the organisation; managers are aware of the complex nature of change and its complexity—change takes place on many levels, usually simultaneously Change means improvement, development; mobilisation of forces, striving at perfection (evolutionary approach) Change is a challenge—individual and organisational; it arouses anxiety	Changes are indispensable, but lead to tensions; they give rise to uncertainty, although they are intriguing Change is a dynamic, complex, multidimensional process, lack of change is just as dangerous as incessantly initiated or unfinished changes Small impact on the nature of major change; managers initiate only less significant changes in the company

Source: own study.

Managers' opinions on the strengths and weaknesses of their companies in the context of preparation and implementation of change were another issues subject to scrutiny. In particular, the most characteristic statements are presented in the following two tables. It can be concluded that managers of both companies indicate that openness, orientation on development and the use of the knowledge and experience of other employees definitely are strengths of both companies.

Table 2. Strengths of Companies A and B

Company A	Company B
Awareness of the multifacetedness and complexity of change Innovativeness and expert knowledge of managers Openness and activity, involvement and innovativeness of employees; motivation for working well Zeal of "young" employees; good relationships between people Culture of the organisation based on openness to change; climate that contributes to development of employee competences High elasticity and small distance to the authority	Openness, orientation on development, on reacting to the challenges of the environment Making use of the knowledge and experience of external consultants Making use of the experiences of foreign partners After making the decision, determination in carrying out actions

Source: own study.

As regards the weaknesses in the context of change, as perceived by key managers of the studied enterprises, quite significant differences exist in the image created by the study subjects. There is no doubt that some of the differences result from the formal and organisational conditions, yet not all do. Both managers of Company A and Company B indicate an accumulation of many projects involving changes as a significant drawback of the implementation of change processes; as a result of those accumulations, they proceed simultaneously and overlap. Managers from Company A perceive the source of the weakness mainly in the lack of laying a foundation for change, while managers of Company B clearly point to the "style of change management," which they assess as prescriptive, hardly subject to consultations, based on an imposed directive. At the same time, managers of Company B consider passivity and reactivity to be the weaknesses of their enterprise; they underline the importance and need for activity and innovativeness on the part of employees. As regards the managers from Company A, they highlight the lack of appropriate rewarding system, incorporating involvement in the functioning of the company, including commitment to the change implementation process in particular.

Table 3. Weaknesses—comparison of Company A and Company B

Company A	Company B
Lack of alignment between specific companies and within them	Acting under the pressure of current affairs—"extinguishing fires" rather than planned operations
The size of the company weakens the effectiveness of the change implementation process	Changes are initiated at the top— they are imposed; poorly consulted with the employees affected; too radical
The complexity and intensity of change occurring on many levels simultaneously leads to the sense of lack of control	Employees are not initiators, but executors of commands—the sense of empowerment and influence on the decisions which are important for the company is missing
Discouragement and tiredness caused by the high quantity and intensity of change	Too many changes introduced simultaneously lead to chaos in the company
Lack of change schedule and efficient communication	Quick pace of the change inctroduction, lack of its anchoring it, leads to tiredness and unwillingness of the employees to be involved in later undertakings
Too slow a process of adjusting the organisational culture of specific companies	Introduction of too many changes is attempted at without completion and summary of the change processes which have been initiated previously
Lack of satisfactory rewards for employees involved in the change	
Frequent changes in the direction of transformation as a manifestation of lack of consistency of the management	Lack of consistency, disorder and passivity—expectation that a solution will come from outside
	Chaotic, inconsistent actions cause loss of faith in the sense of becoming involved in actions beneficial for the company
Lack of explicit change leader	Lack of a comprehensive change action plan
Division of managers into "new" and "old"	Lack of clearly defined tasks and conditions of implementation of change—change schedule is required

Source: own study.

Other issues subject to the analysis were the manifestations and causes of resistance to change and the ways of coping with it. Mangers of both companies agree on defining resistance to change as a result of anxiety and loss of sense of security of employees. Although managers of Company A point to the weaknesses of the process of communicating as an important cause of resistance to change, Company B managers perceive the following factors to be the causes of resistance to change: poor coordination of planned transformations, lack of sense of influence on its shape (purpose, scope, pace), which, as a consequence, leads to the lack of readiness to get involved in the implementation of the change programme.

Table 4. Resistance to change: comparison of Companies A and B

Company A	Company B
Resistance is understood as an expression of fear of the unknown, threat of loss of position, status, power, workplace	Resistance results from loss of the sense of security, fear of losing the job
	Ill-planned and misguided change causes unwillingness for subsequent change, employees' impatience, undermining the sense of both prior and future change at the planning stage
Resistance is aroused by change that is imposed top-down and has not been discussed by all stakeholders	After a period of intensive introduction of too many changes, there appears stagnation, an atmosphere of waiting for an undefined, better future
Shortcomings and errors in communication lead to the occurrence of resistance to change	A sense of lack of influence can be felt and, as a result, there is a drop in employees' morale

Source: own study.

The opinions of managers of both enterprises with respect to overcoming resistance to change are very similar. They identify the following conditions for coping with resistance: good relationships (within teams, between superiors and subordinates), effective, open communication in the company, as well as efficient pay system and employee support.

Table 5. Overcoming resistance to change–comparison of Companies A and B

Company A	Company B
Good relationship between superior and subordinate is a condition for success—direct contact based on trust; efficient communication; ability to cooperate within and between teams; readiness to compromise	Open communication about the purpose of change, vision of the organisation after the change, information on the stages of change implementation and schedule are necessary
Communication is of key importance—information should be simple, clear, reliable, transparent—submitted on an everyday and current basis	Good relationships within a team are important
	Managers' involvement and conviction about the significance of change are needed
Compromise between control over the employees and their freedom of action is necessary	Setting limits on the responsibility of managers is necessary
Improvement of the motivational system—involving ambitious employees for competitive tasks, and then appropriate remuneration	Appropriate financial rewards are needed
Employee support system is needed	Identification of benefits brought by the change is a condition for belief in the change

Source: own study.

Conclusions

An attempt at a generalisation of the beliefs of key managers of Company A and Company B concerning the essence of the changes in the companies leads to a conclusion that the changes in Company A are of anticipatory nature while the changes in Company B are of consequential nature. At the same time, as regards the views on the essence of the phenomenon of organisational change and overcoming resistance to change, all the opinions of the interviewed managers are remarkably similar. However, the differences concern the causes of resistance to change and opinions on the nature of the weaknesses of the enterprises they represent. Referring to the managerial plane, one may conclude that the interviewed managers are true (real) experts in the area of organisational change; they are aware of the weaknesses and strengths both of themselves and of the companies they manage. However, when it comes to the psychological plane, in the context of relationships between subordinates and coping with emotionally challenging situations, the interviewed managers create a much more diverse picture. Some of them use their emotions to a very high extent in relationships with subordinates, they consciously and directly influence their involvement in the process of implementing change. There are also managers for whom subordinates' readiness and commitment to the process of organisational change is perceived as an expression of appropriate organisational and managerial solutions; they do not consider the quality of the relationship that they build with their subordinates to be a factor which determines the subordinates' commitment to the change process. In the light of the statements of managers, one may conclude that the development of emotional relationships is a continuous challenge that confronts the managers of studied companies.

Bibliography

Barabasz A., Bełz G., *Management Triumvirate in Processes of Corporate Renewal* [in:] *Transformations and Dynamics in Management Concepts and Cases of Corporate Renewal*, ed. by J. Skalik, G. Bełz, Wrocław 2010.

Barabasz A., Bełz G., *Psychodynamiczna perspektywa zarządzania rozwojem przedsiębiorstw*, Wydawnictwo Uniwersytetu Ekonomicznego we Wrocławiu, Wrocław 2017.

Kotter J. P., *Leading Change*, Harvard Business School Press, Boston 1996.

Kübler-Ross E., *Rozmowy o śmierci i umieraniu*, transl. I. Doleżal-Nowicka, PAX, Warszawa 1979.

Meaney M., Pung C., *McKinsey Global Results: Creating Organizational Transformations*, "McKinsey Quarterly" 2008, August.

Probst G., Raisch S., *Organizational Crisis: The Logic of Failure*, "Academy of Management Review" 2005, 19.

Stanleigh M., *Effecting Successful Change Management Initiative*, "Industrial and Commercial Training" 2008, 40, 1.

Coopetition and Its Determinants in a Business Group: Theoretical Considerations*

Prof. Wioletta Mierzejewska, Ph.D.   ⓘ https://orcid.org/0000-0001-9777-4376
SGH Warsaw School of Economics

Anna Krejner-Nowecka, Ph.D.   ⓘ https://orcid.org/0000-0003-2848-1881
SGH Warsaw School of Economics

Abstract

Bringing together the apparently contradictory forces of competition and cooperation into one relationship and interaction is not a new approach, but the body of research in the area of coopetition is fragmentary. A new perspective can open up as a result of studies on coopetition in business groups since this area has not been investigated yet. Empirical and cognitive premises have made us engage in an attempt to theoretically consider the determinants of intensity and nature of coopetition in business groups to find answers to questions concerning the orientation at value appropriation in a dynamic multiple-unit context. The paper enumerates the most important factors that lead to the emergence of competition side by side with cooperation between companies. The analysis covers factors related to business group characteristics, as well as the specificity of business group environment.

Keywords: coopetition, determinants of coopetition, business group

---

* The paper is the result of a research project no. 2017/25/B/HS4/02448 entitled *Coopetition in Business Groups: Scale, Nature, Determinants, and Impact on Effectiveness* [*Koopetycja w grupach kapitałowych – skala, charakter, determinanty i wpływ na efektywność*]; project manager: Prof. W. Mierzejewska Ph.D., financed from the resources of the National Centre of Science.

Introduction

Subject matter literature[1] defines coopetition as operations within the realm of strategic management,[2] relationship marketing,[3] business networks,[4] building industrial quarters or managing the value chain.[5] In the simplest way possible, coopetition is defined as the relationship between companies in which cooperation and competition take place simultaneously.[6] Relational dynamics amongst different actors may take the form of competition, coexistence, cooperation, and coopetition.[7] Coopetition can be distinguished by simultaneous value creation and appropriation.[8] It may happen at different levels, starting from employees and workers of the same enterprise (individual coopetition) through divisions, departments or subsidiaries (intra-organisational coopetition) up to the level of independent enterprises (inter-organisational coopetition).[9] Most publications in the subject matter literature are devoted to inter-organisational coopetition but there are almost no writings available that would examine coopetition within business groups. Coopetition in business groups is treated as intra-organisational coopetition. Research studies in this area are still relatively scarce[10] and in most cases they focus on multinational enterprises (MNE).[11] Yet, by looking at business groups operations we can surely conclude that together with cooperation we can observe the emergence of rivalry amongst companies within particular groups.

---

[1]   *Kooperencja przedsiębiorstw w dobie globalizacji. Wyzwania strategiczne, uwarunkowania prawne*, ed. by J. Cygler, M. Aluchna, E. Marciszewska, M. Witek-Hejduk, G. Materna, Wolters Kluwer, Warszawa 2013, pp. 164–166.

[2]   J. Dyer, H. Singh, *The Relational View: Cooperative Strategy and Sources of Interorganizational Competitive Advantage*, "Academy of Management Review" 1998, 23, 4, pp. 660–679; G. Barbee, T. Rubel, *Co-Opetition in Action*, "The Journal of Business Strategy" 2007, 18, 5.

[3]   A. Palmer, *Co-Operation and Competition: A Darwinian Synthesis of Relationship Marketing*, "European Journal of Marketing" 2008, 34, 5/6, pp. 687–704.

[4]   T. Khanna, R. Gulati, N. Nohria, *The Dynamics of Learning Alliances: Competition, Cooperation, and Relative Scope*, "Strategic Management Journal" 1998, 19, 3; R. Gnyawali, M. Ravindranath, *Cooperative Networks and Competitive Dynamics: A Structural Embeddedness Perspective*, "Academy of Management Review" 2001, 26, 3, pp. 431–445; H. Hakansson, D. Ford, *How Should Companies Interact in Business Networks?*, "Journal of Business Research" 2002, 55, 2, pp. 133–139.

[5]   D. Gilbert, *Co-Opetition*, "Business and Society" 1998, 37, 4, pp. 468–470.

[6]   M. Bengtsson, S. Kock, *"Coopetition" in Business Networks: To Cooperate and Compete Simultaneously*, "Industrial Marketing Management" 2000, 29, 5.

[7]   M. Bengtsson, S. Kock, *Cooperation and Competition in Relationships between Competitors in Business Networks*, "Journal of Business & Industrial Marketing" 1999, 14, 3, pp. 178–194.

[8]   W. Czakon, *Koopetycja – splot tworzenia i zawłaszczania wartości*, "Przegląd Organizacji" 2012, 12, pp. 1–4.

[9]   J. Cygler, *Charakterystyka kooperencji* [in:] *Kooperencja przedsiębiorstw w dobie globalizacji. Wyzwania strategiczne, uwarunkowania prawne*, ed. by J. Cygler, M. Aluchna, E. Marciszewska, M. Witek-Hejduk, G. Materna, Wolters Kluwer, Warszawa 2013, p. 36.

[10] W. Mierzejewska, *Koopetycja w grupach kapitałowych*, "Studia Ekonomiczne Uniwersytetu Ekonomicznego we Wrocławiu" 2018, 14, pp. 121–130.

[11] Y. Luo, *Toward Coopetition within a Multinational Enterprise: A Perspective from Foreign Subsidiaries*, "Journal of World Business" 2005, 40, 1, pp. 71–90.

The paper is intended to present theoretical considerations focused on coopetition and its determinants in business groups based on the examination of subject matter literature. It is divided into three parts which introduce us to the substance of coopetition, examine the phenomenon in the context of business groups, and identify the major determinants of cooperation and competition taking place simultaneously in business groups.

The substance of coopetition

Relationships involved in coopetition are strategic and structural bonds developed by companies to survive in the market. They are defined as combinations of cooperation and competition between companies, which means both types of relationships take place simultaneously. The most often quoted definition of coopetition has been proposed by M. Bengtsson and S. Kock[12] who define coopetition as an arrangement, in which two companies cooperate with each other in some operations but at the same time they compete in other fields.

Thus, coopetition is a situation when two companies cooperate and compete at the same time. An arrangement within which a company competes with one company and cooperates with another cannot be referred to as coopetition. Both relationships must take place at the same time and between the same actors although they often emerge in relation with their different operations. Coopetition is identified as a relationship that brings together interests that are diverse (competition perspective) and convergent (cooperation perspective). On the face of it, coopetition seems an internally contradictory relationship as side by side with bonds that have been built on trust and common interests, mutual links based on conflict and contradictory interests emerge there.[13]

Coopetition focuses on value creation and benefits drawn from it, not only on the substance of relationships between the parties, which is why it is referred to as a strategy of joint value creation in a competitive setting where the created values are shared, some goals are convergent and we have an evolving structure of a positive sum game. Its distinguishing factor is a simultaneous value creation (combining complementary resources and competencies, as well as coherent strategies of at least two players who are independent in organisational and legal terms) and its fair appropriation (when each player involved in cooperation can achieve a value higher than would have been available to him if acting individually).[14]

Amongst the features of coopetition, we can list competition and cooperation taking place simultaneously and separately, mutually beneficial relationship, as well as its

---

[12] M. Bengtsson, S. Kock, *"Coopetition" in Business...*, pp. 411–426.
[13] Ibidem.
[14] W. Czakon, *Koopetycja...*, pp. 1–4.

complexity and changeability over time.[15] The complexity of coopetition relationships can be observed in different paths along which they develop and numerous classifications. Typologies of coopetition are formulated based on criteria, such as the number of partners, intensity of competition and cooperation, number of links in the value chain or the number of geographic markets.

The simplest classification of coopetition distinguishes its types based on the intensity of cooperation and competition. Coopetition relationships can be dominated with cooperation, balanced or dominated by competition.[16]

Coopetition is an extremely complex occurrence that may offer a lot of benefits to companies but, at the same time, it generates threats. It is viewed as an inherent element of a business development strategy pursued by a company.[17] Researchers stress that coopetition relationships are vital elements of business growth as they contribute to enhanced efficiency of its operations and financial performance;[18] they are also seen as a relevant stimulator of business growth and a factor that favours innovation.[19] The development of coopetition between companies[20] is also linked with the increasing complexity of markets, dynamic technological progress, the need to get access to unique resources and knowledge, changing customer taste, and growing environmental awareness. At the same time, coopetition as a strategy of joint value creation and competition in sharing this value is "driven" by the need to maintain strategic flexibility. It is not a development of either competition or cooperation theories but a completely new research area within the framework of strategic management.[21]

Coopetition in business groups

Business groups are multiple-operator organisations set up to accomplish common economic goals.[22] Cooperation between companies that belong to the business group is the key to the survival of the group. However, the observation of operations of these complex structures allows us to conclude that beside cooperation there is also competition between companies within the business group. Often times companies within

[15]   J. Cygler, *Kooperencja przedsiębiorstw. Czynniki sektorowe i korporacyjne*, OW SGH, Warszawa 2009.
[16]   M. Bengtsson, S. Kock, *"Coopetition" in Business...*, pp. 411–426.
[17]   G. B. Dagnino, *Coopetition Strategy: A New Kind of Interfirm Dynamics for Value Creation* [in:] *Coopetition Strategy: Theory, Experiments and Cases*, ed. by G. B. Dagnino, Routledge, London 2009, pp. 45–63.
[18]   M. Bagshaw, C. Bagshaw, *Co-opetition Applied to Training: A Case Study*, "Industrial and Commercial Training" 2001, 33, 4/5, pp. 175–177.
[19]   P. Eriksson, *Achieving Suitable Coopetition in Buyer–Supplier Relationships: The Case of AstraZeneca*, "Journal of Business to Business Marketing" 2008, 15, 4, pp. 425–454.
[20]   Ch. Guardo, M. Galvagno, *The Dynamic Capabilities View of Coopetition: The Case of Intel*, "Apple and Microsoft" 2007, http://ssrn.com/abstract=1013561 (access: 15 February 2019).
[21]   E. Stańczyk-Hugiet, *Koopetycja, czyli dokąd zmierza konkurencja*, "Przegląd Organizacji" 2011, 5, pp. 8–12.
[22]   M. Trocki, *Grupy kapitałowe: tworzenie i funkcjonowanie*, Wydawnictwo Naukowe PWN, Warszawa 2012.

the business group must agree on less favourable operating conditions or sacrifice their own goals to let the group achieve its objectives. Such moments often lead to conflicts between companies—members of such groups or shareholders of companies within the group, which may produce rivalry.

Business groups are complex network mechanisms, in which individual units / companies are linked with multiple financial, personal or contractual arrangements. As a result, within a business group we can observe a cooperation-based relationship that naturally emerges from the goals set for the group side by side with competition. Cooperation and competition in business groups can be found in many areas of their operations. Together referred to as coopetition they include most frequently strategy, internal market, investment policy, and pyramid structures.[23] Cooperation between companies within a business group takes place in areas such as technology, operations, organisation, finance,[24] as well as marketing and staff.[25] Competition, in turn, occurs at two main levels: product-market[26] and resource-competency.[27]

We need to bear in mind that coopetition is rather common in business groups, in particular in international ones. It is also most frequently described in the example of multiunit and multinational corporations. Such corporations consist of subsidiaries, branches, which operate in many countries and often compete for the market but at the same time cooperate in other areas.[28] In multinational corporations coopetition is also revealed in cooperation in diverse areas of the value chain and simultaneous competing for resources. Competition in such units is very important due to their network structure, in which individual companies act as nods linked with the flows of information, products, and other resources.[29]

In complex organisations coopetition can be observed between units which, on the one hand, cooperate in knowledge exchange and learn from each other while, on the other hand, they compete for internal resources and external markets since in most cases they are assessed through the lens of profitability indicators.[30] Some researchers claim that cooperation initiatives generate knowledge while competition-based initiatives

---

[23] M. Aluchna, *Kooperencja w grupach kapitałowych* [in:] *Kooperencja przedsiębiorstw w dobie globalizacji. Wyzwania strategiczne, uwarunkowania prawne*, ed. by J. Cygler, M. Aluchna, E. Marciszewska, M. Witek-Hejduk, G. Materna, Wolters Kluwer, Warszawa 2013, pp. 159–194.

[24] Y. Luo, *Toward Coopetition...*

[25] M. Trocki, *Grupy kapitałowe...*

[26] J. Birkinshaw, M. Lingblad, *Intrafirm Competition and Charter Evolution in the Multibusiness Firm*, "Organization Science" 2005, 16, 6, pp. 674–686.

[27] A. M. Rugman, A. Verbeke, *Subsidiary-Specific Advantages in Multinational Enterprises*, "Strategic Management Journal" 2001, 22, 3, pp. 237–250; Y. Luo, *Toward Coopetition...*

[28] W. Tsai, *Social Structure of "Coopetition" within a Multiunit Organization: Coordination, Competition, and Intraorganizational Knowledge Sharing*, "Organization Science" 2002, 13, 2, pp. 179–190; Y. Luo, *Toward Coopetition...*

[29] A. Zorska, *Korporacje transnarodowe: przemiany, oddziaływania, wyzwania*, PWE, Warszawa 2007, pp. 130–131.

[30] W. Tsai, *Social Structure...*

contribute to its utilisation.[31] The fact that companies which compete on the market need to cooperate fosters the view that nowadays within multiunit organisations not only the dominant player but, first and foremost, the subsidiaries are equipped with strategic resources. The latter include in particular strategic knowledge often generated by subsidiaries rather than by the headquarters. Cooperation between competing companies triggers the horizontal flow of valuable knowledge resources generating benefits to the entire organisation.[32]

Coopetition in business groups is often planned and orchestrated by the parent company, which sees it as a way to coordinate group operations and improve its overall efficiency.[33] On the other hand, to some extent coopetition emerges spontaneously as a result of actions undertaken by top management of individual companies striving to accomplish their own goals by identifying various levels of cooperation and competition between other units within a multinational corporation.[34] In both cases we face the problem of managing tensions generated by this relationship. In coopetition tensions derive from the risk that it involves, mostly the risk of losing the key knowledge and skills. If there are too strong or poorly controlled tensions within the coopetition arrangement, they may undermine potential positive effects.[35]

To sum up, we need to say that within business groups we can surely see competition emerging side by side with cooperation between their member companies. Scarce research studies show that in complex organisations individual units compete to achieve diverse strategic goals and priorities but they also cooperate in the best interest of one and the same organisation to which they belong.[36] Unfortunately, coopetition in business groups is still little explored.

Determinants of coopetition in a business group

In business groups coopetition determinants can be sought in their internal organisation, as well as external conditions. To some extent the same factors determine coopetition between enterprises which are legally, organisationally and financially independent.

---

[31] S. Dorn, B. Schweiger, S. Alber, *Levels, Phases and Themes of Coopetition: A Systematic Literature Review and Research Agenda*, "European Management Journal" 2016, 34, 5, pp. 484–500.

[32] S. Schleimer, A. Riege, *Knowledge Transfer between Globally Dispersed Units at BMW*, "Journal of Knowledge Management" 2009, 13, 1, pp. 27–41.

[33] J. Song, K. Lee, T. Khanna, *Dynamic Capabilities at Samsung: Optimizing Internal Co-opetition*, "California Management Review" 2016, 58, 4, pp. 118–140.

[34] Y. Luo, *Toward Coopetition...*

[35] T. Seran, E. Pellegrin-Boucher, C. Gurau, *The Management of Coopetitive Tensions within Multi-Unit Organizations*, "Industrial Marketing Management" 2016, 53, pp. 31–41.

[36] X. Luo, R. J. Slotegraaf, X. Pan, *Cross-Functional "Coopetition": The Simultaneous Role of Cooperation and Competition within Firms*, "Journal of Marketing" 2006, 70, 2, pp. 67–80.

In addition, we need to stress factors typical of only business groups and linked with the organisation thereof (Figure 1).

Figure 1. Determinants of coopetition in business groups

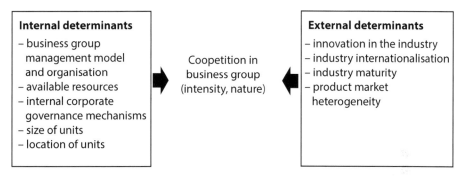

Source: W. Mierzejewska, *Koopetycja w grupach kapitałowych* [*Coopetition in Business Groups*], study under the NCN grant titled *Koopetycja w grupach kapitałowych – skala, charakter, determinanty i wpływ na efektywność* [*Coopetition in Business Groups: Scale, Nature, Determinants and Impact on Efficiency*] [2017/25/B/HS4/02448].

Similarly to inter-organisation coopetition, in a business group the intensity of coopetitive relationships depends on the **industry**[37] in which its units operate. The more **innovative** and prone to technological changes the industry, the more frequent coopetitive relationships between the companies in a business group.[38] It results mainly from the need to exchange knowledge and experience between the units to ensure their better position within the group and vis-á-vis external competitors. At the same time, companies compete for resources, clients and sometimes to win the market for their technological solutions. First and foremost, however, they compete for resources needed to operate in technologically advanced industries which are often capital-intensive.

The internationalisation of an industry is another equally important factor exerting an impact on the intensity of coopetition. Especially in the situation when coopetitive relationships have been rather well described on the example of transnational corporations from globalised sectors/industries.

A globalised industry[39] is dominated by corporations for which the economies of scale connected with possibilities to standardise a product actually matter. Cooperation

[37] J. Cygler, *Kooperencja przedsiębiorstw...*, pp. 88–90.

[38] R. B. Bouncken, S. Kraus, *Innovation in Knowledge-Intensive Industries: The Double-Edged Sword of Coopetition*, "Journal of Business Research" 2013, 66, 10, pp. 2060–2070; L. Dai, *Maximizing Cooperation in a Competitive Environment*, "Competition Forum" 2008, 6, 1, p. 63; P. Dziurski, *Innowacyjność jako determinanta koopetycji*, "Przegląd Organizacji" 2019, 5.

[39] J. Cygler, *Kooperencja przedsiębiorstw...*

between companies in a business group focuses on production and R&D and is aimed at outperforming external competitors. Simultaneously, competition may emerge when strategic domains of business units begin to overlap. The process may stem from the expansion of sales of one of such units. We need to stress that a globalised sector is characterised with a high share of exports and imports which intensify competition between units based in different geographic regions.

Product competition between companies in a business group may also be dictated by **industry maturity**. In industries in early maturity stages competition can be purposefully triggered by the superior unit. An early maturity stage of a sector is characterised by the absence of a leading technological standard or business model. Individual companies can follow different standards and business models (customer care included) while the superior company may allow product competition to see which standard or business model comes out victorious.[40]

Another external determinant of coopetition is also **product market homogeneity** understood as customer preferences. The more diverse customer requirements, the more intense competition between units within a business group. The diversity of customer preferences encourages maintaining a widely diversified product portfolio. If individual product groups are organised in separate units, these units become natural competitors.[41] At the same time, they often cooperate in promoting the entire portfolio of products, using common brand and sometimes in integrating their operations in selected geographic markets.

The **size of units** is the next determinant. Some researchers suggest that smaller units with smaller resources can be more willing to cooperate with larger units with which they also compete. It links with resources available to bigger organisations and their greater opportunities to generate knowledge. At the same time, smaller units may feel threatened since bigger units can dominate the flow of knowledge within a business group.[42]

Geographic proximity is another determinant of cooperation in knowledge exchange between competing units in a business group. Units operating in the same region can be more willing to exchange information about local circumstances. Similar approach can be observed for strategic affinity with respect to business activity areas. Even though closer affinity of strategic operations of units within a business group could be indicative of competition, it also encourages to knowledge exchanges in the core business area.[43]

With regard to resource-based approach, **availability of resources** can determine coopetition in a business group. Diverse resource profiles of companies incline them

---

[40]   J. Birkinshaw, M. Lingblad, *Intrafirm Competition...*
[41]   Ibidem.
[42]   Ibidem.
[43]   Ibidem.

to cooperate[44] but they may also imply competition for access to resources controlled by the dominant company. Uneven availability of resources enforces vertical and horizontal cooperation. Coopetition is also enhanced by technological bonds between companies within a business group.[45]

From the point of view of the management model and organisation of a business group attention should be paid to the **level of centralisation** as a determinant of coopetitive relationships. Research studies have demonstrated that highly centralised operations (in particular in the area of knowledge exchange between competing units) do not favour cooperation within business groups. The above is especially true when it comes to cooperation in knowledge sharing when units compete for external markets. Under such circumstances, informal social relations and decentralisation are much more effective as mechanisms coordinating the flow of knowledge.[46]

We may assume that vertical cooperation prevails in centralised business groups while horizontal cooperation dominates in decentralised ones.

Bigger decentralisation increases the intensity of competition between units within a business group. When decision making is decentralised, managers of individual companies at some point start opting for more attractive areas of market operations. As a result, the domains of two or more companies may overlap generating even stronger market competition between them.[47]

Another factor worth considering as a determinant of types and intensity of coopetitive relationships in a business group relates to **corporate governance internal mechanisms**. The goal of corporate governance lies in building a long-term shareholder value which, in a wider perspective, becomes the stakeholder value. Amongst a number of mechanisms that support the accomplishment of this goal we can identify internal and external ones.[48] Under intensified coopetition, internal mechanisms, such as, e.g., ownership structure, financial links, personal ties or internal monitoring can become dominant. Personal ties between companies in a business group may favour their closer cooperation. Under such circumstances, cooperation may prevail over competition in coopetitive relationships. Also the ownership structure may impact the intensity and nature of intra-organisational coopetition. The concentration of ownership, proportion of institutional investors or managers acting as co-owners are all reflected in the business efficiency of the business group.[49] Different investors have different goals and interests in getting

---

[44] W. Xingxiu, L. Hanmin, Y. Chunxia, *On the Motives for Coopetition in Complex Organizations: An Explorative Analysis*, "Advances in Information Sciences and Service Sciences" 2013, 5, 9, p. 400.

[45] Y. Luo, *Toward Coopetition...*

[46] W. Tsai, *Social Structure...*

[47] J. Birkinshaw, M. Lingblad, *Intrafirm Competition...*

[48] M. Aluchna, *Własność a corporate governance*, Poltext, Warszawa 2015, pp. 22–23.

[49] *Ład korporacyjny*, ed. by D. Dobija, I. Koładkiewicz, Wolters Kluwer, Warszawa 2011.

engaged in operations of individual companies.[50] It may have a meaningful impact on the purposeful shaping of coopetition within a business group and its nature. We may presume that higher share of board members as owners of the company will positively correlate with the choice of coopetition strategy. They should also be more motivated to monitor the environment and changes taking place in it, as well as to select new strategies that would combine contradictory forces in the search for new sources of generating added value.

Due to the complexity of relationships involved in coopetition, some researchers examine the determinants of cooperation and competition as separate sets. Y. Luo[51] demonstrates the determinants of cooperation and competition on the example of multinational groups/corporations. He lists the following cooperation determinants: strategic dependence between units resulting from roles they play in a corporation, their organisational format, and technological links. On the other hand, he sees the following as determinants of competition: the need to adapt to local circumstances and demand of these units for resources, overlapping domains of activities, and declining skills. The above factors lead to the emergence of competition for resources controlled by the parent corporation and for getting its attention. Determinants, together with infrastructure intended to ensure good organisation and cooperation of coopetitive relationships, impact the intensity of competition and cooperation between units within a multinational corporation, which translates into the role a unit plays in one of the four types.

To sum up, we need to observe that the above-mentioned determinants of coopetition in a business group do not add up to make an exhaustive list. There are other factors that impact the intensity of cooperation and competition between companies. They include predominantly management-related factors connected with aspirations and own goals pursued by managers of individual companies. The determinants of coopetition within a business group can also be sought in aspects such as organisational culture and formal or non-formal systems of knowledge management.

Conclusions

Economic growth and an increasing trust in cooperation reduce transaction costs and boost firms' interest in coopetition.[52] The latter has become a strategy often pursued by enterprises operating in a dynamic, innovative, and globalised environment.

---

[50] M. Romanowska, *Planowanie strategiczne*, PWE, Warszawa 2009; S. Douma, R. George, R. Kabir, *Foreign and Domestic Ownership, Business Groups, and Firm Performance: Evidence from a Large Emerging Market*, "Strategic Management Journal" 2006, 27, 7, pp. 637–657.

[51] Y. Luo, *Toward Coopetition…*

[52] P. Eriksson, *Achieving Suitable Coopetition…*

Also complex structures organised in business groups exhibit signs of coopetition at intra-organisational level. Business groups bring together rather differentiated subsidiaries meaning these relationships can potentially develop. Cooperation and competition featured side by side within business groups can exert a positive impact upon the efficiency of subsidiaries on condition, however, cooperation takes primacy over competition.[53] This phenomenon has not been examined sufficiently yet. Research studies on the determinants of the emergence of competition side by side with cooperation between companies in business groups are also missing. The authors seek these determinants in the characteristics of the environment, in which a business group operates, as well as in its internal specificity. While the first ones are characteristic not just of business groups and literature focused on inter-organisational coopetition discusses them at length, the latter group of determinants (internal) needs to be further explored mainly at the empirical level. This paper is an introduction to further quantitative and qualitative studies on the issue, which will try to identify the specificity of coopetition in business groups and its determinants.

Bibliography

Aluchna M., *Kooperencja w grupach kapitałowych* [in:] *Kooperencja przedsiębiorstw w dobie globalizacji. Wyzwania strategiczne, uwarunkowania prawne*, ed. by J. Cygler, M. Aluchna, E. Marciszewska, M. Witek-Hejduk, G. Materna, Wolters Kluwer, Warszawa 2013.

Aluchna M., *Własność a corporate governance*, Poltext, Warszawa 2015.

Bagshaw M., Bagshaw C., *Co-opetition Applied to Training: A Case Study*, "Industrial and Commercial Training" 2001, 33, 4/5.

Barbee G., Rubel T., *Co-opetition in Action*, "The Journal of Business Strategy" 2007, 18, 5.

Bengtsson M., Kock S., *"Coopetition" in Business Networks: To Cooperate and Compete Simultaneously*, "Industrial Marketing Management" 2000, 29, 5.

Bengtsson M., Kock S., *Cooperation and Competition in Relationships between Competitors in Business Networks*, "Journal of Business & Industrial Marketing" 1999, 14, 3.

Birkinshaw J., Lingblad M., *Intrafirm Competition and Charter Evolution in the Multibusiness Firm*, "Organization Science" 2005, 16, 6.

Bouncken R. B., Kraus S., *Innovation in Knowledge-Intensive Industries: The Double-Edged Sword of Coopetition*, "Journal of Business Research" 2013, 66, 10.

Cygler J., *Charakterystyka kooperencji* [in:] *Kooperencja przedsiębiorstw w dobie globalizacji. Wyzwania strategiczne, uwarunkowania prawne*, ed. by J. Cygler, M. Aluchna, E. Marciszewska, M. Witek-Hejduk, G. Materna, Wolters Kluwer, Warszawa 2013.

Cygler J., *Kooperencja przedsiębiorstw. Czynniki sektorowe i korporacyjne*, OW SGH, Warszawa 2009.

---

[53] *Kooperencja przedsiębiorstw...*, pp. 164–166.

Czakon W., *Koopetycja – splot tworzenia i zawłaszczania wartości*, "Przegląd Organizacji" 2012, 12.

Dagnino G. B., *Coopetition Strategy: A New Kind of Interfirm Dynamics for Value Creation* [in:] *Coopetition Strategy: Theory, Experiments and Cases*, ed. by G. B. Dagnino, Routledge, London 2009.

Dai L., *Maximizing Cooperation in a Competitive Environment*, "Competition Forum" 2008, 6, 1.

Dorn S., Schweiger B., Alber S., *Levels, Phases and Themes of Coopetition: A Systematic Literature Review and Research Agenda*, "European Management Journal" 2016, 34, 5.

Douma S., George R., Kabir R., *Foreign and Domestic Ownership, Business Groups, and Firm Performance: Evidence from a Large Emerging Market*, "Strategic Management Journal" 2006, 27, 7.

Dyer J., Singh H., *The Relational View: Cooperative Strategy and Sources of Interorganizational Competitive Advantage*, "Academy of Management Review" 1998, 23, 4.

Dziurski P., *Innowacyjność jako determinanta koopetycji*, "Przegląd Organizacji" 2019, 5.

Eriksson P., *Achieving Suitable Coopetition in Buyer–Supplier Relationships: The Case of AstraZeneca*, "Journal of Business to Business Marketing" 2008, 15, 4.

Gilbert D., *Co-opetition*, "Business and Society" 1998, 37, 4.

Gnyawali R., Ravindranath M., *Cooperative Networks and Competitive Dynamics: A Structural Embeddedness Perspective*, "Academy of Management Review" 2001, 26, 3.

Guardo Ch., Galvagno M., *The Dynamic Capabilities View of Coopetition: The Case of Intel*, "Apple and Microsoft" 2007, http://ssrn.com/abstract=1013561 (access: 15 February 2019).

Hakansson H., Ford D., *How Should Companies Interact in Business Networks?*, "Journal of Business Research" 2002, 55, 2.

Khanna T., Gulati R., Nohria N., *The Dynamics of Learning Alliances: Competition, Cooperation, and Relative Scope*, "Strategic Management Journal" 1998, 19, 3.

Kooperencja przedsiębiorstw w dobie globalizacji. Wyzwania strategiczne, uwarunkowania prawne, ed. by J. Cygler, M. Aluchna, E. Marciszewska, M. Witek-Hejduk, G. Materna, Wolters Kluwer, Warszawa 2013.

Luo X., Slotegraaf R. J., Pan X., *Cross-Functional "Coopetition": The Simultaneous Role of Cooperation and Competition within Firms*, "Journal of Marketing" 2006, 70, 2.

Luo Y., *Toward Coopetition within a Multinational Enterprise: A Perspective from Foreign Subsidiaries*, "Journal of World Business" 2005, 40, 1.

Ład korporacyjny, ed. by D. Dobija, I. Koładkiewicz, Wolters Kluwer, Warszawa 2011.

Mierzejewska W., *Koopetycja w grupach kapitałowych*, "Studia Ekonomiczne Uniwersytetu Ekonomicznego we Wrocławiu" 2018, 14.

Palmer A., *Co-operation and Competition: A Darwinian Synthesis of Relationship Marketing*, "European Journal of Marketing" 2008, 34, 5/6.

Romanowska M., *Planowanie strategiczne*, PWE, Warszawa 2009.

Rugman A. M., Verbeke A., *Subsidiary-Specific Advantages in Multinational Enterprises*, "Strategic Management Journal" 2001, 22, 3.

Schleimer S., Riege A., *Knowledge Transfer between Globally Dispersed Units at BMW*, "Journal of Knowledge Management" 2009, 13, 1.

Seran T., Pellegrin-Boucher E., Gurau C., *The Management of Coopetitive Tensions within Multi-Unit Organizations*, "Industrial Marketing Management" 2016, 53.

Song J., Lee K., Khanna T., *Dynamic Capabilities at Samsung: Optimizing Internal Co-opetition*, "California Management Review" 2016, 58, 4.

Stańczyk-Hugiet E., *Koopetycja, czyli dokąd zmierza konkurencja*, "Przegląd Organizacji" 2011, 5.

Trocki M., *Grupy kapitałowe: tworzenie i funkcjonowanie*, Wydawnictwo Naukowe PWN, Warszawa 2012.

Tsai W., *Social Structure of "Coopetition" within a Multiunit Organization: Coordination, Competition, and Intraorganizational Knowledge Sharing*, "Organization Science" 2002, 13, 2.

Xingxiu W., Hanmin L., Chunxia Y., *On the Motives for Coopetition in Complex Organizations: An Explorative Analysis*, "Advances in Information Sciences and Service Sciences" 2013, 5, 9.

Zorska A., *Korporacje transnarodowe: przemiany, oddziaływania, wyzwania*, PWE, Warszawa 2007.

The Effect of Managerial Ownership and Company Performance on CEO Turnover: Evidence from the Polish Two-Tier Board Model

Prof. Leszek Bohdanowicz, Ph.D.   https://orcid.org/0000-0002-4456-070X
University of Łódź

Abstract

This study is based on the agency theory and seeks to investigate the impact of company performance, managerial ownership, and the activity of supervisory boards on CEO turnover in the Polish system of corporate governance. The results of this study showed that company performance measured by ROA is negatively related to CEO turnover and there is also a weaker relationship between company performance measured by Tobin's Q and CEO turnover. Managerial ownership is also negatively related to CEO turnover. Furthermore, supervisory board activity is positively associated with CEO turnover, showing that these boards are active when the leader of a company is replaced.

Keywords: corporate governance, CEO performance, managerial ownership, CEO turnover

Introduction

Corporate governance literature has paid great attention to CEO turnover and its determinates, focusing especially on company performance, ownership structures, and internal monitoring mechanisms. Particular studies from Anglo-Saxon countries pointed out the importance of external markets for corporate control in changing poorly performing CEOs.[1] They tried to explain how to align the interests

---

[1]   W. H. Mikkelson, M. M. Partch, *The Decline of Takeovers and Disciplinary Managerial Turnover*, "Journal of Financial Economics" 1997, 44, 2; S. N. Kaplan, B. A. Minton, *How Has the CEO Turnover Changed?*, "International Review of Finance" 2012, 12, 1.

of dispersed shareholders and powerful CEOs and cope with the entrenchment effect in public companies. In contrast, Kaplan[2] argued that in Germany concentrated ownership allows shareholders to monitor top managers more effectively than in Anglo-Saxon countries. He underlined the lower costs of dismissing poorly performing top managers. Thus, previous studies showed that institutional context and the type of agency problem affect CEO turnover-company performance sensitivity.

Poland is an interesting example of CEO turnover and its relationship to company performance because of its corporate governance environment. It offers an interesting contrast to that in Anglo-Saxon countries but also in Germany. Company ownership in Poland is concentrated, and managerial ownership plays an important role in ownership structures. Similar to Germany, the board model is a two-tier one, but Polish supervisory boards do not operate subject to the codetermination system, and their members are solely appointed by owners due to their ownership stake. Hence, supervisory boards are controlled by dominant shareholders. In consequence, since top managers have a substantial stake in company ownership, some supervisory boards are, in reality, controlled by them. This raises the opportunity for the entrenchment effect. For this reason, among other things, supervisory boards are viewed as passive in Poland.[3] These internal weaknesses are not mitigated by an active market for corporate control because of limited company contestability through hostile takeovers and underdeveloped capital markets.[4]

Since there are these differences between national systems of corporate governance, our present understanding of the determinants influencing CEO turnover is still full of gaps. Firstly, most previous studies on CEO turnover have been conducted in a one-tier board model[5] and little is known about CEO turnover in the two-tier board model and the role of supervisory boards, i.e. upper boards, in this process. Secondly, CEO turnover is the subject of growing interest for researchers, especially in countries where ownership is dispersed and an efficient market for corporate control exists,[6] whereas only a limited number of studies have been conducted

---

[2]   S. N. Kaplan, *Corporate Governance and Incentives in German Companies: Evidence from Top Management Turnover and Firm Performance*, "European Financial Management" 1995, 1, 1.

[3]   M. Aluchna, *Mechanizmy corporate governance w spółkach giełdowych*, Szkoła Główna Handlowa w Warszawie, Warszawa 2007; J. Jeżak, *Ład korporacyjny: Doświadczenia światowe oraz kierunki rozwoju*, C.H. Beck, Warszawa 2010.

[4]   M. Aggestam, *Corporate Governance and Capital Groups in Poland*, "Journal for East European Management Studies" 2004, 9, 4.

[5]   J. K. Kang, A. Shivdasani, *Firm Performance, Corporate Governance, and Top Executive Turnover in Japan*, "Journal of Financial Economics" 1995, 38, 1; D. J. Denis, D. K. Denis, A. Sarin, *Ownership Structure and Top Executive Turnover*, "Journal of Financial Economics" 1997, 45, 2.

[6]   Ibidem; S. Mobbs, *CEOs Under Fire: The Effects of Competition from Inside Directors on Forces CEO Turnover and CEO Compensation*, "Journal of Financial and Quantitative Analysis" 2013, 48, 3.

in countries where ownership is concentrated, e.g. in Japan,[7] Italy[8] and Slovenia.[9] Moreover, little is still known about the determinants of CEO turnover in many countries, especially in Central and Eastern European countries, including Poland, where ownership is concentrated, often in the hands of top managers.[10] This study attempts to fill these gaps and its purpose is to investigate the impact of company performance, ownership structures and supervisory boards' characteristics on CEO turnover in Polish listed companies.

Theory and development of hypotheses

Corporate governance in Poland

CEO turnover is better understood in the context of the Polish system of corporate governance. According to Weimer and Pape's[11] taxonomy, this system is generally regarded as a Germanic one,[12] although Aggestam[13] describes it as a mixture of market-oriented (Anglo-Saxon) and network-oriented (Germanic) systems and underlines the short-term time horizon of the economic relationships in Poland. The Polish system of corporate governance is characterised by concentrated ownership. According to various pieces of research, the median of the largest blockholders in Polish listed companies ranges from 42%[14] to 45.8%.[15] Moreover, this research has shown that the largest shareholders in listed companies in Poland are both insiders, that is top managers, and outsiders, i.e. domestic or foreign companies, institutional investors and government. But even in companies with dominant outside investors, managerial ownership is widespread.

The Warsaw Stock Exchange is one of the largest stock exchanges in Central and Eastern Europe, due to the number of listings and market capitalisation. At the end of 2018, 464 companies (including 51 foreign ones) were listed on the WSE,

---

7   J. K. Kang, A. Shivdasani, *Firm Performance…*

8   G. Brunello, C. Graziano, B. M. Parigi, *CEO Turnover in Insider-Dominated Boards: The Italian Case*, "Journal of Banking and Finance" 2003, 27, 6.

9   L. Knežević Cvelbar, *The Relationships between Supervisory Board Structure and CEO Turnover: The Empirical Evidence of Slovenia*, "Nase Gospodarstvo" 2007, 53, 5/6.

10   P. Tamowicz, M. Przybyłowski, *Still Much to Be Done: Corporate Governance in Poland*, "International Journal of Disclosure and Governance" 2006, 3, 4.

11   J. Weimer, J. C. Pape, *A Taxonomy of Systems of Corporate Governance*, "Corporate Governance: An International Review" 1999, 7, 2.

12   J. Jeżak, *Ład korporacyjny…*

13   M. Aggestam, *Corporate Governance…*

14   M. Jerzemowska, A. Golec, A. Zamojska, *Corporate governance: BRIC i Polska na tle krajów rozwiniętych*, Wydawnictwo Uniwersytetu Gdańskiego, Gdańsk 2015.

15   P. Tamowicz, M. Przybyłowski, *Still Much to be Done…*

and its market capitalisation amounted to PLN 1,132,803 million (approximately 299,469 million USD). But with such a high ownership concentration, the market for corporate control in Poland does not exist and mergers and acquisitions are carried out as block transactions. In these circumstances, banks play an important role in providing companies with capital. Therefore, the Polish system of corporate governance can also be described as bank-based according to the taxonomy by Allen and Gale.[16]

The Polish board model is a two-tier one, with corporate boards consisting of two separate boards, i.e. management boards and supervisory boards. Management boards consist of one or more inside members. In accordance with the Code of Commercial Partnerships and Companies of Poland (CCPC), the members of the management board shall be appointed and dismissed by the supervisory board, unless the articles of association provide otherwise. A member of the management board may also be dismissed or suspended from his activities by the general meeting. The supervisory board is composed of only outside directors, and consists of three or more members in private companies, and five or more members in public companies. The members of the management board are not allowed to be the members of the supervisory board and vice versa. Hence, also CEO duality is not allowed.

Both boards have separate responsibilities. Management boards are responsible only for running the company. They are powerful and real decision-making boards, which are responsible for the formulation of strategy and for running companies' operations. According to the CCPC, the special duties of supervisory boards include consideration and approval of the management board report on the operations of the company and of the financial report for the previous financial year, with regard to their conformity with the books and documents, as well as with the actual state of affairs, and proposals of the management board concerning the division of profits or the financing of losses, as well as submitting to the general assembly annual written reports on the results of such evaluation.

Articles of association can extend the responsibilities of supervisory boards. Hence, those typically include entering into contract negotiations with top managers, approving long-term plans and annual budgets, selecting external auditors, representing companies in disputes with their management, approving the issue price of new shares, accepting unified texts of the articles of association, granting approval for the purchase or sale of real estate, giving investment guarantees, purchasing shares of significant value, purchasing or selling movables, establishing or liquidating company divisions, setting up new subsidiaries, and the sale of preferred shares or their exchange for ordinary shares.[17]

---

[16] F. Allen, D. Gale, *Comparing Financial Systems*, MIT Press, Cambridge (Mass.) 2000.
[17] J. Jeżak, *Ład korporacyjny...*

In Europe, a two-tier board model works in countries such as Austria, Germany and Estonia. In certain countries, companies can also choose between a one-tier board model and a two-tier board model, e.g. in Bulgaria, France, Lithuania, Latvia, Romania, Slovenia and Hungary. Although the Polish board system was modelled on the German board system, they differ fundamentally. German companies are stakeholder-oriented and the co-determination rule requires one half of the supervisory board to represent labour, with employee representative directors, while the other half should represent capital, elected by shareholders.[18] Additionally, some representatives of shareholders are elected by large German banks, as company law has entrusted the larger banks with proxy voting rights. Thus, German banks have a profound influence on companies as providers of debt and proxy voters.[19] Meanwhile in Poland, there is no codetermination and the Polish supervisory boards are composed solely of shareholders' representatives unless a privatisation agreement of the company or articles of association implemented it, but this is uncommon. Hence, members of supervisory boards are usually selected in the course of an annual shareholders' meeting by shareholders' representatives and banks only have an impact on companies as providers of debt, unless they have a share in ownership.

Agency theory, managerial ownership, and CEO turnover

The frequency of CEO turnover can be explained as a consequence of the separation of ownership and control. According to agency theory, modern public companies are managed by managers (agents), on behalf of their shareholders (principals).[20] Principals and agents tend to focus on their own interests. Shareholders are eager to get a high return on their investment from their shares in a company, whereas managers seek to obtain high remuneration and maintain their position. This sort of agency problem arises when ownership is dispersed. Concentrated ownership can mitigate the conflict of interests between owners and managers because strong shareholders have incentives to monitor managers and oblige them to act in the interest of the owners.[21] However, this can lead to the principal-principal conflict of interest, because majority shareholders are able to extract personal benefits from control.[22] Hence, when the

---

[18]   T. Steger, R. Hartz, *On the Way to "Good" Corporate Governance? A Critical Review of the German Debate*, "Corporate Ownership & Control" 2005, 3, 1.

[19]   Ch. A. Mallin, *Corporate Governance*, Oxford University Press, Oxford 2010.

[20]   M. C. Jensen, W. H. Meckling, *Theory of the Firm: Managerial Behavior, Agency Cost and Ownership Structure*, "Journal of Financial Economics" 1976, 3, 4.

[21]   R. La Porta, F. Lopez-De-Silanes, A. Shleifer, *Corporate Ownership Around the World*, "The Journal of Finance" 1999, 54, 2 .

[22]   A. Dyck, L. Zingales, *Private Benefits of Control: An International Comparison*, "The Journal of Finance" 2004, 59, 2; A. Renders, A. Gaeremynck, *Corporate Governance, Principal—Principal Agency Conflicts,*

CEO is a substantial owner, it leads to many benefits of control and an entrenchment effect. Thus, Morck et al.[23] stated that managers who control a substantial proportion of a company's equity may have enough influence to guarantee their employment with the company at an attractive level of pay. Similarly, Brunello et al.[24] noted that in Italian companies the probability of turnover when the CEO is also a substantial shareholder is close to zero.

In view of this, most research on the relationship between managerial ownership and CEO turnover has been based on the agency theory. For example, Denis et al.[25] examined a sample of 5,545 American company-year observations involving 1,394 companies over the period 1985–1988 and concluded that larger top executive shareholdings insulate managers from internal monitoring efforts. They also noted that the likelihood of top executive turnover is significantly greater in poorly performing companies with low managerial ownership. Similarly, Mikkelson and Partch[26] scrutinised a random sample of 240 companies traded on the New York and American Stock Exchange, and also recognised that managerial ownership increases the managers' ability to retain their position. In contrast, Weisbach,[27] for example, found no evidence that greater managerial ownership reduced the probability of turnover. In addition, Urbanek[28] studied turnover in listed companies in Poland on a sample of 350 companies listed on the Warsaw Stock Exchange between 2006 and 2009 and mentioned that the position of top managers in companies controlled by managerial ownership is, generally, the most stable. This gives rise to the first hypothesis:

Hypothesis 1. Managerial ownership is positively related to CEO turnover.

Company performance and CEO turnover

The relationship between company performance and CEO turnover is among the more frequently studied topics and is deeply rooted in agency theory. Previous studies assumed that owners dismiss managers when these managers are unable to maximise shareholder value and achieve acceptable performance. Hence, the

and Firm Value in European Listed Companies, "Corporate Governance: An International Review" 2012, 20, 2.

[23] R. Morck, A. Shleifer, R. W. Vishny, Management Ownership and Market Valuation: An Empirical Analysis, "Journal of Financial Economics" 1988, 20, 1–2.

[24] G. Brunello, C. Graziano, B. M. Parigi, CEO Turnover...

[25] D. J. Denis, D. K. Denis, A. Sarin, Ownership Structure...

[26] W. H. Mikkelson, M. M. Partch, The Decline of Takeovers...

[27] M. S. Weisbach, Outside Directors and CEO Turnover, "Journal of Financial Economics" 1988, 20.

[28] P. Urbanek, Rotacje zarządów polskich spółek publicznych w warunkach kryzysu gospodarczego, "Gospodarka Rynkowa" 2010, 1–2.

studies indicate that there is an inverse relationship between company performance and CEO turnover.[29]

Research on the relationship between CEO turnover and company performance has been conducted in various systems of corporate governance and in different institutional environments. For instance, Kang and Shivdasani[30] examined nonroutine turnover in 270 non-financial Japanese companies and found that the likelihood of this turnover is significantly negatively related to company performance measured by industry-adjusted returns on assets, excess returns and pre-tax earnings. They concluded that their results cast doubt on claims that Japanese managers can ignore the effects of corporate actions on company performance and shareholder value. Similarly, Brunello et al.[31] investigated this association on a sample of companies listed on the Italian Stock Exchange between 1988 and 1996. They recognised that, although Italian companies are dominated by insiders, in this environment CEO turnover is also negatively related to company performance. However, this relationship is valid only if the controlling shareholder is not the CEO. Additionally, Maury[32] conducted research on a sample of Finnish non-financial listed companies and noted an increase in CEO, top management and board turnover in response to poor stock price performance and operating losses.

Several similar studies on the relationship between CEO turnover and company performance were carried out in CEE countries. First of all, Frydman et al.[33] stated that the association between management turnover and revenue growth in Czech, Hungarian and Polish companies is negative. Knežević Cvelbar[34] also conducted research on a sample of 211 companies from Slovenia, through the collection of data using questionnaires. Most companies (81%) in the sample were registered as joint-stock companies. However, it was noted that there was an inverse relationship between CEO turnover and the lagged return on assets. Thus, it was shown that there is a higher probability of a CEO being replaced if company performance had dropped in the previous year. Furthermore, Eriksson[35] analysed management replacement in the Czech Republic between 1998 and 2000. He found that management turnover

[29] G. Brunello, C. Graziano, B. M. Parigi, *CEO Turnover...*; M. Lausten, *CEO Turnover, Firm Performance and Corporate Governance: Empirical Evidence from Danish Firms*, "International Journal of Industrial Organizations" 2002, 20, 3.
[30] J. K. Kang, A. Shivdasani, *Firm Performance...*
[31] G. Brunello, C. Graziano, B. M. Parigi, *CEO Turnover...*
[32] B. Maury, *Corporate Performance, Corporate Governance and Top Executive Turnover in Finland*, "European Financial Management" 2006, 12, 2.
[33] R. Frydman, Ch. W. Gray, M. Hessel, A. Rapaczynski, *When Does Privatization Work? The Impact of Private Ownership and Corporate Performance in Transition Economies*, "Quarterly Journal of Economics" 1999, 114, 4.
[34] L. Knežević Cvelbar, *The Relationships...*
[35] T. Eriksson, *Managerial Pay and Executive Turnover in the Czech and Slovak Republics*, "Economics of Transition" 2005, 13, 4.

is negatively and significantly related to company performance measured as gross profits in the previous year. Moreover, this turnover was negatively and significantly related to a change in profits, but in a short period of his research, i.e. only between 1998 and 1999.

In Poland, research on the relationship between company performance and managerial turnover was conducted by Urbanek.[36] He did not, however, find any relationship between market measures of performance and managerial turnover. Urbanek concluded that the Polish system of corporate governance is characterised by concentrated ownership, hence managerial turnover is not influenced by the market for corporate control and, consequently, by market measures of performance. These results are in line with the outcomes of research from other emerging markets. Firth et al.[37] scrutinised the relation between CEO turnover and company performance in Chinese companies. They found that CEO turnover was negatively affected by a company's accounting profitability, but not by stock return. Accordingly, the next hypotheses are:

Hypothesis 2a. CEO turnover is negatively related to company performance measured by accounting measures of performance.

Hypothesis 2b. CEO turnover is related to company performance measured by market measures of performance.

Supervisory board activity and CEO turnover

Supervisory boards in a two-tier board model can potentially more easily replace poorly performing top managers, due to their greater independence than unitary boards.[38] Cadbury[39] stated that there is no conflict of loyalties for supervisory board members in a two-tier board model because the functions of supervision and management are kept distinct and carried out by different players. Hence, there is no overlap of membership between both boards and their members can focus their attention on key tasks. In the unitary board model, the monitoring function is performed by outside directors who are members of the same board as the inside directors. In spite of this, Kaplan and Minton[40] indicated that an important governance function is served by outside directors. Thus, particular research has suggested that outside

---

[36]   P. Urbanek, *Rotacje zarządów...*
[37]   M. Firth, P. M. Y. Fung, O. M. Rui, *How Ownership and Corporate Governance Influence Chief Executive Pay in China's Listed Firms*, "Journal of Business Research" 2007, 60, 7.
[38]   S. N. Kaplan, *Corporate Governance...*; B. Maury, *Corporate Performance...*
[39]   A. Cadbury, *Corporate Governance and Chairmanship: A Personal View*, Oxford University Press, Oxford 2002.
[40]   S. N. Kaplan, B. A. Minton, *How Has the CEO...*

directors perform a better monitoring function and ensure that companies act in the interest of shareholders.[41]

It is reasonable to assume that the work of most boards is connected to routines, meaning they are more reactive than proactive. This concerns, in particular, supervisory boards in the two-tier board model which are only monitoring bodies.[42] However, their activity and dynamics are vital when companies find themselves in a unique situation. As a result, according to previous research, board activity is an important dimension of board operations and is driven by merger and acquisition activity and by accounting restatements.[43] Furthermore, they become more active when they have to protect companies against arising crises.[44] Such situations may undoubtedly include CEO fire-and-hire. Nevertheless, studies on the relationship between supervisory board activity in the two-tier board model and CEO turnover have not been performed, hence the empirical evidence is weak. However, this gives rise to the fourth hypothesis:

Hypothesis 3. There is a positive relationship between supervisory board activity and CEO turnover.

Research method

Sample

The sample consists of Polish public companies listed on the main market of the Warsaw Stock Exchange, encompassing an 8-year period from 2008 to 2015. The start date was influenced by the accessibility of information. Furthermore, data were hand--collected from annual reports, the archives of supervisory boards' annual statements and information available on the WSE web pages. Stock exchange information were used to calculate market performance of companies. Observations with missing data were excluded. Additionally, financial institutions were omitted due to their unique financial structure and the special accounting rules which apply to the financial sector.

---

[41] L. Renneboog, *Ownership of Managerial Control and the Governance of Companies Listed on the Brussels Stock Exchange*, "Journal of Banking and Finance" 2000, 24, 12.

[42] B. Tricker, *Corporate Governance: Principles, Policies, and Practices*, Oxford University Press, Oxford 2009.

[43] N. Vafeas, *Board Meeting Frequency and Firm Performance*, "Journal of Financial Economics" 1999, 53, 1; I. E. Brick, N. K. Chidambaran, *Board Meetings, Committee Structure, and Firm Value*, "Journal of Corporate Finance" 2010, 16, 4.

[44] J. Jeżak, *Rada nadzorcza a sytuacja kryzysowa w spółce* [in:] *Nadzór korporacyjny w warunkach kryzysu gospodarczego*, ed. by P. Urbanek, Wydawnictwo Uniwersytetu Łódzkiego, Łódź 2010.

Financial companies are covered by more regulation, which may have an impact on the value of certain variables.[45] This leaves us with an unbalanced panel sample of 357 companies and 1,690 company-year observations.

Variables

CEO turnover, which in this study is a dependent variable, is measured as a dummy variable and describes the CEO leaving the management board. The value "one" is allocated if turnover takes place and "0" is applied otherwise. The measurement of this variable is inspired by Brunello et al.[46] and, similarly to their research, this variable does not allow the reasons for the turnover to be recognised, for instance, forced resignation, voluntary resignation, death, illness or retirement.

In this study, managerial ownership is measured as the fraction of shares in the hands of all the management board's members. This variable is calculated as direct and indirect voting rights at the general meeting and counted as a decimal number. Moreover, it is calculated as a lagged variable, i.e. at the beginning of the period when the turnover could take place.

Polish listed companies are required to reveal in their annual statements only the proportion of shares held directly and indirectly by management board members, but not the proportion held by other top managers. They have a duty to disclose their shares only when they exceed the 5% threshold.

Institutional ownership is measured as the percentage of shares owned by institutional investors. This includes Polish and foreign banks, insurance companies, brokerages, open-ended pension funds, open-ended and closed-ended investment funds, venture capital and private equity funds. Only blocks of institutionally-held shares which exceed the 5% reporting threshold are calculated. This variable is calculated as voting rights at the general meeting and counted as a decimal number. Moreover, institutional ownership is measured as a lagged variable.

To measure company performance, both accounting and market measures are employed. The accounting measure is a return on assets (ROA), which is calculated as the ratio of the net profit divided by the total assets of the company. The market measure is Tobin's Q, which is calculated as the ratio of the total market value of the company, i.e. the market value of equity plus the book value of total debt to total assets. Both variables are measured as lagged variables.

Moreover, this study also employs supervisory board gender diversity and management board gender diversity. In common with the study by Campbell

[45]   M. Firth, P. M. Y. Fung, O. M. Rui, *How Ownership...*
[46]   G. Brunello, C. Graziano, B. M. Parigi, *CEO Turnover...*

and Minguez-Vera,[47] this diversity is measured with the Blau index using the formula below:

$$BI = 1 - \sum_{i=1}^{n} P_i^2$$

where P_i is the proportion of each category of members on the board (expressed in decimal fractions) and n is the number of categories. In this case, there were two categories—male and female. The values of the Blau index remain in the range of 0 to 0.5. The index takes the highest value if the number of men and women on the board are equal. A considerable advantage of this index is that it considers all studied categories simultaneously. This variable was also counted as a lagged variable.

The next supervisory board variable is supervisory board activity. This variable is measured as the number of meetings held by the supervisory board. Similar to prior studies, this one excludes activities by written consent, telephonic meetings, and video teleconferences, because it is more challenging to fulfill board functions from a distance.[48]

To measure board size, two variables are used, i.e. supervisory board size, which is an independent variable, and management board size, which is a control variable. In research on the one-tier board model, board size is calculated as the total number of unitary board members.[49] But since a two-tier board model is studied, board size is measured by two variables, the total number of directors on supervisory boards and the total number of directors on management boards. Both variables are measured as lagged variables.

Using the available information, two company-level variables for CEOs are constructed, that is CEO age and CEO tenure (which is calculated as the number of years spent on the management board of a given company by the CEO). Both variables are measured as lagged variables.

Company size is used in some research on CEO turnover as a control variable.[50] In this study it is measured by total assets and in addition, total assets are transformed with a natural logarithm.[51] Debt (leverage) controlled by the debt ratio. It is counted as the ratio of total liabilities to total assets. Both variables are measured as lagged variables.

The industry is calculated as a dummy variable, which takes the value of "1" if the company belongs to an industrial sector and "0" if the company belongs to the service sector. The allocation of companies to these two categories is based on the Warsaw Stock Exchange classification of sectors. Moreover, year dummy variables are also employed.

[47] K. Campbell, A. Minguez-Vera, *Gender Diversity in the Boardroom and Firm Financial Performance,* "Journal of Business Ethics" 2008, 83, 3.

[48] N. Vafeas, *Board Meeting...*

[49] Ch. Florackis, A. Ozkan, *The Impact of Managerial Entrenchment on Agency Costs: An Empirical Investigation Using UK Panel Data,* "European Financial Management" 2009, 15, 3.

[50] D. J. Denis, D. K. Denis, A. Sarin, *Ownership Structure...*; G. Brunello, C. Graziano, B. M. Parigi, *CEO Turnover...*

[51] T. Eisenberg, S. Sundgren, M. T. Wells, *Larger Board Size and Decreasing Firm Value in Small Firms,* "Journal of Financial Economics" 1998, 48, 1.

Results

Descriptive statistics

Table 1 shows the number and percentage of CEO turnovers in the sample during the studied period. During this time, CEO turnovers occurred in 263 of the 1,690 observations, which accounted for 15.56%. Most took place in 2012 when 43 turnovers were observed, representing 18.45% of the observations for the year. In 2008, there were 33 CEO turnovers, that is in 22.45% observations for the year. On the other hand, in 2014, there were only 28 CEO turnovers, accounting for 12.28% of the observations for that year. Moreover, CEO turnovers took place in 164 of 357 companies from the sample in the period, accounting for 45.94% of them.

Table 1. The number and percentage of CEO turnover between 2008 and 2015

Years	No. of CEO turnovers	No. of observations	%
2008	33	147	22.45
2009	28	189	14.81
2010	25	192	13.02
2011	30	217	13.82
2012	43	233	18.45
2013	37	234	15.81
2014	28	228	12.28
2015	39	250	15.60
All	263	1,690	15.56

Source: author's calculations based on data extracted from annual reports.

Table 2 reports other descriptive statistics. The mean value of managerial ownership is 0.2225 with a standard deviation of 0.2787 when the maximum is 0.9994. These results indicate that the ownership of Polish companies is concentrated, and a substantial proportion of shares belongs to top managers. This is supported by previous Polish research, e.g. Jerzemowska et al.[52] indicated that the largest group among the dominant shareholders of Polish listed companies are individual insider owners.

---

[52]　M. Jerzemowska, A. Golec, A. Zamojska, *Corporate governance...*

On average, there are approximately 6 directors on the supervisory board and 3 on the management board. To be precise, the mean supervisory board size is 5.7503 and the median is 5 members. The standard deviation of the supervisory board size is 1.3010. Moreover, the mean management board size is 3.0763 and the median is 3 members. The standard deviation of management board size is 1.4565. As previously mentioned, supervisory and management board size are limited by company law in Poland. Polish supervisory boards of listed companies should consist of five or more members and management boards of one or more members. These results show that supervisory boards of many Polish listed companies are composed only of the bare minimum number of members. In contrast, on average, management boards consist of more than the minimum number of members.

The mean value of the supervisory board gender diversity is 0.1786 with a standard deviation of 0.1870. Thus, on average Polish supervisory boards consist of six members, including five male members and one female member. Moreover, the mean value of the management board gender diversity is 0.1051 with a standard deviation of 0.1871. These results show that supervisory boards of Polish listed companies are more diverse than their management boards.

The mean supervisory board meeting frequency, which is the proxy of supervisory board activity, is 6.2272 with a standard deviation of 3.3456. Generally, the average number of supervisory board meetings is lower than the average number of meetings of the board of directors. Furthermore, it supports the view that Polish supervisory boards are rather passive and meet infrequently,[53] though, we must remember that supervisory boards are mostly focused on monitoring and supervising. In contrast, unitary boards are additionally engaged in other functions including strategy formulation, policy-making, and accountability.[54]

Furthermore, the mean CEO age is 48.1538 with a standard deviation of 8.3218 and the mean CEO tenure is 7.2746 with a standard deviation of 6.7739, but the median is only 5 years. Moreover, the mean level of institutional ownership is 0.1254, with a standard deviation of 0.1653. The mean of the return on assets is 0.0181 with a standard deviation of 0.1536. The approximation of Tobin's Q has a mean value of 1.2336, with a standard deviation of 0.7640. This indicates that the average market value of companies in the sample is higher than their average book value. Furthermore, the average debt ratio (leverage) is 0.4737 with a standard deviation of 0.2567. Finally, the mean natural logarithm of total assets (company size) is 19.4627, with a standard deviation of 1.6422.

---

[53]   J. Jeżak, *Ład korporacyjny...*
[54]   B. Tricker, *Corporate Governance...*

Table 2. Descriptive statistics

Variable	Mean	Median	Min.	Max.	S.D.
Managerial ownership	0.2225	0.0515	0	0.9994	0.2787
ROA	0.0181	0.0328	−1.3643	1.1451	0.1563
Tobin's Q	1.2336	1.0358	0.1804	9,9886	0.7640
Supervisory board size	5.7503	5	5	15	1.3010
Supervisory board activity	6.2272	5	1	27	3.3456
Supervisory board gender diversity	0.1786	0.1800	0	0.5000	0.1870
Institutional investors ownership	0.1254	0.0675	0	0.9270	0.1653
Management board size	3.0763	3	1	11	1.4565
Management board gender diversity	0.1051	0	0	0.5000	0.1871
CEO age	48.1538	48	26	74	8.3218
CEO tenure	7.2746	5	1	37	6.7739
Leverage	0.4737	0.4552	0.0004	3.4340	0.2567
Company size	19.4627	19.2975	15.7752	24.9160	1.6422

Source: author's calculations based on data extracted from annual reports.

Regression analysis

Table 3 describes the results of logistic regression for the sample. The data is estimated in two separate panels. In the first panel, the variable which represents company performance is ROA. In the second panel, the variable is Tobin's Q. Other variables in both models are the same.

This analysis identifies relationships between dependent and control variables. First of all, managerial ownership is significantly and negatively related to CEO turnover in the model with ROA ($\beta = -1.4641$, $p < 0.001$) and in the model with Tobin's Q ($\beta = -1.3969$, $p < 0.001$). These results show that managers with a substantial proportion of shares can entrench themselves and guarantee their posts. Thus, they uphold certain previous findings[55] and show that in the two-tier board model, supervisory boards are not able to deal efficiently with this entrenchment problem.

Moreover, company performance measured by ROA is significantly and negatively related to CEO turnover ($\beta = -1.8814$, $p < 0.001$). This relationship is in line with certain

---

[55]   R. Morck, A. Shleifer, R. W. Vishny, *Management Ownership...*; W. H. Mikkelson, M. M. Partch, *The Decline of Takeovers...*

previous research on the relationship between company performance and CEO turnover[56] and support hypothesis 2a. There is also a significant, but weaker relationship between company performance measured by Tobin's Q and CEO turnover ($\beta = -0.1855$, $p < 0.1$). These results support hypothesis 2b. Since Urbanek[57] underlines that CEO turnover in Polish listed companies is mainly dependent on the accounting measures of performance, it seems that these findings are complementary to his conclusions and show that the influence of market measures of performance on CEO turnover exist, but is weaker than the accounting measures of performance.

In addition, supervisory board activity is significantly and positively associated with CEO turnover in both ROA ($\beta = 0.1501$, $p < 0.001$) and with Tobin's Q ($\beta = 0.1546$, $p < 0.001$) models. Thus, hypothesis 4 is supported and the results show that supervisory boards need to be assigned more responsibilities and must be more active when the CEO is released from his/her position. However, data analysis did not support hypotheses 3 and 5.

Additionally, CEO tenure is negatively and significantly related to CEO turnover in both models, that is in the model with ROA ($\beta = -0.1003$, $p < 0.001$), and in the model with Tobin's Q ($\beta = -0.1027$, $p < 0.001$). This inverse relationship means that there is a higher probability that a CEO will be fired if he or she has less tenure. This relationship is also consistent with previous findings.[58] CEO age is positively and significantly related to CEO turnover in the model with ROA ($\beta = 0.0353$, $p < 0.001$), and in the model with Tobin's Q ($\beta = 0.0344$, $p < 0.001$). This relationship is also influenced by the retiring of CEOs.

Furthermore, there is a positive and significant association between leverage and CEO turnover in the model with Tobin's Q ($\beta = 0.6253$, $p < 0.05$). It shows that a higher debt-to-assets ratio increases the probability of CEO turnover. Since higher leverage is associated with higher business risk, CEOs in such companies are more exposed to dismissal.

Company size is negatively and significantly related to CEO turnover in both models, in the model with ROA ($\beta = -0.2024$, $p < 0.001$) and in the model with Tobin's Q ($\beta = -0.2138$, $p < 0.001$). These results are in line with,[59] who stated that there is a higher probability that a CEO will be replaced in companies that are smaller. In addition, year dummy variables affect CEO turnover, but only in the model with ROA.

---

[56] E.g. J. K. Kang, A. Shivdasani, *Firm Performance...*; G. Brunello, C. Graziano, B. M. Parigi, *CEO Turnover...*; M. Lausten, *CEO Turnover...*; L. Knežević Cvelbar, *The Relationships...*

[57] P. Urbanek, *Rotacje zarządów...*

[58] L. Knežević Cvelbar, *The Relationships...*

[59] Ibidem.

Table 3. Logistic regression

Independent and control variables	Dependent variables: CEO turnover	
ROA	−1.8814*** (0.4733)	
Tobin's Q		−0.1855† (0.1063)
Managerial ownership	−1.4641*** (0.3569)	−1.3969*** (0.3527)
Supervisory board size	0.0794 (0.0632)	0.1003 (0.0627)
Supervisory board activity	0.1501*** (0.0202)	0.1546*** (0.0203)
Supervisory board gender diversity	−0.0973 (0.4047)	−0.0351 (0.4031)
Institutional investors ownership	−0.0190 (0.4287)	0.1456 (0.4296)
Management board gender diversity	0.2421 (0.3900)	0.3758 (0.387068)
Management board size	0.0211 (0.0594)	−0.0156 (0.0605)
CEO tenure	−0.1003*** (0.0169)	−0.1027*** (0.0169)
CEO age	0.0353*** (0.0089)	0.0344*** (0.0087)
Leverage	−0.0433 (0.2845)	0.6253* (0.2588)
Company size	−0.2024*** (0.0346)	−0.2138*** (0.0343)
Industry	0.0047 (0.1499)	−0.0154 (0.1499)
Year dummies	Yes	No
Akaike info criterion	0.7663	0.7732
Schwarz criterion	0.8306	0.8380
N	1,690	1,676

Note: † $p < 0.1$; * $p < 0.05$; ** $p < 0.01$; ***$p < 0.001$. Standard error is given in brackets.

Source: author's calculations based on data extracted from annual reports.

Conclusions

This study examines the relationships between managerial ownership, company performance, the activity of corporate boards and CEO turnover in the Polish system of corporate governance. The main features of this system are a concentrated ownership structure, a two-tier board model and the non-existence of an effective market for corporate control. Since previous research was mostly conducted on developed markets, especially in Anglo-Saxon countries, this study gives additional evidence on agency problems in emerging market countries and, as such, it is complementary to previous studies.

Since the relationship between managerial ownership and CEO turnover is negative, this study showed that the share in ownership protects top managers against dismissal and increases their private benefits of control. Hence, this also increases the agency costs for outside investors, because owners-managers can entrench themselves and safeguard their job in comparison to non-owner managers. This relationship also indicates that supervisory boards, which are seen as a key mechanism of corporate governance in insider and network-oriented systems of corporate governance, are not able to safeguard outside shareholders from top managers' entrenchment in companies with high managerial ownership. Thus, it casts doubt on the effectiveness of these mechanisms of internal corporate governance in such companies and shows that managers tend to reduce the monitoring role of boards as soon as their equity ownership increases.

The study also shows that the associations between CEO turnover and both ROA and Tobin's Q are negative, but the first relationship is stronger. These results are in line with the outcomes of research from other emerging markets, e.g. Conyon and He[60] found that Chinese listed companies rely more on accounting performance than on stock market performance when determining CEO turnover. They argued that in developing countries, accounting measures are more informative for shareholders. Also, Urbanek[61] indicated that in the Polish system of corporate governance with concentrated ownership, top managers are most of all evaluated through accounting measures of performance. Both arguments seem to be important in explaining the relationships. Dominant shareholders in systems of corporate governance with concentrated ownership are not so sensitive to price fluctuation, because the expected return on their investment is longer than the expected return of dispersed minority investors. Hence, in network-oriented systems of corporate governance, accounting measures of performance seem to be more informative especially for dominant shareholders, since the incentives of these owners for private control benefit reduce their propensity to listen to the capital market.

---

[60]   M. Conyon, L. He, *CEO Turnover in China: the Role of Market-Based and Accounting Performance Measures*, "European Journal of Finance" 2014, 20, 7–9.

[61]   P. Urbanek, *Rotacje zarządów...*

Moreover, this study finds that the supervisory board activity is significantly and positively related to CEO turnover. This shows that Polish supervisory boards which, in some studies, are perceived as passive,[62] become more active and their members meet more when they have to dismiss an incumbent CEO and hire a replacement. In consequence, since in the Polish system of corporate governance supervisory boards are in majority dominated by shareholders' representatives, these owners become more involved in company affairs when its leader is being changed. These results are also consistent with the findings from a one-tier board model, which pointed out that since the corporate board is the most important authority in the company, it is accountable for ensuring that critical decision are taken and implemented.[63] Since in a two-tier board model, supervisory boards are responsible for the evaluation and if needed the replacement of CEOs, which is a critical decision for companies, they need to meet more frequently and be more active when CEOs are employed and dismissed.

As with all empirical studies, the results of this study are not without limitations. Firstly, the research on corporate governance recognised that country-level institutions play an important role in shaping corporate board practices, structure and CEO-board relationships.[64] Although the Polish system of corporate governance is recognised as a Germanic system, it has also its unique traits which can hinder the generalisation of results. Hence, since the research sample is restricted only to Polish listed companies, there are still concerns whether the findings from a single country can be generalised.

Secondly, the research sheds some light on the determinants of CEO turnover in Poland and is complementary to previous research, but it does not scrutinise, for instance, the consequences of CEO dismissal for company performance and frequency of supervisory boards' meetings in the following years. Although Byrka-Kita et al.[65] obtained negative values of abnormal returns as a shareholders' reaction to the decision of the supervisory board to appoint a new CEO, still little is known on topics such as the moderating effect of managerial ownership in this process. The consequences of CEO dismissal for company performance and for the frequency of supervisory boards' meetings may still constitute an important topic for future research.

Thirdly, this research includes two demographic pieces of information on CEOs (age and tenure), but, due to data limitations, it omits other CEO characteristics, especially CEO gender and CEO education. All these limitations may be the starting point for further research.

[62] M. Aluchna, *Mechanizmy corporate governance...*; J. Jeżak, *Ład korporacyjny...*
[63] B. Tricker, *Corporate Governance...*; B. Kolltveit, B. Hennestad, K. Grønhaug, *The Board: A Change Agent?*, "Baltic Journal of Management" 2012, 7, 2.
[64] J. Grosvold, S. J. Brammer, *National Institutional Systems as Antecedents of Female Board Representation: An Empirical Study*, "Corporate Governance: An International Review" 2011, 19, 2.
[65] K. Byrka-Kita, M. Czerwiński, A. Preś-Perepeczko, *Stock Market Reaction to CEO Appointment—Preliminary Results*, "Journal of Management and Business Administration. Central Europe" 2017, 25, 2.

Bibliography

Aggestam M., *Corporate Governance and Capital Groups in Poland*, "Journal for East European Management Studies" 2004, 9, 4.

Allen F., Gale D., *Comparing Financial Systems*, MIT Press, Cambridge (Mass.) 2000.

Aluchna M., *Mechanizmy corporate governance w spółkach giełdowych*, Szkoła Główna Handlowa w Warszawie, Warszawa 2007.

Brick I. E., Chidambaran N. K., *Board Meetings, Committee Structure, and Firm Value*, "Journal of Corporate Finance" 2010, 16, 4.

Brunello G., Graziano C., Parigi B. M., *CEO Turnover in Insider-Dominated Boards: The Italian Case*, "Journal of Banking and Finance" 2003, 27, 6.

Byrka-Kita K., Czerwiński M., Preś-Perepeczko A., *Stock Market Reaction to CEO Appointment—Preliminary Results*, "Journal of Management and Business Administration. Central Europe" 2017, 25, 2.

Cadbury A., *Corporate Governance and Chairmanship: A Personal View*, Oxford University Press, Oxford 2002.

Campbell K., Minguez-Vera A., *Gender Diversity in the Boardroom and Firm Financial Performance*, "Journal of Business Ethics" 2008, 83, 3.

Conyon M., He L., *CEO Turnover in China: the Role of Market-Based and Accounting Performance Measures*, "European Journal of Finance" 2014, 20, 7–9.

Denis D. J., Denis D. K., Sarin A., *Ownership Structure and Top Executive Turnover*, "Journal of Financial Economics" 1997, 45, 2.

Dyck A., Zingales L., *Private Benefits of Control: An International Comparison*, "The Journal of Finance" 2004, 59, 2.

Eisenberg T., Sundgren S., Wells M. T., *Larger Board Size and Decreasing Firm Value in Small Firms*, "Journal of Financial Economics" 1998, 48, 1.

Eriksson T., *Managerial Pay and Executive Turnover in the Czech and Slovak Republics*, "Economics of Transition" 2005, 13, 4.

Firth M., Fung P. M. Y., Rui O. M., *How Ownership and Corporate Governance Influence Chief Executive Pay in China's Listed Firms*, "Journal of Business Research" 2007, 60, 7.

Florackis Ch., Ozkan A., *The Impact of Managerial Entrenchment on Agency Costs: An Empirical Investigation Using UK Panel Data*, "European Financial Management" 2009, 15, 3.

Frydman R., Gray Ch. W., Hessel M., Rapaczynski A., *When Does Privatization Work? The Impact of Private Ownership and Corporate Performance in Transition Economies*, "Quarterly Journal of Economics" 1999, 114, 4.

Grosvold J., Brammer S. J., *National Institutional Systems as Antecedents of Female Board Representation: An Empirical Study*, "Corporate Governance: An International Review" 2011, 19, 2.

Jensen M. C., Meckling W. H., *Theory of the Firm: Managerial Behavior, Agency Cost and Ownership Structure*, "Journal of Financial Economics" 1976, 3, 4.

Jerzemowska M., Golec A., Zamojska A., *Corporate governance: BRIC i Polska na tle krajów rozwiniętych*, Wydawnictwo Uniwersytetu Gdańskiego, Gdańsk 2015.

Jeżak J., *Ład korporacyjny: Doświadczenia światowe oraz kierunki rozwoju*, C.H. Beck, Warszawa 2010.

Jeżak J., *Rada nadzorcza a sytuacja kryzysowa w spółce* [in:] *Nadzór korporacyjny w warunkach kryzysu gospodarczego*, ed. by P. Urbanek, Wydawnictwo Uniwersytetu Łódzkiego, Łódź 2010.

Kang J. K., Shivdasani A., *Firm Performance, Corporate Governance, and Top Executive Turnover in Japan*, "Journal of Financial Economics" 1995, 38, 1.

Kaplan S. N., *Corporate Governance and Incentives in German Companies: Evidence from Top Management Turnover and Firm Performance*, "European Financial Management" 1995, 1, 1.

Kaplan S. N., Minton B. A., *How Has the CEO Turnover Changed?*, "International Review of Finance" 2012, 12, 1.

Knežević Cvelbar L., *The Relationships between Supervisory Board Structure and CEO Turnover: The Empirical Evidence of Slovenia*, "Nase Gospodarstvo" 2007, 53, 5/6.

Kolltveit B., Hennestad B., Grønhaug K., *The Board: A Change Agent?*, "Baltic Journal of Management" 2012, 7, 2.

La Porta R., Lopez-De-Silanes F., Shleifer A., *Corporate Ownership Around the World*, "The Journal of Finance" 1999, 54, 2.

Lausten M., *CEO Turnover, Firm Performance and Corporate Governance: Empirical Evidence from Danish Firms*, "International Journal of Industrial Organizations" 2002, 20, 3.

Mallin Ch. A., *Corporate Governance*, Oxford University Press, Oxford 2010.

Maury B., *Corporate Performance, Corporate Governance and Top Executive Turnover in Finland*, "European Financial Management" 2006, 12, 2.

Mikkelson W. H., Partch M. M., *The Decline of Takeovers and Disciplinary Managerial Turnover*, "Journal of Financial Economics" 1997, 44, 2.

Mobbs S., *CEOs Under Fire: The Effects of Competition from Inside Directors on Forces CEO Turnover and CEO Compensation*, "Journal of Financial and Quantitative Analysis" 2013, 48, 3.

Morck R., Shleifer A., Vishny R. W., *Management Ownership and Market Valuation: An Empirical Analysis*, "Journal of Financial Economics" 1988, 20, 1–2.

Renneboog L., *Ownership of Managerial Control and the Governance of Companies Listed on the Brussels Stock Exchange*, "Journal of Banking and Finance" 2000, 24, 12.

Renders A., Gaeremynck A., *Corporate Governance, Principal—Principal Agency Conflicts, and Firm Value in European Listed Companies*, "Corporate Governance: An International Review" 2012, 20, 2.

Steger T., Hartz R., *On the Way to "Good" Corporate Governance? A Critical Review of the German Debate*, "Corporate Ownership & Control" 2005, 3, 1.

Tamowicz P., Przybyłowski M., *Still Much to Be Done: Corporate Governance in Poland*, "International Journal of Disclosure and Governance" 2006, 3, 4.

Tricker B., *Corporate Governance: Principles, Policies, and Practices*, Oxford University Press, Oxford 2009.

Urbanek P., *Rotacje zarządów polskich spółek publicznych w warunkach kryzysu gospodarczego*, "Gospodarka Rynkowa" 2010, 1–2.

Vafeas N., *Board Meeting Frequency and Firm Performance*, "Journal of Financial Economics" 1999, 53, 1.

Weimer J., Pape J. C., *A Taxonomy of Systems of Corporate Governance*, "Corporate Governance: An International Review" 1999, 7, 2.

Weisbach M. S., *Outside Directors and CEO Turnover*, "Journal of Financial Economics" 1988, 20.

Effective Management Succession Models in Larger Family Enterprises: Presentation of the Best Practices in the World

Prof. Wojciech Popczyk, Ph.D.   ⓘ https://orcid.org/0000-0001-5833-0449

University of Łódź

Abstract

Management succession appears to be a key success factor for the growth and development of family enterprises, which have to guarantee financial security for successive generations of the family. The aim of the article is to present succession models in larger family enterprises of global, multigenerational nature, recognised as effective units, developing on the basis of good, proven practices identified during consulting and research activities by such institutions as Cambridge Institute for Family Enterprise, FORBES, Spencer Stuart, Harvard Business School. The basic similarities of these proposals may be merged into a platform for creating one common model that will serve as a benchmark for individual, specific succession cases. The differences among the proposals may constitute a complementary added value for the model thus created. The degree of convergence of succession planning in a specific case of family enterprise with the presented model—the benchmark will allow to forecast the effectiveness and success of intergenerational transfer.

Keywords: family enterprises, succession, SME, succession models

Introduction

The topic of succession in family enterprises is the most popular in the scientific literature devoted to the functioning and management of these entities.[1] This popularity results from the key importance of planning and implementing intergenerational management

---

[1]   J. Chrisman, J. H. Chua, P. Sharma, *Current Trends and Future Directions in Family Business Management Studies: Toward a Theory of the Family Firm*, "Coleman Foundation White Paper Series" 2003; J.H. Chua,

and ownership transfer for business growth and development over a long period of time, for generating and using intangible assets, the carrier of which is the owner family, in the process of building and increasing competitive advantage.[2] Unfortunately, the succession of management is a complex, multi-stage, multidimensional process in the vast majority of cases resulting in failure. A share of 30% of family businesses make it through the second generation, 10–15% through the third, and 3–5% through the fourth.[3] For natural and pragmatic reasons scientists, consultants and practitioners are looking for solutions, strategies or models that will increase the probability of success in this area and thus the probability of continuity of management, progress in the scope of growth, development and efficiency of family entities.

In his own search, the author has already presented the anthropological concept of family structure in order to explain the causes and potential sources of failures in planning and succession in family enterprises. In each of the four family structures, the socialisation process of the younger generation takes place in different cultural conditions and creates diverse attitudes of representatives of the family's young generation as well as seniors to the succession of business run by the entrepreneurial family. The author proposed systemic solutions that could counteract threats mainly in micro and small-sized enterprises.[4]

This time, the aim of the article is to present succession models in larger family enterprises of global, multigenerational nature, recognised as effective units, developing on the basis of good, proven practices identified during consulting and research activities by institutions such as Cambridge Institute for Family Enterprise, FORBES, Spencer Stuart, Harvard Business School. The basic similarities of these proposals may be merged into a platform for creating one common model that will serve as a benchmark for individual, specific succession cases. The differences among the proposals may constitute a complementary added value for the model thus created. The degree of convergence of succession planning in a specific case of family enterprise with the presented model—the benchmark will allow to forecast the effectiveness and success of intergenerational transfer.

J. J. Chrisman, P. Sharma, *Succession and Non-succession Concerns of Family Firms and Agency Relationship with Nonfamily Managers*, "Family Business Review" 2003, 16, 2.

[2]   T. G. Habbershon, M. L. Williams, *A Resource-Based Framework for Assessing the Strategic Advantages of Family Firms*, "Family Business Review" 1999, 12, 1; T. G. Habbershon, M. L. Williams, I. C. Macmillan, *A Unified Systems Perspective of Family Firm Performance*, "Journal of Business Venturing" 2003, 18.

[3]   C. Wood, *The Surprising Stats about Succession in Family Business*, "All Strategy" 2018, https://www.allstrategy.net/the-surprising-stats-about-succession-in-family-business/ (access: 12 May 2019).

[4]   W. Popczyk, *Anthropological Family Type and Its Impact on Succession Planning in Family Businesses: Research Report* [in:] *New Challenges in Economic and Business Development—2019: Incentives for Sustainable Economic Growth*, University of Latvia, Riga 2019.

Cambridge Institute for Family Enterprise (US):
A model of management succession for medium-sized family businesses

For four decades, the Cambridge Institute has been supporting succession processes in family enterprises as a part of its advisory and educational missions. Together with entrepreneurial families and company boards, it develops successive plans for them. The accumulated experience has allowed the Institute to work out an effective management succession model in family enterprises.[5] The model was built on the following assumptions: a company is medium-sized (its income does not exceed USD 500 million), private (not a listed company), has a moderate level of complexity (Strategic Business Units number, number of employees, geographical coverage), does not provide for sudden changes in strategic directions, ownership, supervision and will not do so over the next 5 years, the current leader—the founder of the business is competent, healthy, has time to search, select and in the final stage integrate a successor, the controlling package is in the hands of a senior generation, family relations are basically harmonious with a normal, controllable level of rivalry or conflict, the family prefers successors more amongst themselves than outside the family.

The most common bad practices observed in management succession by the Institute are as follows:
- prior to planning succession, the current strategic position of the business is not taken into account, which should influence the decision to sell it or to continue family management,
- it is assumed that the younger generation of the family is interested in organisational leadership, knows how to lead and is enthusiastic about sharing or engaging in a dialogue with the young generation on this subject is rare,
- members of the younger generation are rarely involved in the process of building a vision of leadership and ownership, which can result in their frustration and tensions in the family relationships,
- there is often a belief, that the successor should have views and a style of leadership similar to those presented by the current leader (in extreme cases it is said, that the successor should be a clone of the outgoing leader). Meanwhile, rapid changes in the business environment, the need for the business to move to higher stages of its development related to the renewal of the life cycle require new, valuable leadership competences.

In response to these bad successive practices, the Institute has formulated four principles that form the basis of the proposed model. These are: a) creating the concept

---

5   P. Michaud, C. Collette, J. A. Davis, *CEO Succession in the Family Business. A Better Plan for Success*, Cambridge Institute for Family Enterprise, Cambridge (Mass.) 2017.

of a company map, b) pro-entrepreneurial socialisation of the young generation, c) objectivisation of the succession process by delegating powers in this respect to a consultative council, d) dynamics of succession.

The company's map concept is a visualisation of all financial and social interests of the company located in many areas, which most often comprise potential business, investment and social activities of the family. In addition to the core business activity in regards to which the company is a leader, there are: satellite business units, branches and affiliates forming a capital group, strategic business units and diversified functions in the core business structure, a private investment activity area, an area of philanthropic activity, real estate and other family assets management, an area of developing talents in business, an area of integration policy and organisation of family life. Each of the areas require specific leadership competences, passion and determine the vision, mission and strategic behaviour of the holistically understood enterprise / family enterprise. The map shows, what the senior generation has to offer to the young generation in the sense of their potential employment opportunities and career planning in these areas, which leadership positions can be available to them, how all family members can add value to the family enterprise and build their own and the family's reputation. The author believes, that the family business map is a platform for communication and partnership dialogue between and within generations, which integrates the family, strengthens its social capital, neutralises potential conflicts, especially concerning succession and helps to undertake collectively key, rational decisions serving the enterprise and the family. The members of the family's young generation can identify their predispositions relatively earlier, confront them with the competency profiles desired at particular leadership positions in a broadly understood enterprise and plan a further path for their professional development. The results of scientific empirical research confirm the positive correlation between the number of family members employed in the business and its financial performance.

Pro-entrepreneurial socialisation of the young generation in the family structure is the prelude to every management succession. The key to shaping the desired attitudes, entrepreneurial orientation, moral and emotional intelligence is: learning joy from independence and creativity, making the family's well-being dependent on the business and its condition, creative introduction of the young generation into the business and not on the basis of duty or coercion, involving young people in challenges and enabling their early participation in the benefits generated by the business, presenting to them the business world in a positive light and ensuring there is space there for the older and younger generations to enable intergenerational cooperation based on mutual respect, and finally, developing the need for professionalism in the mentality of young people who should be convinced that business requires professional leaders, excellence, products, internal and external relations (especially with clients) to ensure financial security for the family and their future generations.

In the majority of leadership succession cases, the **objectification** of this process is crucial for success by delegating significant powers to a properly structured supervisory board, or rather a consulting council. Such a council consisting of family representatives, non-family board members and professionals from outside develops a competency profile of the future leader and selects the best of the candidates for the new leader position. When a family candidate does not meet the competence criteria or does not express the will to take over leadership in a holistic family organisation, the council recommends an internal or external non-family candidate. The same council helps the winning candidate adapt to the new role and periodically evaluates his/her achievements, in particular the financial results of the business, and if necessary, it formulates recommendations or makes a decision to replace the leader.

Succession is a fundamental, dynamic, disciplined process, highly individualised in each enterprise-related case, implemented in a planned, formal, transparent, unhurried and uninterrupted manner. It should be a collective effort. A new leader is introduced on average for 3–5 years before the previous one retires from the business. The dynamics of the process means that firstly, the most effective family succession takes place not when the senior generation is ready to retreat, but when the younger generation is ready for leadership and secondly, it means the coexistence of generations on the basis of a partnership and support for ten or more years after the introduction of the new leader. The author calls this **a leverage of competence**, which strengthens the entrepreneurial orientation, professionalism, creativity of the new leader with the experience, social capital resources, influences and personal reputation of an outgoing leader. In practice, the senior takes the place of the chairman of the supervisory or consultative board.

Technically, the proposed model of management succession in a family enterprise consists of the following stages and processes:

Stage I. Formal planning

1. Developing a business vision for the future on the basis of strategic analyses.
2. Identifying a desired competence profile of the leader who will contribute to the implementation of the vision.
3. Developing a family vision in the business, determining who from the family can add value to it, whether the family community in the business will generate a synergy effect, how to fill positions on the company's holistic map.
4. Drawing up a list of potential candidates for the leader, family and non-family ones, comparing their competences with the accepted model competence profile.
5. Choosing the best candidate.
6. Developing a retirement plan for the senior leader.
7. Accepting the schedule for implementing the succession plan.

Stage II. Succession plan implementation

1. Initiating the successor in work in the business, entrusting him/her with various, rotating roles in specific functional areas, commissioning the execution of projects to them such as: process improvement, new products, new markets, organising project teams and managing them, preparing problem-oriented presentations for board meetings and active participation in them.
2. Gradual takeover of increasing senior managerial positions by the successor, ending with assisting the current leader.
3. Periodic evaluations of the successor's work by the consultative council.
4. Formulating recommendations by the consultative council as to the professional development of the successor in order to complete his/her competency gaps.
5. Appointing the successor to the post of the new leader after the final evaluation by the consultative board.

Stage III. Stabilisation after succession

Using the previously described competence leverage, giving dynamism and fluidity to the intergenerational transfer, partnership between outgoing and incoming leaders, communication with internal and external stakeholders, full support for the new leader by the outgoing leader and by all the family members.

FORBES, a management succession model for large family businesses

Dennis Jaffe, one of the pioneers of consulting dedicated to family businesses, was looking for the most effective model of planning and implementing succession in the research of 100 large, multi-generational (the business is controlled by at least the third generation of the family) family enterprises in 20 countries. Because those are enterprises that have been in the hands of founding families for at least 100 years, growing and developing in a model way, it seems to be reasonable to assume that their succession practices should be a guide for all family enterprises struggling with the transfer of management.[6] Jaffe calls the families controlling those enterprises *generative families*, because they generate values and norms continuously through subsequent generations and in this way, they build a strong moral and ethical infrastructure both of the family and the business. In his previous publications, the author of this article described the moral infrastructure as an important element of the family's social

---

[6] D. Jaffe, *If You Want Your Family Business to Last Several Generations*, "The Forbes" 2018, www.forbes.com (access: 15 May 2020).

capital, and as a tool for social control in the enterprise and explained the mechanism of building this infrastructure through communication among the family members based on a partner dialogue. The moral infrastructure cumulated by successive generations is a natural environment for the socialisation of the young generation and a source for building strong interpersonal relationships with internal and external communities of stakeholders.

The model proposed by D. Jaffe has no stage structure, it is built on the following fundamental principles:

Continuity of the intergenerational process of generating commonly shared values and norms. A family business begins its story with a strong sense of the founder's mission and values at least as a business. It was discovered in the research that the continuation of family business by successive generations is possible, when the successors will affirm and even develop those values and declare their attachment to them. In order for the young generation to become a part of the enterprise, they must participate in the process of creating further family norms and values within the framework of the partner dialogue, that constitute the foundation of the company's moral infrastructure. The role of seniors is to create a communication platform of intergenerational nature, to ensure a community of values as well as a business vision and mission. Often, the result of such communication is modifying the vision and mission, so that they may be meaningful, obliging and attractive to the young generation.

Resilience to crises and regular renewal. G families are characterised by the development of adaptive abilities and resistance to crisis situations in their structures, business and the external environment.

Transparency. The first generation of a family in business has one founder-leader who usually does not have the habit of sharing information, ideas or control. The more family members are related, the stronger emotional trust is among them. However, when the second or third generation comes to the fore, siblings, or cousins with weaker emotional relationships who are reflecting on their professional future, need quick access to comprehensive, key information on the business, its financial position and the prospects for its financial results in the future. This means that confidential documents, business plans, and financial statements are always freely available, clear and, if necessary, discussed at the forum of the generative family.

Management professionalisation. As the company grows, it must become more professional, develop skills and raise resources to grow and remain competitive. Each generative family reaches a critical point, in which it ceases to manage the enterprise effectively and is not able to carry it further to the next stage of organisational development. A successful transformation requires that the owner / leader and his / her senior management team develop and acquire new skills along with the company's expansion. According to the theory of hierarchised systems by E. Jaques[7] the ability to acquire new skills and necessary knowledge may depend on their intellectual potential, talent and age. Organisations evolve into a certain and predictable way, and each stage is characterised by specific requirements as to the role foreseen for leaders and their managers at various levels of management. In such a critical point, non-family succession of management is necessary, although it may induce intergenerational tensions, but it means the maturity and responsibility of current leaders for financial security and the well-being of subsequent generations of the family. Changing the status of a managerial family into an owner family becomes a fact. There is always a possibility of returning to the primary status in the case of the emergence of a family candidate for the leader who meets the stakeholders' expectations and will be ready to take up this position.

Intergenerational commitment and cooperation. Subsequent generation changes cause loosening emotional and social ties among family members, which worsens communication among them (siblings, cousins, their spouses, etc.) as well as the erosion of social capital built by the first generation. In generative families, family members from different generations and with a different degree of kinship share the sense, will and value of "tribal" cooperation of the family, based on the principles of mutual respect and a sense of community. There are conflicts even in such families resulting in the departure of individual members or entire family branches from the business, but other individuals in it quickly consolidate and adapt to the new reality.

Offering employment in the broadly understood enterprise for members of the new generation. In generative families, all family members are encouraged to work professionally for the common benefit of the whole family. They have a chance to become not only the leaders of a major business venture, if they have appropriate competences, but also they may become entrepreneurs who will commercialise their innovative ideas in new business units created specifically for this purpose (the creation of a capital group), financiers investing their family savings and managing the family properties, philanthropists and social innovators operating in foundations and associations under the family auspices. Regardless of the path which a family member follows, they can always count on the family's moral and financial support.

Philanthropy. Enterprising generative families have a sense of possessing more resources than they need. They socialise their young generations in terms of material inequality in the world, the negative effects of social exclusion, the vastness of social needs, sensitivity to human woes and the moral obligation to share well-being. They

---

[7]   E. Jaques, *Requisite Organization: Total System for Effective Managerial Organization and Managerial Leadership for the 21st Century*, Gower, London 1997.

perceive philanthropy as a value integrating the family, strengthening its identity, building the reputation of the family and the business and finally, as a career opportunity for their members.

Social responsibility. In addition to philanthropy, generative families display a great concern for loyal employees with long-term experience. In many cases, family members involved in the business form a network of close interpersonal relationships with them, thereby increasing the resources of internal social capital. They strive to strengthen and expand networks of relations with external stakeholders, mainly with target clients and the local community. They show concern for the protection of the environment as well as for the safety and quality of value propositions.

Spencer Stuart: A management succession model for medium and large enterprises

Spencer Stuart is one of the leading consulting companies in the world, seeking empirically the best practices in the field of leadership in organisations, including management succession planning in family enterprises. Based on many years of experience in cooperation with business practice and contacts with family business leaders in the world, Spencer Stuart has worked out a successful management succession model for medium and large enterprises.[8] It consists of the following components: a) a process approach to succession guaranteeing the continuity of management, b) a competence profile of a potential successor drawn up on the base of strategic development plans of the enterprise, c) an independent supervisory board and family council—as the bodies responsible for preparing and implementing the management succession plan, d) broadening the spectrum of potential candidates for the successor for professionals from outside the family, e) support for the new leader by internal stakeholders.

- The process approach to succession means a continuous concentration of a succession committee, specially established by the supervisory or consultative body, on succession planning. At least once or twice a year the committee determines whether there is a person for the successor who will ensure continuity of management in the case of surprise scenarios: a sudden and unexpected departure of the current leader, sets the conditions and time of his/her planned retirement, selects the target candidate for the successor, finally supervises the implementation of the provisions.
- Business vision, growth and development strategies are the basis for creating the competence profile of the future leader by the succession committee. A planned expansion into new geographic and product markets, the growing scale, diversity

---

[8]   S. Spencer, *Beyond the Family Tree: Succession Planning for Family Businesses*, 2010, www.spencerstuart. com (access: 15 May 2020).

and scope of the company's operations, dynamics of changes in the sector's power balance and ways of competing are associated with challenges that require the leader's specific skills, expertise, talent, experience, entrepreneurial orientation (innovation, pro-activity, a lack of risk aversion). A good practice in this regard is that the competence profile is updated every three to five years, if necessary.

- The succession committee is appointed by the supervisory or consultative board and should have a procedural character. It should include professionals who are most independent of the owner's family, who are on the supervisory board, consultative board and management board. The family council is also responsible for planning succession in the sense that it creates a consensus among family members who are involved in the enterprise management and those who only participate in the ownership structure in matters of importance to business, including succession. Candidates for management successors reported by the family council are evaluated by the succession committee according to the criteria resulting from the pre-deter- mined competence profile. If the committee finds competence gaps in the candidate / candidates, it recommends a procedure and time to fill them.

- Expanding the group of potential candidates for the management successor to professionals outside the family makes deep sense due to the importance of the competence profile. However, if the competence criteria are met by family candidates at a satisfactory level, they have the priority over professionals from outside the family. This results from the possibility of preserving and increasing the resources of the family's social capital in the organisation and beyond it, and the best fit of the new leader to the given organisational culture. The candidate evaluation procedure takes into account the criteria resulting from the competence profile, the benchmark of profiles of all candidates with respect to one another and the benchmark of the best profiles to competence profiles of leaders of the most successful companies in the sector. The lack of family candidates in general, a weak interest in taking over management by the existing or their poor competences, which cannot be completed, provide for initiating the search for professionals from outside the family, whose additional competence should be sensitivity to the specifics and dynamics of the family enterprise.

An external successor who is able to move the enterprise to a higher level of development, renew its life cycle, but who does not fit culturally into the organi- sation, may cause confusion and concern among its main stakeholders and lead to the eruption of family-accumulated social capital, which is a major competitive advantage of family enterprises over non-family entities. The desirable sensitivity of a professional from the outside to the specifics of a family business should manifest itself in the culture of stewardship, diplomacy in communicating with the family, integrity culture, readiness to increase the family's reputation and culture as well as internal and external social capital resources, a positive attitude to cooperation with the family council, willingness to use the intellectual potential of the family members in the company's activities while demonstrating a strong personality but without an excessive ego.

Spencer Stuart notes an upward trend in the interest of professional managers in taking the positions of general directors or presidents in large family enterprises. This can be explained by exerting lesser pressure on quarterly financial results and less surveillance from external stakeholders (stock exchange, media, investors), a greater focus on the value of a family enterprise in the long run, and greater freedom, flexibility in implementing product, process, market or organisational changes in these types of entities. Such working conditions compensate slightly lower considerations in family enterprises as compared to non-family stock companies.

- Support for the new leader must come primarily from the outgoing senior and other members of the owner's family remaining on the board. They should not enter into the competence of the new leader, disturb him and take actions that undermine his/her authority. For that purpose, they should communicate to the internal and external stakeholders their support and trust in the new leader.

Harvard Business School: A succession management model for large, global family enterprises

Claudio Fernández-Aráoz works for a Swiss, global consulting company Egon-Zehnder conducting research in the field of management and leadership in large enterprises and is a board member of Harvard Business School. On the basis of surveys of 50 large global family enterprises, he has established an effective model of management succession, which increases the likelihood of maintaining family control, and continuing business development in the long run.[9] All the surveyed companies used the following principles:

- corporate governance providing for a professional supervisory board neutralising nepotic practices,
- the principle of gravity of the family and its values,
- the possibility of choosing a candidate for the new leader from outside the family,
- the presence of a formal selection procedure for the candidate for the management successor.

The surveyed enterprises generated revenues of at least EUR 500 million, and came from various sectors of North and South America, Europe and Asia. Interviews were conducted with their family and non-family leaders.

---

[9]   C. Fernández-Aráoz, S. Iqbal, J. Ritter, *Leadership Lessons from Great Family Businesses*, "Harvard Business Review" 2015, 93, 4.

Large family businesses have no chance to properly manage internal (family and non-family) talents or attract outside professionals without implementing good corporate governance practices that separate the owner family and business systems and provide a strong supervision of a professional body in the form of an independent supervisory board over the management board. Almost 25% of the surveyed leaders from outside the family mentioned the following concerns about corporate governance before starting work in a family business: uncertainty about the level of a leader's autonomy, hidden intentions of the owner's family, a lack of dynamics of operational activities and finally nepotic threats and the irrationality of made decisions. A share of 94% of the surveyed family enterprises were controlled by supervisory or consultancy/advisory boards consisting of nine members on average. They were represented by owner-families in 46% on average in Europe, 28% in the Americas and 26% in Asia. There was a significant separation of family and business systems in those enterprises. One of the surveyed companies with a supervisory board introduced such a solution that only branches of the family that do not have their representatives on the management board delegate them to the supervisory board and a professional from the outside belongs to each family member in the board. A share of 6% of the surveyed companies did not have any supervisory or consultative body in their structures. Those were enterprises fully managed by families but planning to establish such independent bodies in the future. Ensuring a rational decision-making process and the best management practices is fundamental to the company's position, regardless of whether it is a stock exchange company or not, if the strategic investor is a private equity or whether it remains under the control of the owner's family.

The **family gravity principle** preserves the family nature of the enterprise. Although family businesses should resemble their non-family counterparts in terms of the corporate governance structure and take advantage of opportunities for professional growth, they must remember not to lose what makes them unique and is their source of competitive advantage over other entities, namely maintaining and increasing the family social capital—internal and external. This phenomenon is called the gravity of a family and determines the long-term success of the business. The surveyed enterprises usually have one key family member (up to a maximum of three) occupying a central position in the organisation bodies (management or supervisory boards). These people personify the corporate identity and adapt different interests to the clearly defined values and shared vision (family and business). They focus not on quarterly results but on the next generation of leaders. They guard the strategy in the centre of which there are employees, clients and social responsibility. They are the face of their organisations, have strong personalities and charisma, gather talented individuals around themselves and are able to motivate them.

Enterprises with a transparent and substantive structure of corporate governance and with substantial social capital resources of the family do not have problems with gaining leaders from or outside the family. All candidates should be assessed according to their competences, development potential and value system. The most desirable competences necessary to achieve organisational success are: strategic orientation, knowledge of the market and sector, marketing orientation and focus on the needs of target customers, orientation on results, the ability to interact, having influences and networks of extensive interpersonal relationships, fulfilling a leadership role in the team and in the process of initiating changes. No less important is the development potential—the ability to change, learn and grow in the direction of performing even more complex and demanding roles that will appear in the future. For the owners' families, the additional competence of a candidate for the leader is understanding the expectations and dynamics of the owner's family, respecting the right of the family generations to apply for employment in the enterprise, social sensitivity and readiness to take actions oriented towards sustainable growth. Empirical studies have shown that the values presented by the candidates are decisive after they meet the competence and development criteria. Exceptional 95% compliance has been detected in the understanding and expression of the corporate ethos by family leaders and professionals from outside the family. A vast majority used the same terminology: respect, integrity, quality, humbleness, passion, modesty, ambitions. In the interviews, the family members emphasised the importance of matching the candidate to the organisational culture of the business. In 40% of the surveyed enterprises, the members of the young generation of the owner's family already occupied lower-level managerial positions. In many cases, they started their business careers outside the family business, achieved successes there, gathered experience and added value to the family business on their return. The best surveyed enterprises decided on a strategy of an early selection of young, talented family, non-family candidates and even such outside the business, and then intensively invested in their competence development. When they achieved the desired competence and cultural maturity, they became formal leaders.

Management succession should follow a formal procedure introduced in the enterprise. The results of the research prove that the most successful plans are those, which follow the formal procedure of an exceptional priority and exceptional compliance discipline, predicting the selection of the best candidate among the group of registered family members, talented non-family workers and professionals from outside the family and the enterprise.

The model enterprises in terms of succession formalisation followed procedures consisting of three stages described in Table 1.

Table 1. The model of management succession in large global enterprises

Stage I. Communication with shareholders		
Communicating the start of succession process, presenting the succession committee appointed by the supervisory board and possible scenarios of the process	Shareholders' meeting to update the company's strategic growth and development plans	Developing the new leader profile based on the vision, strategic goals, strategic plans as well as on other desired competences, development potential and value system
Stage II. Candidate selection		
Preparing and evaluating a list of internal and external candidates for the new leader	Reviewing references and other candidate documents, interviews, initial selection	Reaching an agreement on the choice of one or two finalists, starting negotiations with the selected management successors
Stage III. Successor's integration and professional development		
A trial period, a result plan for the first months of employment, a selection of a new management board	Assessing the new leader, drawing up his/her professional development plan, if necessary, a result plan for the next two years	Discussion and decision on the renewal of the contract with the leader

Source: C. Fernández-Aráoz, S. Iqbal, J. Ritter, *Leadership Lessons from Great Family Businesses*, "Harvard Business Review" 2015, 93, 4, pp. 82–88.

The supervisory board appoints a succession committee responsible for implementing the succession process in accordance with the adopted procedure. The Committee develops the competence profile of the successor, starts completing the list of internal and external candidates, conducts interviews with the candidates, verifies their references and assesses their competences. After the initial selection, the Committee submits a short list of candidates to the supervisory / consultative board and the management board, which decide on the successor and the family council approves it.

Summary

Overlapping the presented four versions of the succession model in large family enterprises leads to the creation of one holistic model that can and should be a benchmark for the succession plans and activities of specific family enterprises. Its basic structure includes the following processes:

Pre-succession stage

- Socialising the family's young generation towards entrepreneurial orientation, developing their need for professionalism in managerial and business activities as well as their moral and emotional intelligence.
- Creating job opportunities for all young generation members in the family enterprise and encouraging them to benefit from the opportunities by getting them acquainted with **the map of a widely understood family enterprise**.
- Creating a platform for intergenerational communication based on partner dialogue by seniors, in order to maintain the continuity of the process of generating norms and values in the family, as well as in the business, and to modify the business vision and family vision in it, which will be attractive to the young generation (generative families).

Succession stage

- Ensuring independence of the supervisory board or, in the absence thereof, the consultancy / advisory board, which will be obliged to introduce a formal succession procedure in a company with a high priority and a compliance discipline, guaranteeing the selection of the new leader among the best family and non-family candidates based on competence profile criteria. The supervisory board appoints a succession committee that performs the technical activities provided for in the procedure.
- Nurturing the principle of family and its values gravity in order to maintain and increase the family's social capital resources in the enterprise, which are a source of competitive advantage over non-family entities.
- Evaluating the match of a non-family candidate for the new leader to the organisational culture of the company is an additional criterion of his/her choice.
- Developing a senior leader's retirement strategy.
- Managing the competence development of a candidate for the leader.

Post-succession stage

- Frequent assessments of activities and results of the new leader during the trial period of employment by the independent body (a committee or a board).
- Demonstrating support for the ideas and actions of the successor by the outgoing leader and other family members and the board.
- Using the intergenerational competence leverage.

An important conclusion resulting from the review of literature and reflections on the effective succession model in family enterprises is the inevitability of the transformation of managerial families actively involved in business management into ownership families limited only to the supervisory and control functions in multigenerational large family enterprises. The effect of "the gravity of the family and its values" in the enterprise allows to maintain a unique organisational culture based" on the family's moral infrastructure, even in the conditions of the family members' withdrawal from active leadership. The values of the owner's family may continue to set the pattern of behaviours in such organisations.

Therefore, insisting on the narrow definition of a family enterprise, in which the family dominates simultaneously in management and ownership structures for the needs of research and knowledge on functioning family entities is unjustified and inappropriate, as this approach limits family enterprises only to the sector of small and medium-sized enterprises and stands in overt contradiction with the paradigm of growth and organisation development in management and quality sciences. The narrow definition of a family enterprise is anachronistic, detrimental to its image, hindering effective succession processes, guaranteeing financial security for subsequent generations of the family. Thus, the most appropriate definition appears to be that adopted in the USA, Japan and other developed countries which reads that: "it is an enterprise of any legal form, the entire or substantial capital of which is in the possession of the family, at least one of its members exerts a decisive influence on the management or fulfils the managerial function with the intention of permanently maintaining the enterprise in the hands of the family."[10]

Bibliography

Chrisman J., Chua J. H., Sharma P., *Current Trends and Future Directions in Family Business Management Studies: Toward a Theory of the Family Firm*, "Coleman Foundation White Paper Series" 2003.

Chua J. H., Chrisman J. J., Sharma P., *Succession and Non-succession Concerns of Family Firms and Agency Relationship with Nonfamily Managers*, "Family Business Review" 2003, 16, 2.

Fernández-Aráoz C., Iqbal S., Ritter J., *Leadership Lessons from Great Family Businesses*, "Harvard Business Review" 2015, 93, 4.

---

[10]　P. A. Frishkoff, *Understanding Family Business: What Is a Family Business?*, Oregon State University, Austin Family Business Program 1995; W. Popczyk, *Zarządzanie przedsiębiorstwem rodzinnym. Osiągnięcia młodej specjalności w naukach o zarządzaniu w Polsce* [in:] *Stan i perspektywy rozwoju nauk o zarządzaniu. Wybrane problemy*, ed. by A. Zakrzewska-Bielawska, Wydawnictwo Towarzystwa Naukowego Organizacji i Kierownictwa Dom Organizatora, Toruń 2016.

Frishkoff P. A., *Understanding Family Business: What Is a Family Business?*, Oregon State Uniwersity, Austin Family Business Program 1995.

Habbershon T. G., Williams M. L., *A Resource-Based Framework for Assessing the Strategic Advantages of Family Firms*, "Family Business Review" 1999, 12, 1.

Habbershon T. G., Williams M. L., Macmillan I. C., *A Unified Systems Perspective of Family Firm Performance*, "Journal of Business Venturing" 2003, 18.

Hoffman J., Hoelscher M., Sorenson R., *Achieving Sustained Competitive Advantage: A Family Capital Theory*, "Family Business Review" 2006, 19, 2.

Jaffe D., *If You Want Your Family Business to Last Several Generations*, "The Forbes" 2018, www.forbes.com (access: 15 May 2020).

Jaques E., *Requisite Organization: Total System for Effective Managerial Organization and Managerial Leadership for the 21st Century*, Gower, London 1997.

Michaud P., Collette C., Davis J. A., *CEO Succession in the Family Business. A Better Plan for Success*, Cambridge Institute for Family Enterprise, Cambridge (Mass.) 2017.

Popczyk W., *Anthropological Family Type and Its Impact on Succession Planning in Family Businesses: Research Report* [in:] *New Challenges in Economic and Business Development—2019: Incentives for Sustainable Economic Growth*, University of Latvia, Riga 2019.

Popczyk W., *Kapitał społeczny w firmach rodzinnych. Struktura i mechanizm kreowania kapitału rodziny*, "Przedsiębiorczość i Zarządzanie" 2014, 7, 15.

Popczyk W., *The Structure and Creating of Family Social Capital in Business* [in:] *New Challenges of Economic and Business Development*, University of Latvia, Riga 2018.

Popczyk W., *Zarządzanie przedsiębiorstwem rodzinnym. Osiągnięcia młodej specjalności w naukach o zarządzaniu w Polsce* [in:] *Stan i perspektywy rozwoju nauk o zarządzaniu. Wybrane problemy*, ed. by A. Zakrzewska-Bielawska, Wydawnictwo Towarzystwa Naukowego Organizacji i Kierownictwa Dom Organizatora, Toruń 2016.

Spencer S., *Beyond the Family Tree: Succession Planning for Family Businesses*, 2010, www.spencerstuart.com (access: 15 May 2020).

Wood C., *The Surprising Stats about Succession in Family Business*, "All Strategy" 2018, https://www.allstrategy.net/the-surprising-stats-about-succession-in-family-business/ (access: 15 May 2020).

Management of Family Businesses in View of the Challenges of Modern Economy

Agnieszka Thier, Ph.D. https://orcid.org/0000-0002-5915-2071
Cracow University of Economics

Prof. Marcin Łuszczyk, Ph.D. https://orcid.org/0000-0001-7337-0668
Opole University of Technology

Abstract

This paper is poised to present the issue of family businesses and the specific role they play in the modern economy as well as to describe the ways in which those businesses deal with the challenges of modern civilisation. Among numerous issues related to the functioning and development of the researched sector, the author focused on the following: the definition, functioning and tasks dealt with by family businesses, the number, the structure as well as the social and economic significance of such firms in comparison to other countries, succession within family businesses, exemplary oldest and largest family businesses in the world, life cycle stages of family businesses as well as the determinants of their development and the directions thereof. Finally, the main challenges faced by those businesses in Poland and the European Union. The argument has been supported by statistical data and the results of questionnaires.

Keywords: family business, functions of family businesses, succession in family businesses, external and internal factors of family business development, life cycle of a family business, a new business model

Introduction

A family business is the oldest and the most popular form of economic activity. Within the framework of centrally managed economy, with the predominant presence of state-owned enterprises, the role of family businesses was marginal. Fortunately, this is becoming a thing of the past, both in Poland as well as in other Eastern European former socialist states. In the broad perspective, family businesses constitute 80% of all enterprises in the USA and Canada, approximately 75% in the EU, and 36–40% in Poland. The latter figure is still on the rise.[1] According to other statistics, family businesses account for approximately 66% of enterprises in the world, employing 80% of total workforce.[2]

This paper is poised to present the specific attributes and functions of family businesses as well as some issues that emerged in the directions of their development over the past few years.[3] It appears those businesses have to face the growing consequences of the 3rd and 4th industrial revolutions (information and digital) as well as other new challenges of civilisation.

The substance and the functions of family businesses in the economy

The substance of a family business consists in the conjunction of two factors, a family and a firm, that is a union of two separate environments represented by business and family life.[4] A family is a social institution involved in the functioning of a household while a firm is an economic entity that engages in business. It is independent in legal and economic terms, and its function is to manufacture products or provide services to external customers. Despite their diversity, those two environments or subsystems are mutually connected. That is because, as Sigismund Freud put it, the relations between love and work must be in balance. Hence, a specific feature of a family business is the concentration of property, control and key management positions in running such a business in the hands of a single family.

In terms of terminology, *family enterprise* is by far a more common name than *family business*. However, in common language, the words "enterprise" and "firm" are used interchangeably, which is not always proper. That is because "the firm" has two denotations; the logo, i.e. the trademark (by the commercial code) and the enterprise whose owner is also the manager or a member of the board, i.e. an entrepreneur. Hence, although that name is associated with a family enterprise it has not much in common with a large joint-stock company. The owners/stockholders of the latter with dispersed shareholders have negligible, or even no influence on the decisions of the board represented by hired managers.

---

[1]   A. Lewandowska, E. Więcek-Janka, A. Hadryś-Nowak, M. Wojewoda, *Model 5 poziomów definicyjnych firm rodzinnych. Podstawy metodyczne i wyniki badań firm rodzinnych w Polsce*, Instytut Biznesu Rodzinnego, Poznań 2016, pp. 12, 21.

[2]   J. Jeżak, *Rozwój przedsiębiorczości rodzinnej w Polsce na tle tendencji światowych*, "Przegląd Organizacji" 2016, 4, p. 53.

[3]   A. Thier, *Przedsiębiorstwa rodzinne* [in:] R. Borowiecki, B. Siuta-Tokarska, A. Thier, K. Żmija, *Rozwój małych i średnich przedsiębiorstw w Polsce wobec wyzwań gospodarki XXI wieku*, Uniwersytet Ekonomiczny w Krakowie, Kraków 2018, pp. 168–260.

[4]   J. Jeżak, W. Popczyk, A. Winnicka-Popczyk, *Przedsiębiorstwo rodzinne. Funkcjonowanie i rozwój*, Difin, Warszawa 2004, p. 20.

Although the notion of a family business is relatively easy to recognise in common language, yet it proves to be hard to understand in the statistics and publications due to diverse organisation and legal frameworks enterprises may have. Besides, it is not always easy to identify their owners. What is more, in practice the criteria for identification of family enterprises are not uniform and they vary between the authors and with the purpose of identification. For that reason, depending on the adopted criteria, the number of such enterprises and their share in the total of enterprises in a region or a country may differ substantially. In the definition of a family enterprise, the organisational and legal framework is not much of substance, yet the main criterion is the degree of engagement of a family in running the business. The capital aspect plays the major role, that is to say a family must be the owner or a majority stakeholder in the business.

Going further, apart from the stake of family members in the assets, their part in supervision and management is also considered. Hence, a *narrow* definition assumes a majority stake, strategic control and full management to be in the hands of a family, as well as a multi-generation succession. *Indirect* definitions take into account control shares, exercising strategic control and taking part in enterprise management as well as envisaging family succession. *Broad* definitions speak only of a substantial family stake, minimum strategic control and no anticipation of succession, i.e. the involvement of the family in the operation of the enterprise and management are negligible. In extreme cases, the self-assessment of management, i.e. identification with the family enterprise becomes a major criterion as it appears that quite frequently young entrepreneurs do not admit that, or are reluctant to admit it. In the USA alone, more than a half of family enterprises are identified with the broad definitions which accounts for their large share in the total of enterprises. However, for many authors multi--generation management of an enterprise is a prerequisite as it makes impact on strategic decisions. Caring for enterprise goodwill is another important feature.

Hence, it is worth selecting three criteria defining a family enterprise: ownership and management, family succession and organisational culture. In practical terms, it is difficult to come up with a succinct and clear measure, yet some attempts have been made. To give an example, SFI (Substantial Family Influence) indicator proposed by Sabina Klein[5] or F-PEC (Family—Power, Experience and Culture Scale) includes succession and organisational culture of a family enterprise.[6] In Poland, the SFI factor has already been applied as a sum of three coefficients: family stake in the business, participation in the supervisory board and the Board of an enterprise.[7]

---

[5] S. B. Klein, *Family Business in Germany. Significance and Structure*, "Family Business Review" 2000, 3, pp. 157–181.

[6] M. Stradomski, *Finansowanie obce firm rodzinnych na rynku niedoskonałym*, PWE, Warszawa 2010, p. 45.

[7] J. Wieczorek, A. Wyzuj, *Charakterystyka finansowa firm rodzinnych*, "Debiuty Naukowe Wyższej Szkoły Bankowej" 2015, 15.

In a family enterprise, two or more family members own at least 51% stake in the business, and at least one of them holds a key managerial position, which they try to bequeath to the next generation.[8] In turn, the frequently quoted definition by Pricewater Coopers is quite similar, yet it highlights the fact that family members constitute a majority in the Board and they operate the enterprise on a day-to-day basis. The intention of keeping the enterprise in the hands of a family is written in the Articles of Association of the Institute of Family Enterprises and supported by the Polish Agency for Entrepreneurship Development. The author of this paper condones the narrow definition. It is worth mentioning that there are other definitions in use and we wish to present one of them, which has been based on the succession criterion and has been applied in the empirical research in Poland. The definition is structured on five definition levels for family enterprises:[9]

1. Multi-generation family enterprise (at least for the second generation),
2. A family enterprise with a clear intent of succession (at the threshold of succession).
3. A one-generation family enterprise (at least one owner engaged in operational management).
4. An enterprise considered to be family type by the owners (forming identity of a family enterprise).
5. An enterprise with a potential to become a family enterprise as it is owned by a family (property of a natural person to be inherited by the children coming of age).

Family enterprises fulfil diverse **functions and tasks**. A large number of such enterprises is conducive to employment and the generation of GDP. The foremost function entails a long-term objective which is sustaining property and bequeathing it to the generations to come. That particular function is important not just for families, but also for the development of the national economy. Other functions and macroeconomic features include the following:

- making use of the concentration of assets and power for increasing fixed assets by way of prudent investment decisions;
- operating in market niches and realising special orders;
- building resilience to economic downturns and crises in the closest environment and making a contribution to the stabilisation of the local economy;
- caring for the brand and goodwill which translates into a high quality of products and loyalty of suppliers and customers;
- building a specific enterprise culture including integrity, care for tradition, CSR;
- overall engagement in social activity, sponsoring local initiatives and giving support to charities.

---

[8] D. Jaffe, *Working with Ones You Love: Conflict Resolution and Problem Solving Strategies for Successful Business*, Conari Press, Berkeley 1990; W. Piekarski, J. Rudzińska, *Znaczenie sukcesji w polskich firmach rodzinnych*, "Logistyka" 2012, 4, p. 1200.

[9] A. Lewandowska, E. Więcek-Janka, A. Hadryś-Nowak, M. Wojewoda, *Model 5 poziomów...*, pp. 17–18.

In turn, the macroeconomic and social functions and features of family enterprises can be listed as follows:

- integrating the enterprise sphere with that of a family, i.e. merging professional and family matters;
- generating the image of the company in keeping with the tradition and family values;
- quite frequent transforming of an enterprise into a family hub;
- providing a family structure to the enterprise irrespective of the characteristics of the environment;
- larger responsibility of the enterprise owners for the family, workers and local community; greater care for the workers and their families;
- providing jobs to those family members who have little prospects for employment elsewhere.

All in all, the functions of family enterprises listed above can be considered beneficial and positive. Nonetheless, such enterprises may breed various kinds of trouble such as conflicts among family members, nepotism and emotional reactions, alienation of those workers who do not belong to the family, weaker innovation and creativity, entering the grey zone (hiring workers without contracts, cooking the books, tax evasion) which is particularly common in small service companies. Innovation in small family enterprises is fairly rare, especially under the circumstances when the production is stable and there is a steady demand for it. Still, it is known that many patents and inventions originate in such enterprises. Garage firms are a special case; they are accommodated in very modest facilities, yet with their innovation potential they may find place in large hi-tech companies or in the manufacture of not necessarily modern products which belong to the high opportunity category on the market.

The importance of family enterprises in Polish economy

According to the estimates of a team of University of Łódź scholars, among 2831.5 thousand economic entities registered by the Main Census Office as of 1 January 2010, 1172.4 thousand belonged to the family enterprise category (41.4%). In view of the authors of this paper, this figure is much lower than the statistics for Germany (78%) and other European countries. The total number of enterprises in Poland should be considered with caution, since the current figures released by MCO quote for that period not 2.83 million, but almost 3.91 million economic entities (Table 1). Once we deduct state-owned companies, State Treasury partnerships, co-operatives and foreign capital partnerships, the final figure will drop by no more than 200 thousand.

Table 1. National economy entities registered by the REGON register in Poland 1990–2016 (as of 31 December 2016)

Specification	1990	2000	2015	2016	2016 as percentage of 2000	Structure in % 1990	Structure in % 2016
State owned enterprises	8,454	2,268	151	144	6.3	0.7	0.0
Total partnerships;	–	464,018	746,038	791,688	170.6	–	18.7
commercial law partnerships	36,267	159,660	456,910	501,056	313.8	3.0	11.8
including foreign capital entities	–	43,737	85,552	91,125	208.3	–	0.2
Civil law partnerships	–	302,717	286,759	288,209	95.2	–	6.8
Co-operatives	18,575	19,011	17,561	17,633	92.8	1.5	0.4
Natural persons companies	1,135,592	2,500,952	2,972,144	2,968,786	118.7	93.2	70.1
Other entities	–	699,359	448,515	459,440	65.7	–	10.8
Total	121,839	3,685,608	4,184,409	4,237,691	115.0	100.0	100.0

Source: prepared by the author based on MCO yearbooks.

On the other hand, according to the estimates of the Family Business Institute of Poznań, the share of family enterprises which claim to belong to that category is at 36%, which is lower than the Łódź assessment. A similar estimate (36%) was provided by the State Agency for Entrepreneurship Development (SAED). Yet, their estimate included solely the sector of small and medium companies, which translated into 219 thousand of family enterprises.[10] A similar index of 33–35% for that sector may be found in other publications.[11] Once the 33–35% index is adopted for the total number of economic entities (following the author's update), there would be 1.25–1.33 million family enterprises as of 2010. This estimate would correspond to the University of Łódź figure. There would be 1.32–1.45 million family enterprises as of 2016, and once we adopt higher growth dynamics, that figure would climb to over 1.5 million. Hence, it might be assumed that there are almost 2 million family enterprises on the market.

---

[10] *Firmy rodzinne w polskiej gospodarce – szanse i wyzwania*, PARP, Warszawa 2009.

[11] A. Surlej, K. Wach, *Przedsiębiorstwa rodzinne wobec wyzwań sukcesji*, Difin, Warszawa 2010, p. 7; *Barometr Firm Rodzinnych*, 2014, http://firmyrodzinne.pl/ (access: 10 June 2020).

Family enterprises in Poland can be predominantly found in the sector of small and medium companies. Unlike the western European countries, medium and large companies note merely minority holding. As of 2015, the structure of family enterprises by the number of employed workers was as follows (figures provided by the Institute for Family Business):

- Micro enterprises (mostly run by natural persons, up to 9 workers): 81%
- Small enterprises (10–15 workers): 12%
- Medium enterprises (51–250 workers): 6%
- Large enterprises: 1%

The structure of family enterprises by their legal framework is also important. Clearly, the largest share belongs to natural persons performing business activities (over 70%), and then to partnerships of natural persons (see Table 2). The differences in figures of successive studies are not as much attributable to the methods of assessment but rather to the growth of that sector of economy in time, particularly to the transformation of enterprises of natural persons into partnerships.

Table 2. The structure of family enterprises by their legal form criterion (in %)

Specification	Łódź Institute study of 2009	Institute for Family Business study of 2015
Natural persons enterprises engaged in economic activity	85.5	70.5
Civil law partnerships of natural persons	8.2	13.6
Limited Liability Enterprise	3.1	10.1
General partnerships	2.7	4.7
Joint-stock partnerships	0.2	0.2
Other entities	0.3	0.9
Total	100.0	100.0

Source: J. Jeżak, W. Popczyk, A. Winnicka-Popczyk, *Przedsiębiorstwo rodzinne. Funkcjonowanie i rozwój*, Difin, Warszawa 2004, p. 31; A. Lewandowska, E. Więcek-Janka, A. Hadryś-Nowak, M. Wojewoda, *Model 5 poziomów definicyjnych firm rodzinnych. Podstawy metodyczne i wyniki badań firm rodzinnych w Polsce*, Instytut Biznesu Rodzinnego, Poznań 2016., pp. 27–28.

Table 3 presents the structure of family enterprises in Poland and the EU by the number of workers. Clearly such enterprises are much smaller in Poland.

Table 3. The structure of family enterprises by headcount in %

Number of employees	Poland	European Union
Over 50 workers	77	39.5
50–249	20	32.5
250–1,000	2	16.5
over 1,000	1	11.5
Total	100	100.0

Source: *Barometr Firm Rodzinnych*, 2017, http://firmyrodzinne.pl/ (access: 10 June 2019), p. 28.

Table 4 presents the sectorial breakdown of family enterprises. It is apparent that in comparison to non-family companies, family enterprises are mostly engaged in industry and commerce, and rarely in services. In addition, they promote progress and innovation in their manufacturing activity.

Table 4. The structure of family enterprises in Poland (in %)

Specification	University of Łódź study from 2009	The Institute of Family Business study from 2015
Industrial processing	8.4	16.3
Construction	5.2	11.9
Commerce	39.3	32.3
Services	46.9	–
Other branches	0.2	39.5
Total	100.0	100.0

Note: Including "professional activity" 10.6%

Sources: prepared by the author based on previously quoted publications.

As shown by the European Family Business statistics, family enterprises provide 50–80% of jobs in most EU member states. That figure is much lower in Poland, and it pertains mostly to the sector of small and medium companies. According to Polish Agency of Development of Entrepreneurship, those companies employ approximately 1.3 million people, i.e. 21% of the people employed. There are some indications that that index has already reached 33%. As shown by the University of Łódź report of 2009, in that year 50% of family enterprises chose not to hire external workers. Another 37.4% of companies hired 1 to 5 persons (just like micro companies) and merely 7% of companies gave jobs to minimum 10 workers. Another conclusion drawn from the research shows that, as a rule, family enterprises hire more workers than similar non-family companies, and that employment tends to be more stable.

The most difficult issue is to assess the share of family enterprises in the generation of domestic product. Early assessments show approximately 10.5% of GDP within 2009–2010 timeframe. Apparently this figure is much higher now with the growing number of family enterprises in the medium and large companies sector.

Succession in family enterprises

Generational transition among property holders and the changes in family enterprise management are the most difficult issues, just like the launch and growth stage, for the survival of an enterprise. In those companies the time comes to cede power to a younger generation at a certain stage of the life cycle of an enterprise. In most cases the transition occurs when the owner reaches retirement. Quite frequently this is a critical moment due to the threats and opportunities involved in the change of management and possibly in the system of management. In family enterprises, succession consists in yielding property and power by the owner to a chosen successor. In other words, it is a process poised at ensuring the continuation of a family enterprise or, to put it bluntly, survival on the market. Succession brings changes to the ownership structure and alters the style of management despite the fact that the power still remains with the family. The transfer of property, power and knowledge to the younger generation should be conducted so as to uphold the values which are important for the family and the branch of business.[12]

An entrepreneur who is at the helm of a family enterprise should be aware of the significance of succession and prepare the roadmap for the transfer of property and power as well as knowledge to his successor. That is because the absence of such a plan may breed chaos and cause slowdown in production and sales, and in the extreme cases bring an enterprise down. Nonetheless, numerous family enterprises do not have such plans due to negligence or the deference of this issue for later, the lack of interest among the potential successors (a succession plan might induce them to take over) as well as the insufficient qualification of successors. It is also important to be aware of the fact that a succession is not a quick event or a ceremony of bestowing power to the successor, but rather a process which may take a few years. That process should be conducted in line with the changes taking place in the environment and consider prerequisites for the functioning of the family so that to prepare a new leader to run a business.

The European Commission has been working on the legislation to provide uniform succession regulations. Such work is necessary due to the fact that within the EU, about

---

[12]   A. Lewandowska, *Kody wartości, czyli jak efektywnie przejść przez sukcesję w firmach rodzinnych*, Lewandowska i Partnerzy, Poznań 2015, p. 80.

20–40% of enterprises are taken over by new owners every decade, and each year over 650 thousand companies with approximately 3 million workers are affected. For that reason, in 1993, the European Commission organised the First EU Symposium on the subject of generational change in family enterprises, and it followed with the guidelines for property transfer in 1994. In 2003, the EC published the Handbook of Good Practice in Transferring Ownership of Enterprises. Finally, in 2007, the *Expert Group on Family Business* was set up. In the opinion of the EC, the young generation is not much interested in taking over family businesses. For that reason, in planning succession the option of selling an enterprise to its workers or a third party should be taken into account. In Poland, the National Council for Entrepreneurship at the Ministry of Economy has put succession on its agenda. In 2016, the Polish Agency for Entrepreneurship Development launched a pilot project to support succession in family enterprises. The Institute of Family Business and the Firm Initiative Association have been discussing the issues of succession with a view of making family entrepreneurship more popular.

There are many family enterprises with a long record in countries with stable economy and a firm political situation. The oldest family enterprises can be found in Japan; the Kongo Gumi construction enterprise has survived over 40 generations since its foundation in 578, and Hoteliers Ryokan Houshi Onsen Chojukan have been operating since 718. There are over 3 thousand companies with more than a 200-year tradition in that country. In France, the vineyard and wine shop Chateau Goulaine and Italian Foundry of Bells Marinelli have been in business since 1000.

Table 5 presents vital information about 15 large family enterprises which are either familiar to Polish people or have their subsidiaries in Poland, e.g. Aldi, Auchan, Santander Bank, Fiat, Mittal. The shares of most companies, especially those in the motor industry, are traded publicly. It poses a threat of a hostile takeover, yet many companies show incredible resilience to economic crises, a respect for tradition and upholding of family values.

Table 5. Examples of the largest family enterprises in the world (as of 2010)

Enterprise name	Founders	Country	Year of foundation	Industry	Employment— thous. of workers	Annual revenue— billion USD
Wal-Mart Stores	Walbon	USA	1962	Discount stores	2,100	380
Toyota Motor Corporation	Toyota	Japan	1937	Motor industry	320	260
Ford Motor Corporation	Ford	USA	1903	Motor industry	250	175
Koch Industries	Koch	USA	1918	Conglomerate	80	110

Enterprise name	Founders	Country	Year of foundation	Industry	Employment—thous. of workers	Annual revenue—billion USD
Samsung Group	Lee	South Korea	1938	Conglomerate	270	200
Arcelor Mittal	Mittal[b]	Luxemburg	2006	Steel foundries	300	110
Banco Santander	Botin	Spain	1857	Banking	150	90
PSA Peugeot Citroen	Peugeot	France	1810 1970	Motor industry	210	90
Fiat	Angelli	Italy	1899	Motor industry	180	90
BMW[c]	Quandt	Germany	1913	Motor industry	110	85
Hyunday Motor	Chung	South Korea	1967	Motor industry	75	75
Robert Bosch GmbH	Bosch	Germany	1886	Car parts	270	70
Groupe Auchan	Mullier	France	1997	Retail trade	190	55

[a] Food and electronics. [b] Lakshmi N. Mittal of India founded Mittal Steel partnership in 1976, and Arcelor partnership in 2002. In 2006, foundries from 60 countries merged; operating capacity 100 million tons of steel. [c] BayerischeMotorenWerke AG.

Source: *Przedsiębiorstwo rodzinne w gospodarce globalnej*, ed. by R. Sobiecki, Szkoła Główna Handlowa, Warszawa 2014, pp. 224–225.

Determinants of the development of family enterprises and the directions of development

In the analysis of the determinants of company development, one should consider the resources, links to the environment as well as the sources of funding investment projects. It is recommended to analyse the stimulating or impeding factors with a holistic approach, e.g. the *enterprise life cycle*. There are three stages in a typical cycle: launch and formation, maturity and stabilisation, and a decline, i.e. disintegration or a hostile takeover which translates into a legal (or even physical) liquidation or a rebirth. The life cycle of a family enterprise is somewhat different due to a different impact which the ownership exerts on the enterprise development. That is attributable to the connection between the owner's life cycle and the life cycle of his family. This connection is not always discernible. Hence, there are four stages of a family enterprise life cycle:[13]

1. **Pioneer stage**, the foundation of the company due to the involvement, enterprise and innovation of its owner;

---

[13] K. Leszczewska, *Przedsiębiorstwa rodzinne. Specyfika modeli biznesu*, Difin, Warszawa 2016, pp. 61–63.

2. **Growth stage**, visible especially after the takeover of the company by the successor; sometimes a transformation from a natural person business to a limited liability company takes place;
3. **Maturity stage**, sometimes divided into sub-stages of co-operation, control and formalisation. This is the stage of setting up procedures and making management more professional by organisational and legal changes, as well as hiring people from the outside of the family. Usually it lasts to the 2nd generation;
4. **Decline stage**, entailing a crisis of power or a successful succession. Usually in the 3rd generation by evolving into a joint-stock company beyond the power of the family, or sale. Takeover by the successor and passage to the 4th generation of a family enterprise are less likely.

There are manifold internal factors with varying impact that may stimulate the growth of a company. It is worth analysing them and / introducing them into the development programme or principles of operating management. Some of them have been listed below. They are relatively well known, yet regrettably rarely implemented in a consistent way:
- Formation and implementation of the development strategy giving preference to long-term objectives and company sustainability;
- Greater focus on the product and service quality, goodwill and customer care;
- Development of company's own research capacity;
- Intensification of the provision of options for the development of qualifications;
- Streamlining the structure of the company (fewer levels in the hierarchy) and introducing project teams to make management more flexible;
- More open attitude to the environment, launching on more distant markets, more aggressive import of supplies (which seems to contradict prudence and risk aversion);
- Taking part in international fairs, closer co-operation with foreign partners;
- Extending fixed assets base and greater propensity to invest (in comparison to non-family enterprises);
- Making decisions to use robots, manipulators and other artificial intelligence devices, or preparing the implementation of such in the near future;
- Offering the service of purchased products, also in the time of their exploitation (with the use of a calculation cloud);
- Earlier designation of a successor.

The internal factors that lower productivity or impede the development of a family enterprise are as follows:
- The absence of a precise mission statement and strategy of development due to the insufficient involvement or weakness of the owner;
- Exaggerated cultivation of tradition by overt conservatism and risk aversion;
- Difficulties in finding firm/family life balance;

- Insufficient professional background and experience and authoritarian style of management by the owner;
- Family conflicts in day-to-day management of the enterprise and during the succession period;
- Nepotism by giving preference to family members to man managerial positions, incompetent people in key positions;
- Excessive wish to retain control which impedes the use of external sources of financing;
- No confidence in staff members and advisors who are not family, even under the circumstances when this is a prerequisite to enterprise development;
- Low innovation of the managerial staff attributable to complacency and routine;
- Entering the grey zone by lowering turnover, pumping up expenses and hiring staff illegally without the necessary contracts.

External factors include changes in the international situation or state economic policy, which may be dramatic or unexpected. Sometimes those changes are beneficial, e.g. new preferential subsidies, loans and loan guarantees for environmental protection or innovation. However, entrepreneurs are more likely to complain about frequent changes in taxation, muddled or complicated tax procedures than tax increases which are announced in good time and provided with a rational explanation.

The external factors which the entrepreneurs consider detrimental include the following:
- High cost of labour, in particular the cost of social insurance and other charges involved in employment (a positive change was stopping the criticism of increasing remuneration by raising the minimum wage not just owing to the fact that it compared negatively to the pay rates offered in western European countries, but also it was necessary in view of the aggravating shortage of workforce);
- Insufficient capital for investment attributable to high rates for bank credit;
- Inflexible labour law and inflexible employment procedures;
- Unfair access to support programmes and insufficient information about the available forms of financial support;
- Difficulties in collecting debts, particularly on the part of small companies;
- Competition from the grey zone by offering cheaper products and services;
- Economic barriers attributable to the changes in EU legislation and aggressive competition on the international markets.

Regrettably, the set of detrimental factors is quite varied and extensive. Poland has started investigating liquidations of companies due to the wrong decisions of the owner or the manager, and the results of research are presented in Table 6. As shown by the study results, wrong managerial decisions are mainly attributable to the absence of a company development strategy, then the lack of experience and an insufficient appreciation of innovation. Table 7 presents the challenges to be faced by family enterprises both in Poland and in the EU member states. The survey was made by KPMG in the second half of 2017 and it shows the top challenge to be the rising costs of labour, followed by political instability, changing regulations and growing competition. Within the EU, we see a shortage of qualified workers (Poland is going to experience it shortly), growing competition and the rising costs of labour.

Table 6. The reasons for liquidation of small companies due to wrong decisions taken by the owner

Specification	Breakdown in %
Absence of vision and strategy	20.2
Lack of experience in the sector and management skills	13.5
Ignoring the importance of innovation	10.2
Absence of knowledge management	9.7
Reluctance to consult external advisors	9.7
Overt optimism and propensity to take risk	9.3
Mistakes at the launch stage	7.7
Absence of logistics management	6.7
Owner's personal problems	6.6
Reluctance to resign from the set goals	6.4
Total	100.0

Source: *Wyzwania i perspektywy zarządzania w małych i średnich przedsiębiorstwach*, ed. by M. Matejun, C. H. Beck, Warszawa 2010, p. 203.

Table 7. Challenges and the most difficult issues faced by family enterprises in Poland and the EU

Specification	Poland	The EU	Poland when EU = 100
Rising labour costs	60	32	193.7
Political instability	41	30	136.7
Growing competition	35	37	67.6
Acquisition of qualified staff	29	43	67.4
Rising taxation	27	10	270.0
Management instruments			
Formal Board	51	70	72.9
Family council	29	33	87.9
Remuneration principles to managers from the outside	30	30	100.0

Source: *Barometr...*, 2017, pp. 4–36.

Rising payroll costs and other charges involved in employment, in particular social insurance and Labour Protection costs, are the most acute issues. That is attributable to declining human resources, in particular the shortage of highly qualified workers. As the society is ageing and the economy moves into the fourth generation of industry characterised by computerisation and automation based on artificial intelligence, there are new challenges and higher demands for the infrastructure and HR management. On the whole, family enterprises in Poland are much smaller than those in Western Europe, which is another factor impeding the implementation of new technologies. The situation is complicated even further by political instability and the absence of satisfactory government solutions in the area of employment of foreigners and admission of refugees. To supplement the information included in the bottom part of Table 7, it is worth quoting the results of research by Blackpartners conducted among small family enterprises. The outcomes show an even lower index of enterprises having a formal board or family council. It might be concluded that the entrepreneurs are not always aware of the fact that the functioning of management instruments does not rely only on the size of a company but it is a contributing factor to the development of any family enterprise.

New directions for the development of family enterprises in Poland do not solely reflect the global trends in economic development. Neither do they merely mirror the transition of Central-Eastern European countries towards the market economy. They also prove—what is most significant—the self-organisation of the family business sector. Most family enterprises are registered with the organisations catering for such entities (approximately 70%). There are already a few organisations dealing with family business and they are becoming more and more proficient in monitoring the functioning of family enterprises, postulating amendments to economic and family legislation, organising training workshops in building the strategy of corporate development, the principles of financing development, CSR, etc. There are many indications that Poland excels in the area of NGO activity, bringing to life social economy and developing civil society. The foregoing aspects make a certain impact on the engagement of family enterprises and their associations both in upgrading the system of company management and upholding business ethics.

In terms of changes in the structure of the branches of industry, the main direction of changes may be defined as increasing the share of the production plants, especially industrial ones. Increasing the role of industry is not just the consequence of the EU and domestic plans of reindustralisation of the economy,[14] but also of

---

[14] In the mid-20th century, highly industrialised countries moved to the post-industrial stage. At that time, the share of the service sector in employment and generation of domestic product reached 60–70%. As a result, the share of farming and mining, and also of the processing industries declined. By no means does the term "post-industrial stage" stand for the decline of industry—even though obsolete plants are being shut down—but it diminishes its relative significance. More advanced machinery and products are prerequisite for better provision of more and more diversified services, and they are manufactured

the fact that remuneration, qualifications and the character of work are continually appealing for seeking employment in a factory. Those factors, parallel to the challenges of technological development and demand for innovation, encourage entrepreneurs to launch production in advanced industries, i.e. mostly in the electromechanical and chemical industries which are considered to be the carriers of technical development for the whole economy. It has been demonstrated that many small and medium enterprises launch the manufacture of modern electronic and electrotechnical products, including control and measurement equipment for the industry and other hi-tech products. In turn, other companies focus on the manufacture of "high opportunity" products which are characterised by fair price and high demand. As a rule, they are customised products matching the expectations of certain consumers found in niche markets.

The most significant changes are to be noticed in the attitudes of younger-generation family enterprise owners. There are several reasons for this: better education and foreign internships, a social atmosphere that promotes work on one's own and entrepreneurship, the development in the organisation of family business. The most conspicuous changes are taking place within the business model, i.e. the way of doing business and managing a company. Needless to say, there are still conservative attitudes, particularly in micro-companies, yet changes are both gradual and decisive. Although the new business model has not been researched thoroughly, it is possible to describe its manifestations:

- Greater importance of customer relations;
- Faster and more active reaction to changes in the external environment, and more anticipatory attitudes;
- More attention to organisational, product and process (technological) innovation and the emergence of social innovation;
- Networking and work in the industrial clusters;
- Propagation of CSR.

The government and territorial institutions have been trying to provide support to family business. Yet, there are numerous postulates for streamlining the process of family enterprise management which are forwarded to government institutions and branch chambers or the associations of those companies. Table 8 presents the results of a survey in that area conducted by the auditing firm KPMG in Poland and 25 other EU member states.

---

by the industry. That is why programmes of reindustralisation were launched related to the Fourth Industrial Revolution (digital), i.e. Industry 4.0.

Table 8. Postulated changes in the economic policy towards family enterprises (in % of indications)

Specification	Poland	European Union	Poland when EU = 100
Simpler tax regulations	36	27	133.1
Lower taxes	33	32	103.1
Lowering non-payroll cost of labour	31	27	114.8
Facilitating taxation and procedures during succession	22	25	88.0
More flexible legislation on the labour market	18	39	46.2
Better education and training	17	15	113.3
Lowering administrative load	10	33	30.3
Easier access to finance	10	9	111.1
State support in seeking finance	10	4	250.0
Development of infrastructure	6	18	33.3

Source: *Barometr...*, 2017, p. 22.

The tone of the postulates of Polish enterprises is similar to the opinions voiced by Western-European countries. A lower percentage of indications suggesting making the labour market in Poland more flexible is surprising since it is clearly demanded by entrepreneurs of non-family enterprises (that need is not so strongly supported by small family businesses). Even greater disparity of indications was noted in the need for the development of the infrastructure. This might be the consequence of the fact that small companies predominate in Poland, and their requirements in the area of technical infrastructure and automation are lower.

Conclusions

In summary, the following issues are the key problems in the management of family enterprises and their development:
- Proper structure of the financing of investment projects;
- Preparation of the successor and orderly succession process including the transfer of property, power and knowledge,
- Making enterprise management more professional in line with care for tradition and company sustainability with reducing the influence of family conflicts on company management.

Observing the trends in the development of family enterprises to date, both in Poland and in Western Europe, it might be most convenient to envisage that within that category small companies registered as a natural person engaged in economic activity will prevail (the index reaching 80%). The number of natural person enterprises will oscillate around 3 million. That is because even though new companies are continually being founded, every year the same number is liquidated or taken over by other entrepreneurs. In case of family businesses, companies are becoming larger and the differences between the Polish and Western European firms are being alleviated gradually. This is followed by a tendency to change the organisational and legal structure, that is, the transformation of natural person establishments into companies, including limited liability companies and—more cautiously—joint-stock companies. It is also connected with the growing openness of family enterprises to cooperation with the environment and the use of external sources of financing.

Bibliography

Barometr Firm Rodzinnych, 2014, 2017, http://firmyrodzinne.pl/ (access: 10 June 2020).

Firmy rodzinne w polskiej gospodarce – szanse i wyzwania, PARP, Warszawa 2009.

Helping the Transfer of Business. A Good Practice Guide of Measures for Supporting the Transfer of Business. New Ownership, European Commission, Brussels 2003.

Jaffe D., *Working with Ones You Love: Conflict Resolution and Problem Solving Strategies for Successful Business*, Conari Press, Berkeley 1990.

Jeżak J., Popczyk W., Winnicka-Popczyk A., *Przedsiębiorstwo rodzinne. Funkcjonowanie i rozwój*, Difin, Warszawa 2004.

Jeżak J., *Rozwój przedsiębiorczości rodzinnej w Polsce na tle tendencji światowych*, "Przegląd Organizacji" 2016, 4.

Klein S. B., *Family Business in Germany. Significance and Structure*, "Family Business Review" 2000, 3.

Leszczewska K., *Przedsiębiorstwa rodzinne. Specyfika modeli biznesu*, Difin, Warszawa 2016.

Lewandowska A., Więcek-Janka E., Hadryś-Nowak A., Wojewoda M., *Model 5 poziomów definicyjnych firm rodzinnych. Podstawy metodyczne i wyniki badań firm rodzinnych w Polsce*, Instytut Biznesu Rodzinnego, Poznań 2016.

Lewandowska A., *Kody wartości, czyli jak efektywnie przejść przez sukcesję w firmach rodzinnych*, Lewandowska i Partnerzy, Poznań 2015.

Piekarski W., Rudzińska J., *Znaczenie sukcesji w polskich firmach rodzinnych*, "Logistyka" 2012, 4.

Przedsiębiorstwo rodzinne w gospodarce globalnej, ed. by R. Sobiecki, Szkoła Główna Handlowa, Warszawa 2014.

Stradomski M., *Finansowanie obce firm rodzinnych na rynku niedoskonałym*, PWE, Warszawa 2010.

Surlej A., Wach K., *Przedsiębiorstwa rodzinne wobec wyzwań sukcesji*, Difin, Warszawa 2010.

Thier A., *Przedsiębiorstwa rodzinne* [in:] R. Borowiecki, B. Siuta-Tokarska, A. Thier, K. Żmija, *Rozwój małych i średnich przedsiębiorstw w Polsce wobec wyzwań gospodarki XXI wieku*, Uniwersytet Ekonomiczny w Krakowie, Kraków 2018.

Wieczorek J., Wyzuj A., *Charakterystyka finansowa firm rodzinnych*, "Debiuty Naukowe Wyższej Szkoły Bankowej" 2015, 15.

Wyzwania i perspektywy zarządzania w małych i średnich przedsiębiorstwach, ed. by M. Matejun, C.H. Beck, Warszawa 2010.

The Development of Instruments for Financial Security Management of Households

Prof. Anzhela Kuznyetsova, Ph.D.   https://orcid.org/0000-0003-3590-7625
Banking University

Prof. Oleksiy Druhov, Ph.D.   https://orcid.org/0000-0003-1987-187X
Banking University

Marta Zvarych, Ph.D. student   https://orcid.org/0000-0002-7367-911X
Banking University

Abstract

The instruments for financial security management of households have been proposed, which are divided into three directions: financial planning (financial plans, financial goals, and financial forecasts), financial saving (reducing unproductive costs), and financial investing (financial products, investment funds, real estate investments). A range of banking products are proposed to increase household activity in saving and investing. Practical recommendations for households during the process of real estate are given. The characteristics and advantages of creating a financial "security buffer" for a household are described. The importance of financial consulting and financial coaching for personal financial security management is presented.

Keywords: financial security, financial instruments, household savings, household investments, financial planning

Introduction

Today the person-centred paradigm of globalisation processes is gaining in popularity, which represents a model focused on maximising the disclosure of each person's potential and society as a whole, creating decent conditions for the realisation of all intellectual, cultural, and creative possibilities of a person. A significant contribution to the study of the issues of financial security has been made by such Ukrainian and foreign scholars as: O. I. Baranovsky, M. Yu. Vorobyov, V. V. Voroshilo, O. O. Dragan, R. G. Snishchenko, L. Tvardovska, K. E. Dynen, A. Atkinson, J. Y. Campbell, A. Finney, D. Hayes. At the same time, it should be noted that despite in-depth investigation of the topic of financial security, mainly the strategy for managing the financial security of the state or enterprise is emphasised, whereby much less attention is paid to performing financial security management of households.

The policy of encouraging financial security management of households should take a prominent place in the state strategies of all countries, since under the current conditions the world economic system is characterised by a propensity for fundamental changes, which affects the well-being of households. However, it is impossible to create a reliable basis for people's living standards without their own participation. Therefore, the aim of the research is to define and develop a series of instruments for financial security management of households.

Working on issues such as personal financial security, investments and retirement savings will help to properly manage the personal capital of a household. The investigation of financial and legal borrowing issues, as well as familiarisation with the features of budget planning will help households to protect themselves against risks.

The necessary actions for ensuring the financial security of households are:[1]

- rational use of financial resources;
- forecasting and planning of costs;
- effective management of the home budget;
- the adoption of optimal and rational decisions in financial matters;
- assessment of expenditures effectiveness.

The instruments for financial security management of households include three directions: financial planning, financial saving and financial investing.

Figure 1. Instruments for personal financial security management

Source: prepared by the author.

---

[1] N. Papusha, *Financial Security of a Person: Genesis*, "Scientific Works of the Kirovohrad National Technical University. Economic Sciences" 2011, 19, pp. 230–234.

Financial planning as a key tool for providing financial security for households

Financial planning is a process of developing financial plans, setting financial goals, defining financial forecasts in order to increase the level of the household's financial security. The precise planning of a home budget, given the economic situation in the country, allows to prioritise spending and control cash flows.

The introduction of household's financial planning is necessary due to a number of reasons: 1) the household's need to be aware of the availability of cash for its life; 2) the ability to synchronise the existing cash flows to ensure financial security; 3) the ability to provide the necessary resources; 4) the ability to use cash resources rationally; 5) the household's control over its own receipts and use of funds.[2]

Personal financial planning involves a series of consecutive steps, namely:
1. definition of own current financial condition;
2. formation of financial goals;
3. identification of alternative strategies for achieving goals;
4. evaluation of alternatives;
5. creation and application of a personal financial plan;
6. revision and improvement of a financial plan.

The rule "50 + 20 + 30" proposed by Alex von Tobel[3] consists in the division of the monthly budget into three parts: the first part—50% of the expenses should be directed to daily needs (food, transport) and payment for utility services or house rent; the second part—20% of expenses are placed into a bank account to a deposit or simply saved and the third one includes 30% of expenses, which remain for entertainments, rest, sports—expenses that exist, and are not necessary but desirable. This scheme of personal budget distribution is valuable in its simplicity and flexibility, since it does not talk about the exact distribution of costs, and the proportion may change for better balancing. In addition, the described scheme favours consistency in managing own funds, which is extremely useful for students, especially when it comes to confidence in one's "tomorrow" and a full-fledged life today.

There is another rule of the so-called "four envelopes," aimed not only to rationally distribute costs, but also to save a certain amount of money. This approach recommends to save 10% of total revenue per month. From the rest of the sum it is necessary to

---

[2]   A. Atkinson, M. Flore-Anne, L. Rabinovichii, J. Yoongii, *Financial Education for Long-term Savings and Investments: Review of Research and Literature*, OECD Working Paperson Finance, Insuranceand Private Pensions, No. 39, OECD Publishing, Paris 2015.

[3]   D. Schawbel, *Alexa Von Tobel: How to Be the Master of Your Financial Future*, "Forbes" 2014, https://www.forbes.com/sites/danschawbel/2014/01/20/alexa-von-tobel-how-to-be-the-master-of-your-financial-future/#6a0e34f74a68 (access: 5 June 2019).

deduct the main and largest items of expenses—utility payments, repayment of credit, payment of tuition and other. The remaining amount of money needs to be divided into four equal parts, each of which is used for expenditure within one week. Exceeding the limit destroys the main idea of this scheme, so it is necessary to keep a weekly amount of the budget. In the case of extra funds remaining at the end of the week, they can be added to the next, or form one more reserve of funds for unforeseen events, such as: repair of equipment, treatment, etc. Thus, this method encourages the planning of personal finances, the rational use of funds and savings of a certain amount of money.

The importance of financial saving in the process of financial security management of households

Households can independently develop tools for ensuring financial security, including in the direction of saving financial resources. Financial saving is the process of optimising the household budget by reducing unproductive costs. In case of unforeseen circumstances, such as: loss of employment, accident, loss of a breadwinner, the household has a chance to continue a normal livelihood by creating the so-called financial "security buffer" in advance. It should be a certain amount of savings that can be used by household members in times of crisis. However, it is important that the funds be sufficient not only for the minimum satisfaction of basic needs, but for a full-fledged life of the household, including the costs for education, entertainment, recreation. It is expedient to create a financial "buffer of security" for a period of minimum 6 months, because during this period the household is able to find a stable source of income: able-bodied people can get a job or open their own business.

To form such a financial "security buffer" firstly it is necessary to calculate the average amount of the household's spending in the last few months that includes all aspects of life of its members: the purchase of food and clothing, payment for housing, car maintenance, tuition, entertainment, etc. The size of the financial "security buffer" may be calculated by multiplying the average monthly costs by the number of months of the planned financial "security buffer." The next stage is the definition of the deductions amount for the formation of a buffer, which can fluctuate in the range of 15–20% of the household's income. As a rule, each household can reduce its monthly spending by at least 20% without abrupt changes in lifestyle, which will not affect its quality. Thus, in a few years, the household can accumulate funds to form a financial "security buffer" that can help to survive easily during financially difficult times and feel more confident in the future.

At the same time, the following rules should be taken into account: the funds forming the given financial "security buffer" should be intact, as much as possible, protected from losses (the optimal option is a deposit in a bank) as it reduces the probability of their depreciation. In any case, the financial "security buffer" is not intended to be stored at home, because there is a risk of spending it on constantly emerging needs or of theft. Regarding the investing of the financial "security buffer" in a variety of financial instruments, this may result in the inability to quickly withdraw funds from investment projects without loss or limiting quick access to these financial resources.

Financial investing by households: New financial products and tools

After planning own financial flows, learning how to save, the household must think about ways to invest their funds. Financial investing is a process of saving financial resources in the form of investments by placing them on the financial market, in investment funds or investing in real estate.

First of all, considerable attention should be paid to the role of banking institutions in the process of financial investing by households as the most popular investment destination among the Ukrainian population is placement in bank deposits.[4] Accordingly, the creation of new banking products and the improvement of existing ones can have a significant impact on households' activity in saving and investing. One of the promising ways of expanding the client base for the bank and raising the level of the population's financial literacy is the involvement of school-age children as potential clients by offering their parents an account for their child.

Such a bank product can be in the form of an individual bank account for children from 6 to 18 years old with the ability to place funds on a deposit account with an attractive interest rate but with a certain limit of the deposit amount. It is imperative to develop an internet-based platform specifically for children, filled with educational videos in the form of cartoons. On this website, children should have the opportunity to use online banking services under adult supervision with a special focus on saving, managing personal finances, choosing a page design to their own taste, receiving virtual rewards for reaching a certain level of deposit value. In addition, banks should occasionally organise creative contests for children, their parents and teachers in order to disseminate information about this banking product.

An important aspect in this process of children's financial education is the involvement of parents who must have access to their child's account. Thus, there is a comprehensive coverage of the child's environment, which helps to master the peculiarities of personal finances.

In the case of families expecting to have a child, which involves changes in their financial situation, it would be advisable to create a banking product in the form of an investment deposit with a certain purpose. Accordingly, a young spouse could save money for a future child with the help of a financial intermediary, who in turn, would transfer these funds to investment and innovation projects of companies operating in

---

4   T. Odintsova, *Savings of the People as a Source of Investment Resources of the Ukrainian Economy*, "Business Inform" 2014, 7, pp. 89–92.

the economic sectors of strategic importance to the state's socio-economic development. The purpose of such a deposit may vary depending on the particular needs of a household, or simply become a deposit called the "Financial Reserve." According to the activity of the Bank's Management Funds, banks can trust the assets accumulated within the framework of this programme and make target payments to the beneficiaries in the case of a necessity. The given financial product will be an incentive to invest savings, and this transformation of savings into investments will allow households to receive additional revenues that will lead to an increase in consumer demand and an increase in the population's quality of life. Growing consumer needs will encourage enterprises to increase production, which will stimulate payments to the budget and extrabudgetary funds in the form of taxes, duties, and obligatory payments. In addition, tax liabilities of individuals will grow due to an increase in the tax object, which will raise the revenue part of the budget. Thus, the transformation of unorganised household savings into investments will increase the income of the population, the revenue part of the state budget of the country, profits of economic entities, which in turn will contribute to GDP and welfare growth.[5] The ultimate goal of this financial product is to provide the financial security of households, regardless of any factors of influence, possible threats or unpredictable events.

Along with the placement of funds on deposit accounts, the population invests in real estate by making purchases on the primary or secondary market, including acting as a participant in construction financing funds and real estate funds.

Increasing the households' financial security in the process of investing money in real estate can be presented from two points of view, since the provision of financial security relies not only on the responsibility of the state, as a guarantor of citizen's rights, but also depends on the household itself, whose duty is to deepen personal knowledge and skills in the financial sphere to achieve personal well-being. Unfortunately, households are often not able to make a free and optimal choice in the financial sphere because of the lack of knowledge, qualifications, experience, as well as the complexity of financial information, which requires a thorough understanding and detailed analysis.

At the same time, successful investing in real estate involves, first of all, the investor's conscientious analysis, information covering the activities of the developer, the construction object and the real estate sales contract. Due to the presence of different schemes for investing in real estate, it is necessary to investigate what scheme is used by the developer to make sure it is transparent and does not foresee any "pitfalls" for the investor.

In order to explain to households the importance of financial security management, it is necessary to intensify the activity of consulting companies. The issue of establishing or expanding home business, searching for sources of attraction and placement of financial resources, helping to develop financing schemes or creating household

---

[5]   E. Nosova, *Households Savings as a Source of Investment Resources in Ukraine*, "Bulletin of the Taras Shevchenko National University of Kyiv. Economics" 2015, 2, pp. 73–80.

budgets, and disclosing information on opportunities in the financial market are areas of personal finance management that can be covered by financial advisers.

The scope of competence of financial advisers should include:

- search for free money investment options for households to gain passive income;
- recommendations for a quick and effective exit from debt and burdensome debts;
- search for a reliable and profitable method of target saving (child education, retirement, real estate purchase, etc.);
- permanent analysis of the household's financial status, investment strategies, etc.

Along with the services of financial advisers financial coaching is also gaining in popularity. Especially when a household needs not just access to information about a particular financial product, but a sort of a guide that can help to establish financial goals and outline the way how to achieve them. Financial coaching is a relatively new area of financial education, and is especially relevant for those who do not have access to professional financial advisors or experienced financial advisers among relatives or friends.

By asking questions, the coach uses his knowledge of financial services that help clients set or improve goals. The client and coach work together to develop plans for achieving these goals. A financial coach can continue to support the client for a long time following the achievement of successes. The coach uses each individual client target as a starting point for his work, in contrast to a series of predefined steps. Accordingly, financial coaches do not usually offer or promote the purchase of specific financial products.

Therefore, financial coaching involves a holistic and individual approach to each client. Its goal is to make customers become more capable of managing their financial resources on the market. Coaching helps households understand what they do well and how to improve what they want to do better. Focusing on strengths potentially motivates clients to be confident in their knowledge and better manage their personal finances.

Given the direct influence of private consultants, consulting companies and financial coaches on the financial security of their clients, it is necessary to ensure their competence and professionalism, and therefore, a normative regulation of market entry and activity of these financial advisers is required. Thus, it would be advisable for regulatory authorities to introduce a licensing or accreditation procedure for consulting intermediaries in order to create a segment of genuine specialists in this field.

Conclusion

Financial security management of households is provided by members of the household, but conditions for the implementation of instruments for ensuring such financial security are created by the state through a system of government bodies. Given that the needs of people, including financial needs, grow quantitatively and change qualitatively, their satisfaction remains one of the priorities of the state policy. Thus, a financial system built on improving financial security management of households will help families acquire skills for creating and maintaining a household budget, setting long-term goals, and effectively choosing financial products and services.

Bibliography

Atkinson A., Flore-Anne M., Rabinovichii L., Yoongii J., *Financial Education for Long-term Savings and Investments: Review of Research and Literature*, OECD Working Paperson Finance, Insurance and Private Pensions, No. 39, OECD Publishing, Paris 2015.

Campbell J. Y., *Household Finance. Presidential Address to the American Finance Association*, "Journal of Finance" 2006, 61, 4.

Finney A., Hayes D., *Genworth Index: Measuring Consumer Financial Security and Vulnerability*, http://www.bristol.ac.uk/geography/research/pfrc/themes/credit-debt/genworth-index.html (access: 5 June 2019).

Klapper L., Lusardi A., Oudheusden P., *Financial Literacy around the World: Insights from the Standard & Poor's Rating Services Global Financial Literacy Survey*, http://gflec.org/wp-content/uploads/2015/11/Finlit_paper_16_F2_singles.pdf (access: 5 June 2019).

Nosova E., *Households Savings as a Source of Investment Resources in Ukraine*, "Bulletin of the Taras Shevchenko National University of Kyiv. Economics" 2015, 2.

Odintsova T., *Savings of the People as a Source of Investment Resources of the Ukrainian Economy*, "Business Inform" 2014, 7.

Papusha N., *Financial Security of a Person: Genesis*, "Scientific Works of the Kirovohrad National Technical University. Economic Sciences" 2011, 19.

Schawbel D., *Alexa von Tobel: How to Be the Master of Your Financial Future*, "Forbes" 2014, https://www.forbes.com/sites/danschawbel/2014/01/20/alexa-von-tobel-how-to-be-the-master-of-your-financial-future/#6a0e34f74a68 (access: 5 June 2019).

Snishchenko R., *Financial Security of Households in the Period of Instability of the Economy*, "Bulletin of the Kremenchuk Mykhaylo Ostrogradsky National University. Economic Sciences" 2014, 1.

Tvardovska L., *The Problem of Determining the Economic Security of Households in a Market Economy*, "Scientific Notes of the National University of Ostroh Academy. Economic Sciences" 2012, 19.

Benefits of Competition and Cooperation among Local Government Units within Polish Metropolitan Areas

Prof. Piotr Bartkowiak, Ph.D.   ⓘ https://orcid.org/0000-0001-9678-3465
Poznań University of Economics

Maciej Koszel, Ph.D.   ⓘ https://orcid.org/0000-0003-1613-2334
Poznań University of Economics

Abstract

Development strategies of metropolitan areas take into account the relations between the local government units that form them. Nowadays, city-to-city or community-to-community relations are shaped by simultaneous competition and cooperation[1]–coopetition. Inter-organisational collaborations become an important part of a development strategy to cope with faster business dynamics, higher uncertainties and environmental complexity. The present unstable economic and business developments in the form of market globalisation, aggressive competition (hypercompetition) and intensive know-how diffusion among cities are one of the most important causes of the occurrence of coopetition.

Keywords: governmental units, competitiveness factors of local government units, governmental units competition

The conducted empirical studies have served to characterise coopetition occurring between communities in Polish metropolitan areas. The study covered 345 self-government units and cities in 8 metropolitan areas in Poland. One of the examined aspects of coopetition was the benefits of separate competition and cooperation. Responses obtained from 137 representatives of the highest authorities of local government units were used for the purposes of comparative analysis of the benefits of both competition and cooperation. Questionnaire survey was used to gather empirical data.

---

[1]   P. J. Taylor, *On City Cooperation and Competition* [in:] *International Handbook of Globalization and World Cities*, ed. by B. Deruder, M. Hoyler, P. J. Taylor, F. Witlox, Edward Elgar Publishing Ltd., Cheltenham 2012.

Data gathered from the representatives of local government units in Polish metropolitan areas demonstrate that the average level of cooperation benefits is higher than the level of competition benefits. The obtained results show that cooperation is much more often used as an approach in the relationships shaping among local government units within metropolitan areas in Poland. Most of the researched units declared a high level of cooperation, which is connected with participation in expected benefits—mostly connected with the improvement of the units' effectiveness (e.g. public utility services, investment in infrastructure).

Cooperation and competition among local government units within metropolitan areas, as well as their benefits, are strictly connected with the features of the researched unit—its type, location, affiliation and number of inhabitants. Future research should focus on the significance of cooperation and competition benefits as one of the factors determining the relational strategies within metropolitan areas.

Introduction

The dynamic development of metropolitan areas in Poland and the whole European Union in the last 25 years[2] has contributed to the accumulation of high quality resources: physical, human and organisational which can be considered as a source of competitive advantage.[3] Nowadays, it is believed that also relational resources are relevant in this context.[4] In the field of functioning of local government units among metropolitan areas, relational resources are associated with socio-economic and functional relationships between these units.[5] In the case of metropolitan areas, as a complex systems consisting of many local government units, it is more desirable to realise convergent objectives from the perspective of individual units. Especially when there are rational premises, mainly connected with the challenges of public utility

---

[2]   B. Jałowiecki, *Polish Cities and Metropolisation Processes*, "Studia Regionalne i Lokalne" 2006, 2, 64, pp. 75–84; S. Krätke, *Metropolisation of the European Economic Territory as a Consequence of Increasing Specialisation of Urban Agglomerations in the Knowledge Economy*, "European Planning Studies" 2007, 15, 1, pp. 1–27; E. Zuzańska-Żyśko, *Shaping of Metropolization Process in Poland: Theoretical Aspect*, "Studia Regionalia" 2015, 41–42, pp. 95–114.

[3]   J. B. Barney, *Firm Resources and Sustained Competitive Advantage*, "Journal of Management" 1991, 17, 1, pp. 99–120; J. J. Parysek, *Development of Polish Towns and Cities and Factors Affecting This Process at the Turn of Century*, "Geographia Polonica" 2005, 78, 1, pp. 99–115; E. Barth Eide, *The Competitiveness of Cities: A Report of the Global Agenda Council on Competitivensess*, Cologny, World Economic Forum, Geneva 2014.

[4]   M. Wittmann, S. Hunt, D. Arnett, *Explaining Alliance Success: Competence, Resources, Relational Factors, and Resource-Advantage Theory*, "Industrial Marketing Management" 2009, 38, 7, pp. 743–756.

[5]   T. Komornicki, P. Korcelli, P. Siłka, P. Śleszyński, D. Świątek, *Powiązania funkcjonalne pomiędzy polskimi metropoliami*, Wydawnictwo Akademickie Sedno, Warszawa 2013.

services—tasks entrusted to local government units in Poland.[6] One of the possible solutions is cooperation within metropolitan areas. It is particularly important in the case of those units, which struggle with numerous relevant developmental problems— their limitation or even complete elimination can stand for main objectives of urban and municipal strategies as well as those of whole metropolitan areas. The Polish law ensures different forms of cooperation between local government units. On the other hand, in practice particular business of individual self-governments contributes to competitive behaviour.[7]

The increasing role of self-governmental projects, especially in supra-local level, contributes to a tightened cooperation between local government units. The present financial perspective of the EU focuses on regional projects—more than 40% of the total sum can be potentially used by voivodship self-government units in Poland. The most important needs are associated with the functioning of metropolitan areas—investments of both tangible (e.g. infrastructure) and intangible character (e.g. competencies). Does the increasing importance of cooperation between local government units contribute to a decrease in the significance of competition be- tween self-governments? Research conducted in 2016[8] shows that the phenomenon of coopetition (simultaneous competition and cooperation) is common and the connections between coopetition's approach and the level of socio-economic devel- opment (its sustainable dimension) are rather relevant—the units that diversify their inter-self-government relations reach a higher level of sustainable development. The article deals with the issue of shaping inter-organisational relationships in Polish metropolitan areas between local government units. The main objective of the research is to identify the dominant approach in relational strategy from the perspective of benefits gained as a result of overlapping relationships between network participants. The basic question is what kind of relationship is more advantageous—competition or cooperation in the context of the benefits of the municipalities declared by the representatives of the local self-government authorities. CAWI was conducted on a group of 345 self-government units—a return rate of 39.7%. The results obtained contribute to further research on the functioning of metropolitan areas and the shaping of inter-municipal relationships. The main motivation for the conducted study was to identify the benefits of both cooperation and competition among local government units. The research questions are as follows:

---

[6]   The Polish National Parliament, *The Act on Commune Self-government of 8th March 1990*, Warsaw 1990; The Polish National Parliament, *The Act on Municipal Services Management of 20th December 1996*, Warsaw 1997.

[7]   P. Swianiewicz, A. Gendźwiłł, J. Krukowska, M. Lackowska, A. Picej, *Współpraca międzygminna w Polsce. Związek z rozsądku*, Wydawnictwo Naukowe Scholar, Warszawa 2016.

[8]   M. Koszel, *Coopetition in Sustainable Development of Metropolitan Areas in Poland*, unpublished doctoral dissertation, Poznań University of Economics and Business, 2016.

- What are the benefits of cooperation and competition among local government units within metropolitan areas?
- Which of the benefits are most important from the perspective of the local government units' authorities?
- What are the types of coopetition (relational strategies) among local government units within metropolitan areas concerning the criteria for the level of cooperation and competition?
- What are the possible directions of future research in the field of relational strategies within metropolitan areas?

The presented research results are part of a study conducted in 2016 for the purposes of a doctoral dissertation.[9]

Relations between local government units in Polish metropolitan areas

Cooperation of self-government units within metropolitan areas

Local government units are increasingly opting for cooperation.[10] Partnerships, agreements and associations are created to serve strategic objectives.[11] An interesting example of inter-municipal cooperation is the agreement concluded in metropolitan areas, whose development in the last two decades is flourishing.[12]

Cooperation between self-government units within metropolitan areas is conducive to achieving results that would not be feasible within the autonomous activities of individual municipalities.[13] The specificity of metropolitan areas shows a very strong relationship within them. The integration of actions, broader programmes that group them and the overall approach of the strategy accelerates the socio-economic development of not only individual municipalities but also the whole metropolitan area. The diversity and, above all, the complementarity of functions performed by particular municipalities of the metropolitan area makes them one of the most attractive fields from three perspectives: 1) investment, 2) place of residence, 3) tourism and recreation. Potential residents expect a relatively high standard of living (access to specialist

---

9   Ibidem.
10   H. Buis, *The Role of Local Government Associations in Increasing of Effectiveness of City-to-City Cooperation*, "Habitat International" 2009, 3, 2, pp. 190–194.
11   *Formy współdziałania jednostek samorządu terytorialnego*, ed. by B. Dolnicki, Wolters Kluwer Business, Warszawa 2012.
12   *Współpraca JST w Polsce. Stan i potrzeby*, ed. by A. Porawski, Wydawnictwo Związek Miast Polskich, Poznań 2013, p. 48.
13   A. Kajumulo Tibaijuka, *City-to-City Cooperation: Issues Arrising from Experience*, United Nations Centre for Human Settlements (Habitat) & United Towns Organisation (UTO/FMCU), Nairobi 2001.

services, high quality infrastructure, career opportunities, access to cultural institutions, education and sports). Companies are interested in the right climate for running and developing their business (specialised infrastructure, absorptive markets, qualified human capital, proximity of contractors). On the other hand, visitors expect a strong intensity of tourist value with considerable potential.

Awareness of the common interest of local government units forming a metropolitan area is crucial from the perspective of pursuing a targeted policy of shaping conditions conducive to attracting potential investors. This is reflected in enhancing the internal capacity of municipalities through the development and acquisition of key resources. The benefits generated by locating a new business in a municipality do not only affect the area. Municipalities of the metropolitan area establish very intense and tight relations between them. The group of the relationship participants is not limited to self-government units themselves. It is important to point out the significant role played by businesses, organisations and institutions, and increasingly the local community itself. This latter group of stakeholders is actively involved in shaping the development of local governments. The social participation of the inhabitants of communes, who express their expectations regarding the quality of life, is becoming more and more important nowadays.

Art. 9 of The Act on Commune Self-Government[14] foresees that municipalities, in order to carry out their tasks, may conclude agreements with other entities, including non-governmental organisations. In the remainder part of the Act, there are three basic, permanent forms of cooperation between municipalities, which are identified with a "set of activities aimed at achieving a specific situation."[15] These are:

- intentional communal (municipal) partnerships created for the purpose of joint performance of public tasks—performance of public service tasks, including water and sewerage services, heat and power generation and distribution, waste management, public transport,[16]
- municipal agreements—on entrusting one of the municipalities being part to the agreement to the public tasks referred to therein,[17]
- associations of municipalities created to defend common interests—are governed by association law.[18]

---

[14]   The Polish National Parliament, *The Act on Commune Self-government...*
[15]   *Prawo administracyjne*, ed. by J. Boć, Kolonia Limited, Wrocław 2013, p. 4.
[16]   The Polish National Parliament, *The Act on Commune Self-government...*, Art. 64–73.
[17]   The Polish National Parliament, *The Act on County Self-government of 5ᵗʰ June 1998*, Warsaw 1998, Art. 74–75.
[18]   The Polish National Parliament, *The Act on Voivodeship Self-government of 5ᵗʰ June 1998*, Warsaw 1998.

Table 1. Forms of formal cooperation between self-government units in Poland

Level of self-government	Local self-government	County self-government	Voivodship self-government
Local self-government	Self-government partnership Communal agreement Self-government association Commercial company Local action group Local tourist organisation	Agreement with the local self-government Self-government association Commercial company Local action group Local tourist organisation	Entrustment agreement on public tasks of self-government from voivodship Self-government association Commercial company
	County self-government	County partnership County agreement Self-government association Commercial company Local action group Local tourist organisation	Entrustment agreement on public tasks of self-government from voivodship Self-government association Commercial company
		Voivodship self-government	Association of self-government units Commercial company

Source: own work.

Competition of self-government units within metropolitan areas

Competition as an approach of shaping relationships between self-government units within metropolitan areas can contribute to an increase in competitiveness, which is also referred to as attractiveness in the functioning of municipalities and cities. The model approach assumes an increase in competitiveness and, as a consequence, an improvement in the competitive position—the situation of the individual unit against its neighbours treated as direct competitors. This is possible thanks to the development of competitive advantages based on a set of valuable, rare, difficult to imitate and well-organised resources—sources of competitive advantage. The essence of cross--border competition is to compete for these resources, which contribute into an improved strategic position—competitiveness in a narrow sense. It must be distinguished from the competitive potential—access to valuable and rare resources is not always equivalent with their conscious use and management in the process of shaping local development. From the inhabitants' perspective, quality of life should be taken under consideration as one or the most important effects of city-to-city competition.[19]

The overall importance of competitiveness relates to the ability to succeed in economic competition.[20] The competitiveness of local self-government units is often identified with the competitive potential, competition strategy and competitive position of the municipality.[21] The challenges that arise in the economic, social, ecological and spatial spheres contribute to this. Competitive are those local governments that have at their disposal resources to improve the standard of their inhabitants' living quality. Equally important is the shaping of conditions conducive to the development of entrepreneurship at various levels—both individual entrepreneurial attitudes and large-scale entrepreneurship (the sphere of activity of large enterprises).[22]

Góralski and Lazarski[23] indicate that the term of competitiveness is valuatory. It determines a certain desired condition and depending on the research goal, the concept can be specified or generalised. Competitiveness can mean the ability to participate in the competition in the present and in the future. The authors present four elements that can be considered as key:
• life quality of inhabitants,
• business conditions of enterprises,
• ability to attract investors,
• location of institutions and events of national and international level.

Regional competitiveness, but also at lower levels, can be considered in three dimensions:
• spatial, which takes place using the resources with which the area is equipped,
• economic and social, which takes place from the perspective of the behaviour of the region's users of resources and the effects of their activities,
• organisational as a responsibility for local authorities, which has a significant impact on the quality of social life.[24]

---

[19] D. A. Rondinelli, J. H. Johnson, J. D. Kasarda, *The Changing Forces of Urban Economic Development: Globalization and City Competitiveness in the 21st Century*, "Emerging Issues of Urban Development" 1998, 3, 3, pp. 71–105; R. J. Rogers, *Quality of Life and City Competitiveness*, "Urban Studies" 1999, 36, 5–6, pp. 969–985.

[20] D. R. Kamerschen, R. B. McKenzie, C. Nardinelli, *Economics*, Houghton Mifflin Company, Boston 1989, p. 47.

[21] B. Szałko, *Konkurencyjność w świetle badań atrakcyjności inwestycyjnej gminy* [in:] *Samorząd terytorialny a polityka lokalna*, ed. by P. Laskowski, Wydawnictwo WWSZiP, Wałbrzych 2014, p. 142.

[22] D. Twardowski, *Konkurencyjność w ujęciu regionalnym – istota, czynniki oraz jej kształtowanie* [in:] *Samorząd terytorialny a polityka lokalna*, ed. by P. Laskowski, Wydawnictwo WWSZiP, Wałbrzych 2014, p. 127.

[23] P. Góralski, M. Lazarek, *Czynniki kształtujące konkurencyjność regionów*, "Polityki Europejskie. Finanse. Marketing" 2009, 1, 50, p. 307.

[24] M. Piotrowska-Trybuł, *Istota i czynniki konkurencyjności regionu* [in:] *Konkurencyjność regionów w okresie przechodzenia do gospodarki rynkowej. Międzynarodowa analiza porównawcza Białoruś, Litwa, Łotwa i Polska*, ed. by W. Kosiedowski, Wydawnictwo Uniwersytetu Mikołaja Kopernika, Toruń 2004, p. 23.

Local governments compete for investors, organisation of significant events (cultural, sports, others), external funding, access to national and international infrastructure (motorways, airports), other significant organisations and institutions that are likely to localise its headquarters in the municipality or finally, highly qualified human capital. The acquisition of these factors requires the possession of a significant internal potential. On the other hand, their acquirement will be accompanied by a strengthening of their current competitive position. This situation, however, favours the formation of disparities between regions as well as within them in relation to the centre-periphery relationship.

The region, the metropolitan area or the municipality is competitive when it allows to:
- generate a high level of employment, with a low unemployment rate,
- increase labour productivity,
- sustainably increase the standard of the community's living conditions,
- succeed in economic competition—against its competitors,
- adapt rapidly to changing environmental conditions,
- absorb and generate innovation,
- create and use strategic resources.[25]

The wider scope of competitive factors of local government units is shown in Table 2.

Table 2. Competitiveness factors of local government units

Factors	Examples
Location rent	proximity of international transport routes central location—high transport accessibility proximity of transport nodes—seaports, airports, railway nodes, traffic cords near the border location
Economic factors	diverse sectoral structure of the economy level of internal and external relations between enterprises high share of service sector in the economy entrepreneurship development foreign direct investment situation on the labour market
Demographic factors	age and sex structure population growth in the region, county, municipality
Human capital	highly qualified and educated human capital prone to lifelong learning knowledge and competencies

---

[25] Z. Przygocki, *Procesy terytorializacji przedsiębiorstw – poszukiwanie zasobów specyficznych w regionie łódzkim* [in:] *Przedsiębiorczy i konkurencyjny region w teorii i polityce rozwoju regionalnego*, ed. by A. Klasik, KPZK, Warszawa 2005, p. 174.

Factors	Examples
Social capital ·	tendency of people to associate participation in electoral decisions in the state, region, municipality sense of local and regional ties and identity
Innovations	presence of research and development institutions and higher education institutions ability to produce and absorb innovation stakeholders relations in region
Quality of environment and tourism development	landscape differentiation high quality of soil, water and air richness of forests, the presence of protected natural sites (valuable ecosystems) biodiversity presence of a high-standard tourism infrastructure and its use
Cultural factors	cultivating traditions, customs, beliefs
Business environment	presence of business environment institutions organising fair trades, especially international ones
Technical infrastructure	expansion and diversification of transport network investments in "environmental" infrastructure (water supply, sewerage, waste water treatment plants)
Social infrastructure	efficient education system efficient service of healthcare network
Self--government activity	the tendency of associations in special purpose relationships cooperation between cities, municipalities, regions territorial marketing availability of public institutions strong leadership
National situation	economy and social situation political climate adopted model of regional policy, sectoral policies, state finances
International factors	state obligations under contracts and membership of international organisations ability to use foreign funds level of economy internationalisation

Source: own work.

The wide range of factors that local government units compete for can result in a fierce rivalry between them. It should be emphasised, however, that this rivalry concerns primarily those resources that can be characterised by a high level of mobility. An approach whereby communities are competing and co-operating with one another is increasingly common and is referred to as coopetition.

Coopetition as a new form of relation between local government units

Nowadays, the strategies for inter-organisational relations are explained on the basis of the theory of coopetition. In the recent years, a growing emphasis has been placed on coopetition by research and business practice.[26] The term was first introduced in the 1980s by Ray Noorda and later followed by a first conceptualisation made by Brandenburger & Nalebuff.[27] Lado et al.[28] completed the first academic study on coopetition by explaining this strategy from a theoretical perspective. However, they never used the term "coopetition" instead of the phrase "syncretic rent-seeking behaviour." The first academic study using the word "coopetition" was conducted in 1999 by Bengtsson & Kock. They ground their work in the network theory[29] and the resource-based view.[30]

Coopetition represents the notion of competing activities and cooperative activities merged together. A coopetitive relationship includes both cooperative and competitive activities at any level of analysis.[31] Coopetition is regarded as a complex phenomenon, occurring both within an organisation and between companies. The recent literature refers to coopetition as "a paradoxical relationship between, two or more actors, regardless of whether they are in horizontal or vertical relationships, simultaneously involved in cooperative and competitive interactions."[32]

It is also possible to use coopetition as the main assumption in the field of the functioning of local government units within metropolitan areas. Coopetition assumes a simultaneous competition and cooperation between independent organisations—in this case: cities and communities. The intensity of the relation, their number, spatial

---

[26] K. Walley, *Coopetition: An Introduction to the Subject and Agenda for Research*, "International Studies of Management & Organization" 2007, 37, 2; G. Padula, G. B. Dagnino, *Untangling the Rise of Coopetition: The Intrusion of Competition and Cooperation Game Structure*, "International Studies of Management & Organization" 2007, 37, 2; M. Bengtsson, J. Eriksson, J. Wincent, *Co-opetition Dynamics: An Outline for Further Inquiry*, "Competitiveness Review: An International Business Journal" 2010, 20, 2; M. Bengtsson, S. Kock, *Coopetition—Quo vadis? Past Accomplishes and Future Challenges*, "Industrial Marketing Management" 2014, 43, 2; R. B. Bouncken, M. Bogers, J. Gast, S. Krauss, *Coopetition: A Systematic Review, Synthesis and Future Research Directions*, "Review of Managerial Science" 2015, 9, 3; A. Tidström, A. Rajala, *Coopetition Strategy as Interrelated Praxis on Multiple Levels*, "Industrial Marketing Management" 2016, 58; S. Dorn, B. Schweiger, S. Albers, *Levels, Phases and Themes of Coopetition: A Systematic Literature Review and Research Agenda*, "European Management Journal" 2016, 34, 5.

[27] A. M. Brandenburger, B. J. Nalebuff, *Co-opetition*, Doubleday, New York 1996.

[28] A. A. Lado, N. G. Boyd, S. C. Hanlon, *Competition, Cooperation, and the Search for Economic Rents: A Syncretic Model*, "Academy of Management Review" 1997, 22, 1.

[29] M. Granovetter, *The Strength of Weak Ties*, "American Journal of Sociology" 1973, 78, 6; S. Borgatti, P. Foster, *The Network Paradigm in Organizational Research: A Review and Typology*, "Journal of Management" 2003, 29, 6.

[30] J. B. Barney, *Firm Resources...*

[31] M. Bengtsson, J. Eriksson, J. Wincent, *Co-opetition Dynamics...*

[32] M. Bengtsson, S. Kock, *Coopetition—Quo vadis?...*, p. 180.

range and time horizon are the most important features of coopetition.[33] For the purposes of the thesis it is assumed that coopetition is a commonly occurring phenomenon within metropolitan areas in Poland from the perspective of local government units, but varies depending on: specific metropolitan area, type of local government unit, number of habitants, its location. Coopetition has the potential to provide major benefits or losses to participating organisations—enterprises or local government unit. For the purposes or the article it was decided to identify the most common benefits of coopetition as a simultaneous stream of competition and cooperation between communities in Polish metropolitan areas.

The overriding principle of the functioning of local government units and the whole of metropolitan areas is their sustainable development.[34] Sustainable development is a constitutional rule;[35] which assumes fair satisfaction of local community needs that respects the balance and harmony between economic, social, ecological and spatial orders. It is important to satisfy the needs of the current generation without limitation of that possibility from the point of view of future generations. The assumption of balance and harmony is connected with the parity principle—realisation of the objectives of sustainable development cannot interfere and limit the potential of other aspects. What is more, such a development should be characterised by durability and effectiveness from the perspective of local government units as well as local community and other stakeholders. These criteria can be considered as superior in the context of the evaluation of actions taken under sustainable development of self-government units and metropolitan areas.[36]

Methodology

The research tool used to gather data serving to identify the benefits of competition and interregional cooperation in Polish metropolitan areas was survey. The study was of qualitative nature. Both traditional survey questionnaire and electronic questionnaire (CAWI, Computer-Assisted Web Interview) were used. Further data analysis (including comparative analysis) enabled to identify the key benefits. The study covered

---

[33] P. Chiambaretto, H. Dumez, *Toward a Typology of Coopetition: A Multilevel Approach*, "International Studies of Management and Organization" 2016, 46, 2–3.

[34] L. Mierzejewska, *Rozwój zrównoważony miasta. Zagadnienia poznawcze i praktyczne*, Wydawnictwo Naukowe UAM, Poznań 2010.

[35] The Polish National Parliament, *Constitution of the Republic of Poland of 2nd April 1997*, Warsaw 1997, Art. 5; D. Szymańska, J. Chodkowska-Miszczuk, *Endogenous Resource Utilization in Shaping Sustainable Development in Poland*, "Renewable and Sustainable Energy Reviews" 2011, 15, 3.

[36] M. Thorz, *Konstytucyjna zasada rozwoju zrównoważonego jako podstawa tworzenia i stosowania prawa* [in:] *Partnerstwo publiczno-prywatne jako instrument zrównoważonego rozwoju*, ed. by M. Urbaniec, S. Dolata, Wydawnictwo Educator, Częstochowa 2009.

the representatives of the highest authorities (city mayors and presidents or their deputies) of local government units in eight Polish metropolitan areas. Questionnaires were sent to 345 local government units in the following Polish metropolitan areas (MA): Gdańsk MA, Katowice MA, Kraków MA, Łódź MA, Poznań MA, Szczecin MA, Warszawa MA and Wrocław MA. The selection of units was deliberate—the study covered all localities in metropolitan areas in Poland.

The spatial extent of metropolitan areas was determined on the basis of delimitation carried out by voivodship spatial planning offices for the purposes of elaborating voivodeships' spatial plans. The selection of the examined units in terms of methodology of their delimitation thus meets the criteria of reliability and uniformity.

The survey questionnaire comprised a total of seven question blocks covering the following issues: 1) role of local self-government in the region, 2) approach to resource management, 3) formation of inter-municipal relations, 4) inter-municipal competition, 5) inter-municipal cooperation, 6) benefits of inter-municipal competition, 7) benefits of inter-municipal cooperation. For the purpose of the article, the research results will be presented in the last two aspects—the benefits of competition and inter-municipal cooperation in metropolitan areas in Poland. The research questionnaire contains questions concerning the benefits connected with both competition and cooperation, and the benefits specific to a particular type of relationship—competition or cooperation.

The evaluation of the benefits linked to competition and inter-municipal cooperation was carried out by examining opinions of the representatives of the highest self-government authorities on the level of formation of the specified advantages of competition and inter-communal cooperation within the metropolitan area. The research questions used a five-step response scale, in which the variants were: 1—strongly disagree, 2—disagree, 3—agree, 4—strongly agree, 0—no opinion. On the basis of the responses given, the average level of competition and cooperation benefits was determined according to the following criteria:

- metropolitan area affiliation (Gdańsk, Katowice, Cracow, Łódź, Poznań, Szczecin, Warsaw, Wrocław),
- number of inhabitants (under 5 thous., 5–10 thous., 10–25 thous., 25–50 thous., 50–100 thous., over 100 thous.).
- type of local government unit (urban, urban-rural, rural),
- location within metropolitan area (central zone, zone two, periphery),

For formal reasons, only aggregate results are presented in the article.

Research results

A total of 137 units took part in the survey conducted at the turn of 2015 and 2016—the return rate was 39.71% (Table 3).

Table 3. Structure of researched units

		Gdańsk MA [%]	Katowice MA [%]	Kraków MA [%]	Łódź MA [%]	Poznań MA [%]	Szczecin MA [%]	Warszawa MA [%]	Wrocław MA [%]	Total [%]
type	urban	28.0	100.0	4.0	23.1	16.0	27.3	20.0	22.2	24.1
	urban-rural	8.0	0.0	32.0	23.1	28.0	36.4	35.0	11.1	23.4
	rural	64.0	0.0	64.0	53.8	56.0	36.4	45.0	66.7	52.6
location	central	32.0	55.6	24.0	23.1	32.0	54.5	20.0	22.2	30.7
	second	64.0	44.4	60.0	61.5	48.0	36.4	60.0	55.6	55.5
	peripheral	4.0	0.0	16.0	15.4	20.0	9.1	20.0	22.2	13.9
number of inhabitants	below 5 thous.	12.0	0.0	0.0	0.0	0.0	27.3	5.0	22.2	6.6
	5–10 thous.	24.0	0.0	44.0	53.8	24.0	9.1	25.0	33.3	28.5
	10–25 thous.	32.0	0.0	40.0	23.1	52.0	18.2	35.0	22.2	32.8
	25–50 thous.	24.0	0.0	12.0	7.7	16.0	27.3	30.0	11.1	17.5
	50–100 thous.	0.0	33.3	0.0	7.7	4.0	9.1	0.0	0.0	4.4
	above 100 thous.	8.0	66.7	4.0	7.7	4.0	9.1	5.0	11.1	10.2

Source: own work.

Prior to the presentation of detailed results on the benefits of competition and inter-
-municipal cooperation, reference should be made to the identification of types of coopetition—simultaneous competition and cooperation between municipalities within
metropolitan areas. It was decided for the purpose of the article to use assumptions
made on the field of the functioning of companies and characterised in scientific
literature by Lado et al.,[37] Luo,[38] and Cygler et al.[39] Considerations of this authors con-
centrate on the fundamental typologies based on the criteria concerning the level of
competition and cooperation. Typology established on this criteria distinguishes four
types of coopetition (more precisely—types of "coopetitors"): "integrator," "partner,"
"warrior," "solitary." The performed data analysis shows that the "partner" type was
identified in the case of 57 local government units. The "partner" type of coopetition
is characterised by a low level of competition and a high level of cooperation. In the

---

[37] A. A. Lado, N. G. Boyd, S. C. Hanlon, *Competition, Cooperation...*

[38] Y. Luo, *A Coopetition Perspective of Global Competition*, "Journal of World Business" 2007, 42, 2.

[39] *Kooperencja przedsiębiorstw w dobie globalizacji. Wyzwania strategiczne, uwarunkowania prawne*,
      ed. by J. Cygler, M. Aluchna, E. Marciszewska, M. Witek-Hejduk, G. Materna, Wolters Kluwer Business,
      Warszawa 2013.

case of 55 self-government units, an "integrator" type of coopetition was identified (high level of competition and cooperation). Sixteen units were identified as a "solitary" type of coopetition (low level of competition and cooperation), and 9 units were identified as a "warrior" type of coopetition (high level of competition and low level of cooperation)—Figure 1.

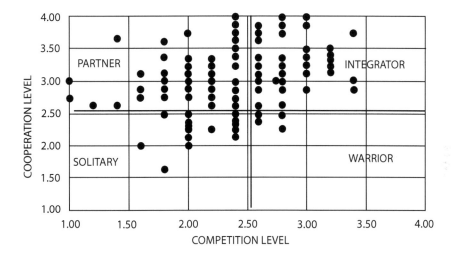

Figure 1. Types of coopetition among local government units in Polish metropolitan areas

Source: own work.

In order to assess the benefits of cross-border cooperation and competition in Polish metropolitan areas, respondents (representatives of the highest authorities of researched local government units) were asked to rate distinguished benefits—separately for competition and cooperation. The first nine statements were identical in both cases. Subsequent statements referred to the specific benefits of competition and cooperation. There was also an open variant—"other, please specify?" Due to the low rate of response and the lack of specification, the results were not included in the interpretation and discussion of deliverables—the obtained findings in this variant were statistically insignificant. Figure 2 demonstrates a comparative assessment of the benefits of competition and inter-municipal cooperation (the same statements) in order of decreasing average value of cooperation benefits. The overall average for the surveyed population in all nine cases is higher for the benefits of inter-municipal cooperation. In all cases, the significance of individual benefits was indicated (average score above 2.50 indicating that the respondents "agree" or "strongly agree").

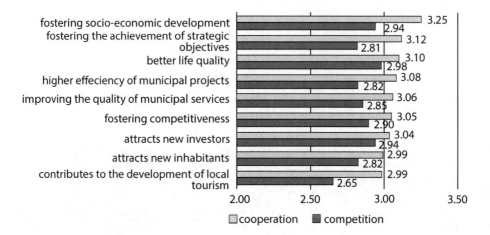

Figure 2. The average level of competition and cooperation between local government units within Polish metropolitan areas—2016

Source: own work based on own research.

In the case of inter-municipal cooperation, the most important benefits (also indicated in the case of cross-border competition) were: 1) fostering socio-economic development (3.25), 2) fostering the achievement of strategic objectives (3.12), and 3) better life quality (3.10). To the smallest extent, inter-municipal cooperation contributes to the benefits of: 1) attracting new investors (3.04), 2) attracting new residents (2.99) and 3) developing local tourism (2.99).

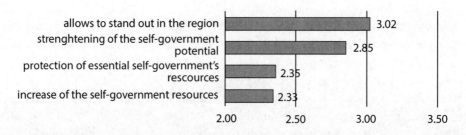

Figure 3. The average level of specific competition benefits between local government units among Polish metropolitan areas—2016

Source: own work based on own research.

The most important benefits of inter-municipal competition are the following: 1) better life quality (2.98), 2) fostering socio-economic development (2.94), and 3) attracting new investors (2.94). The lowest rates were received by the following benefits: 1) fostering the achievement of strategic objectives (2.81), 2) attracting new inhabitants (2.82), and 3) higher efficiency of municipal projects (2.82).

In the case of competition, four specific benefits were identified. The average overall results are shown in Figure 3. Among the benefits of cross-border competition, the most important was that it allows stand out in the region (3.02—improving competitive position, increasing attractiveness) and that competition contributes to strengthening of the self-government potential (2.85). Competition among local government units contributes to the protection of essential self-government resources (among the surveyed communes there is a greater tendency to exchange resources). Competition also contributes to the increase of self-government resources.

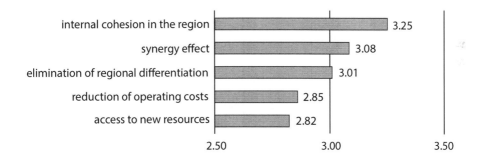

Figure 4. The average level of specific cooperation benefits between local government units within Polish metropolitan areas

Source: own work based on own research.

The respondents also identified specific benefits of inter-municipal cooperation. The most important from their point of view was internal cohesion in the region (3.25) and synergy effects (3.08). A significantly less important benefit was the reduction of the municipality's operating costs (2.85) and access to new resources (2.82)—Figure 4.

From the perspective of benefits, the level of cooperation and competition, it is clear, that a more desirable approach in relationship shaping among local government units within metropolitan areas in Poland is cooperation strategy. It can be explained on the basis of the measured level of comparable benefits, which were higher in the case of cooperation—Figure 2. What is more important, data analysis identifies an integrator and partner type of coopetition in 112 local government units, which means that the average level of cooperation is higher than the competition level.

For the purposes of the research it was decided to verify the obtained results in the context of unit features such as: type (urban, urban-rural, rural), location (central zone, second zone, peripheral zone), number of inhabitants (very large, large, medium, small, very small) and its belonging to a particular metropolitan area (Gdańsk, Katowice, Kraków, Łódź, Poznań, Szczecin, Warszawa, Wrocław). A higher level of cooperation was declared by the authorities of urban units located in central zone of the metropolitan area, of very large, large and medium size by the number of inhabitants—for instance, the units of metropolitan areas of Poznań and Warszawa. On the other hand, a higher level of competition was declared by the representatives of rural units, located in the second and peripheral zone of the metropolitan area, and in the case of small and very small size, especially units of the metropolitan area of Katowice.

The measurable benefits of both cooperation and competition are probably one of the most important factors that determine inter-municipal relationships within metropolitan areas. Further directions of research should focus on factors influencing relational strategies among local government units and the particular role of the potential (expected) and obtained (real) benefits.

Conclusions

The research conducted on the challenge of development of inter-communal relations within metropolitan areas in Poland demonstrates that the benefits of cooperation significantly outweigh the benefits of competition. Although most municipalities and cities base their relationships on a high level of cooperation and low level of competition (partner type of coopetition), a higher level of socio-economic development is achieved by individuals who "diversify" their approach through extending the scope of co-operation. Similar conclusions emerge with regard to the benefits of cooperation and competition—a "higher" level of benefit is achieved by "integrators." Noticeably worse outcomes in terms of socio-economic development level are achieved by those municipalities and cities which focus on competition "warriors"). As with the "solitary" type, the benefits of competition and cooperation are limited. It should be pointed out that these are mainly rural communities, small, located in peripheral parts of the metropolitan area, in areas where formal inter-communal cooperation is not yet developed. The final conclusion is related to the need for research and ongoing monitoring of the situation, as both the determinants of co-operation and inter-communal competition within metropolitan areas are changing dynamically.

Bibliography

Barney J. B., *Firm Resources and Sustained Competitive Advantage*, "Journal of Management" 1991, 17, 1.
Barth Eide E., *The Competitiveness of Cities: A Report of the Global Agenda Council on Competitiveness*, Cologny, World Economic Forum, Geneva 2014.

Bengtsson M., Eriksson J., Wincent J., *Co-opetition Dynamics: An Outline for Further Inquiry*, "Competitiveness Review: An International Business Journal" 2010, 20, 2.

Bengtsson M., Kock S., *Cooperation and Competition in Relationships between Competitors in Business Networks*, "Journal of Business and Industrial Marketing" 1999, 14, 3.

Bengtsson M., Kock S., *Coopetition—Quo vadis? Past Accomplishes and Future Challenges*, "Industrial Marketing Management" 2014, 43, 2.

Borgatti S., Foster P., *The Network Paradigm in Organizational Research: A Review and Typology*, "Journal of Management" 2003, 29, 6.

Bouncken R. B., Bogers M., Gast J., Krauss S., *Coopetition: A Systematic Review, Synthesis and Future Research Directions*, "Review of Managerial Science" 2015, 9, 3.

Brandenburger A. M., Nalebuff B. J., *Co-opetition*, Doubleday, New York 1996.

Buis H., *The Role of Local Government Associations in Increasing of Effectiveness of City-to-City Cooperation*, "Habitat International" 2009, 3, 2.

Chiambaretto P., Dumez H., *Toward a Typology of Coopetition: A Multilevel Approach*, "International Studies of Management and Organization" 2016, 46, 2–3.

Dorn S., Schweiger B., Albers S., *Levels, Phases and Themes of Coopetition: A Systematic Literature Review and Research Agenda*, "European Management Journal" 2016, 34, 5.

Formy współdziałania jednostek samorządu terytorialnego, ed. by B. Dolnicki, Wolters Kluwer Business, Warszawa 2012.

Góralski P., Lazarek M., *Czynniki kształtujące konkurencyjność regionów*, "Polityki Europejskie. Finanse. Marketing" 2009, 1, 50.

Granovetter M., *The Strength of Weak Ties*, "American Journal of Sociology" 1973, 78, 6.

Jałowiecki B., *Polish Cities and Metropolisation Processes*, "Studia Regionalne i Lokalne" 2006, 2, 64.

Kajumulo Tibaijuka A., *City-to-City Cooperation: Issues Arrising from Experience*, United Nations Centre for Human Settlements (Habitat) & United Towns Organisation (UTO/FMCU), Nairobi 2001.

Kamerschen D. R., McKenzie R. B., Nardinelli C., *Economics*, Houghton Mifflin Company, Boston 1989.

Komornicki T., Korcelli P., Siłka P., Śleszyński P., Świątek D., *Powiązania funkcjonalne pomiędzy polskimi metropoliami*, Wydawnictwo Akademickie Sedno, Warszawa 2013.

Kooperencja przedsiębiorstw w dobie globalizacji. Wyzwania strategiczne, uwarunkowania prawne, ed. by J. Cygler, M. Aluchna, E. Marciszewska, M. Witek-Hejduk, G. Materna, Wolters Kluwer Business, Warszawa 2013.

Koszel M., *Coopetition in Sustainable Development of Metropolitan Areas in Poland*, unpublished doctoral dissertation, Poznań University of Economics and Business, 2016.

Krätke S., *Metropolisation of the European Economic Territory as a Consequence of Increasing Specialisation of Urban Agglomerations in the Knowledge Economy*, "European Planning Studies" 2007, 15, 1.

Lado A. A., Boyd N. G., Hanlon S. C., *Competition, Cooperation, and the Search for Economic Rents: A Syncretic Model*, "Academy of Management Review" 1997, 22, 1.

Luo Y., *A Coopetition Perspective of Global Competition*, "Journal of World Business" 2007, 42, 2.

Mierzejewska L., *Rozwój zrównoważony miasta. Zagadnienia poznawcze i praktyczne*, Wydawnictwo Naukowe UAM, Poznań 2010.

Padula G., Dagnino G. B., *Untangling the Rise of Coopetition: The Intrusion of Competition and Cooperation Game Structure*, "International Studies of Management & Organization" 2007, 37, 2.

Parysek J. J., *Development of Polish Towns and Cities and Factors Affecting This Process at the Turn of Century*, "Geographia Polonica" 2005, 78, 1.

Piotrowska-Trybuł M., *Istota i czynniki konkurencyjności regionu* [in:] *Konkurencyjność regionów w okresie przechodzenia do gospodarki rynkowej. Międzynarodowa analiza porównawcza Białoruś, Litwa, Łotwa i Polska*, ed. by W. Kosiedowski, Wydawnictwo Uniwersytetu Mikołaja Kopernika, Toruń 2004.

Prawo administracyjne, ed. by J. Boć, Kolonia Limited, Wrocław 2013.

Przygocki Z., *Procesy terytorializacji przedsiębiorstw – poszukiwanie zasobów specyficznych w regionie łódzkim* [in:] *Przedsiębiorczy i konkurencyjny region w teorii i polityce rozwoju regionalnego*, ed. by A. Klasik, KPZK, Warszawa 2005.

Rogers R. J., *Quality of Life and City Competitiveness*, "Urban Studies" 1999, 36, 5–6.

Rondinelli D. A., Johnson J. H., Kasarda J. D., *The Changing Forces of Urban Economic Development: Globalization and City Competitiveness in the 21ˢᵗ Century*, "Emerging Issues of Urban Development" 1998, 3, 3.

Swianiewicz P., Gendźwiłł A., Krukowska J., Lackowska M., Picej A., *Współpraca międzygminna w Polsce. Związek z rozsądku*, Wydawnictwo Naukowe Scholar, Warszawa 2016.

Szałko B., *Konkurencyjność w świetle badań atrakcyjności inwestycyjnej gminy* [in:] *Samorząd terytorialny a polityka lokalna*, ed. by P. Laskowski, Wydawnictwo WWSZiP, Wałbrzych 2014.

Szymańska D., Chodkowska-Miszczuk J., *Endogenous Resource Utilization in Shaping Sustainable Development in Poland*, "Renewable and Sustainable Energy Reviews" 2011, 15, 3.

Taylor P. J., *On City Cooperation and Competition* [in:] *International Handbook of Globalization and World Cities*, ed. by B. Deruder, M. Hoyler, P. J. Taylor, F. Witlox, Edward Elgar Publishing Ltd., Cheltenham 2012.

The Polish National Parliament, *Constitution of the Republic of Poland of 2ⁿᵈ April 1997*, Warsaw 1997.

The Polish National Parliament, *The Act on Commune Self-government of 8ᵗʰ March 1990*, Warsaw 1990.

The Polish National Parliament, *The Act on County Self-government of 5ᵗʰ June 1998*, Warsaw 1998.

The Polish National Parliament, *The Act on Municipal Services Management of 20ᵗʰ December 1996*, Warsaw 1997.

The Polish National Parliament, *The Act on Voivodeship Self-government of 5ᵗʰ June 1998*, Warsaw 1998.

Thorz M., *Konstytucyjna zasada rozwoju zrównoważonego jako podstawa tworzenia i stosowania prawa* [in:] *Partnerstwo publiczno-prywatne jako instrument zrównoważonego rozwoju*, ed. by M. Urbaniec, S. Dolata, Wydawnictwo Educator, Częstochowa 2009.

Tidström A., Rajala A., *Coopetition Strategy as Interrelated Praxis on Multiple Levels*, "Industrial Marketing Management" 2016, 58.

Twardowski D., *Konkurencyjność w ujęciu regionalnym – istota, czynniki oraz jej kształtowanie* [in:] *Samorząd terytorialny a polityka lokalna*, ed. by P. Laskowski, Wydawnictwo WWSZiP, Wałbrzych 2014.

Walley K., *Coopetition: An Introduction to the Subject and Agenda for Research*, "International Studies of Management & Organization" 2007, 37, 2.

Wittmann M., Hunt S., Arnett D., *Explaining Alliance Success: Competence, Resources, Relational Factors, and Resource-Advantage Theory*, "Industrial Marketing Management" 2009, 38, 7.

Współpraca JST w Polsce. Stan i potrzeby, ed. by A. Porawski, Wydawnictwo Związek Miast Polskich, Poznań 2013.

Zuzańska-Żyśko E., *Shaping of Metropolization Process in Poland: Theoretical Aspect*, "Studia Regionalia" 2015, 41–42.

Practical Experience in the Formation of Entrepreneurial Competencies among Students

Prof. Natalia Trifonova, Ph.D.   https://orcid.org/0000-0003-0697-8846
St. Petersburg State University of Economics

Marina Vlasova, Ph.D.   https://orcid.org/0000-0002-5049-4219
St. Petersburg State University of Economics

Irina Borovskaya, Ph.D.   https://orcid.org/0000-0002-7869-0684
St. Petersburg State University of Economics

Alexandra Proshkina, Ph.D. student   https://orcid.org/0000-0003-0976-5686
St. Petersburg State University of Economics

Abstract

The article focuses on the solution to an important research task—the formation of entrepreneurial competencies and identification of the motivational basis of a young entrepreneur. One of the conditions for the formation of a competitive economic system is to enhance the country's technological security. The key factor in ensuring the country's ability to develop lies in the transformation of science and technology within the modern educational organisation which faced the task not only and not so much to support the educational process as to form the entrepreneurial competencies of the student. This year the International Business Department of SPbSEU is occupied by the task of developing a methodology concept for technological entrepreneurship of the young people in Russia. The implementation of the model adopted at the department is based on the involvement of students into research activity with the aim of forming and introducing particular managerial processes. Our approach is adapted to suit the educational programmes of SPbSEU and provides a methodological basis for the formation of entrepreneurial competencies among students.

Keywords: entrepreneurial competencies, research work, youth technological entrepreneurship, motivational basis

Introduction

One of the factors for the formation of a competitive economic system is to enhance the country's technological security. According to the *Strategy for Scientific and Technological Development of the Russian Federation* the transformation of science and technology is a key factor in ensuring the country's ability to meet the big challenge effectively, that is to deal with the problems and threats that require state intervention, which is one of the main priorities formulated in the Strategy of National Security of Russia.[1]

According to the RAS academician L. I. Abalkin, the technological component of national security is integral to the economic security of the state, however, the innovation potential of Russian science has practically no effect on the development of the domestic economy, since there is a problem of interaction between science and business, scientific achievements and real economy—innovations are not mastered by the economy to the extent that is necessary for the sustainable development of Russia.[2] In science there is a shortage of specialists—managers in the field of commercialisation of innovations and integration of research results into the production process.

The modern scientific world and technological sphere has significantly higher rates of the appearance of new technologies: the frequency of technology change is equal to the frequency of the generation change. Among the main problems of the RF's technological lagging behind the leading industrial countries we can identify:

- shortage of personnel for work in priority areas for Russia, which is also caused by the "brain drain;"
- low demand for innovation from the Russian industry, which is connected with both a lack of proprietary competitive technologies and a lack of interaction between the spheres of science and real economy, as well as with bans of transfer of technologies under sanctions;
- limited credit facilities for small- and medium-sized businesses under the present inefficient system of planning technological priorities, which is implemented mainly on large-scale projects, for example Skolkovo and Rusnano.

As a result, there is a high level of import dependency of the leading industries in Russia: the share of machinery, equipment and vehicles in the import commodity structure of the Russian Federation is 47%, whereas in the machine-tool industry it amounts up to 80%.

---

[1] L. I. Abalkin, *Economic Security of Russia*, "Bulletin of the RAS" 1997, 67, 9; T. H. Byers, T. H. Dorf, A. J. Nelson, *Technology Ventures: From Idea to Enterprise*, McGraw Hill, Columbus 2011.

[2] Decree of the President of the Russian Federation of 31 December 2015, No. 683 *On the National Security Strategy of the Russian Federation*, http: //www.consultant.ru/document/cons_doc_LAW_191669/ (access: 9 February 2018).

This situation has led to the fact that so far, according to the dynamics of innovation development, the Russian industry lags 4–6 times behind the leading industrial countries. For example, in Switzerland, 60.2% of companies use innovations, in Germany—58.9%, in France—46.5%, in Great Britain—45.7%, in Poland this figure is 18.6% of industrial enterprises, in Hungary—18.8%.[3]

To overcome the current situation, Russia needs to enhance interaction between the government, science and business as the leading powerhouse of the economy through the formation of new types of ecosystems, which will consider the best foreign experience and the specific character of Russia.

Universities in entrepreneurial ecosystems

Daniel J. Isenberg, professor of management, the author of the idea of entrepreneurial ecosystems, stresses that the creation of an effective ecosystem does not tolerate patterns. Each newly created ecosystem must fit organically into the existing conditions, taking into account a set of local factors.[4]

Today there are examples of effective cooperation of the government, science and entrepreneurship. Technologically developed countries apply a management system based on the university model, which concentrates the efforts of scientists, small enterprises and government institutions. The NASA Agency, with the support of the federal budget, has formed an extensive research ecosystem that includes about 80 US universities and hundreds of small innovative enterprises with 10–15 employees. Thus, in 2015 the evaluation of the results of their activities using an expert methodology that included 536 different indicators revealed that, without taking into account additional effects in the form of launching new products, research and development at the firm level, the conversion degree of government investments was 2.6 times.[5]

In this format, ecosystems are formed by the convergence of government organisations and the private sector with the scientific sphere and can be regarded as independent economic institutions that take national peculiarities of the country into consideration (Figure 1) and are created on the basis of leading Russian Universities.

---

[3]   D. Isenberg, *Introducing the Entrepreneurship Ecosystem: Four Defining Characteristics*, https://www.forbes.com/sites/danisenberg/2011/05/25/introducing-the-entrepreneurship-ecosystem-four-defining-characteristics/#1cf409155fe8 (access: 9 February 2018).

[4]   *Россия наращивает технологическое отставание* [*Russia is increasing the technological gap*], https://news.rambler.ru/scitech/39457868-rossiya-naraschivaet-tehnologicheskoe-otstavanie (access: 4 April 2019).

[5]   A. A. Yanik, *Peculiarities of Commercialization of Results of Private Sector Research and Development for NASA: Experience of the Small Business Innovation Research Program*, "Space Exploration" 2017, 2, pp. 126–136.

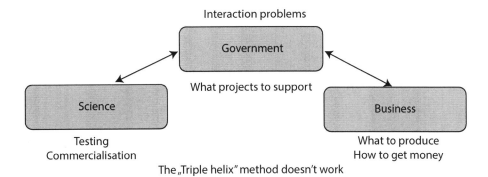

Figure 1. Problems and opportunities for interaction between business, science and the government

Source: prepared by the author.

Therefore, the modern educational organisation now has an ambitious research task of not only and not so much supporting the educational process as forming the entrepreneurial competencies of the student.

Research work as a base for entrepreneurial competencies formation

A number of centres have been set up in Russian universities in order to encourage self-motivated young people who are eager to try or to take a challenge in business. Currently, there are several types of such interactions, each of which has its own advantages and disadvantages: Centre for Technology Entrepreneurship, Business Accelerators, Business Incubators, Technoparks, etc. However, all of them focus on enterprising young people who can already demonstrate entrepreneurship.

The model of identification of entrepreneurial skills and formation of entrepreneurial competencies used in the educational process at the Department of International Business of SPbSEU includes organisation, methodology and implementation of the assigned task (Figure 2). The implementation of this model is based on the involvement of students in research activities and includes the formation and introduction of such managerial processes as the formulation of research topics, specification of the conditions of the discussion, attracting students, selecting and filtering ideas, documenting the results of discussion, the possibility and search of ways to commercialise the research result etc. This approach differs from the regular educational process (Table 1).

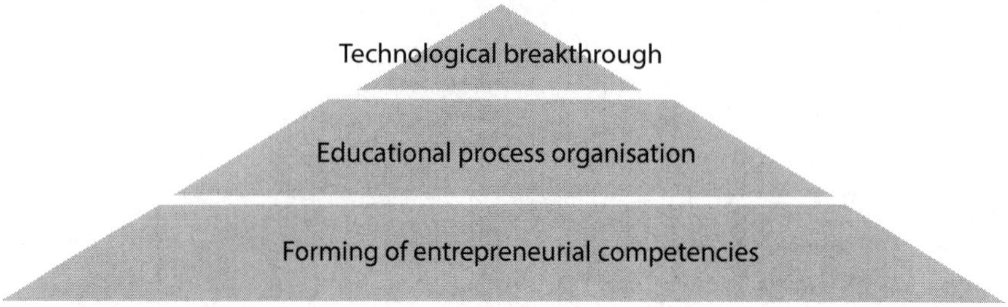

Figure 2. The process of forming entrepreneurial competencies of the student at the International Business Department of the SPEU

Source: prepared by the authors.

Table 1. Model of use of the students' research work

Rule	How we use it at the department
1. Choose the model correctly	The purpose can be both educational (for testing the skills of working with particular sites, programmes), and research (testing the skills of working with a large array of information and data, the ability to summarise collected material and draw conclusion.
2. Choose the target group correctly	We take into account the area of the educational programme
3. Choose the right reward	Identifying the motivational basis: from the willingness to try their hand at realising a particular business project to taking part in competitions of student works at different levels
4. Keep notifications of dismissal in the desk drawer (that is, the "crowd" cannot do all the work)	We are always honest with students, we explain why it is necessary to fulfil the assignment
5. Consider the silence of the "crowd" (that is, observe the principle of the benevolent dictatorship)	Active participation of the teacher and adjustment of directions of further research are necessary
6. Simplify the assignment and divide it into parts	The problem is divided into small steps

Each student, taking into account their abilities, gets a specific assignment |
7. Remember the law of Sturgeon, which is named after the science fiction writer Theodore Sturgeon and says that 90% of all information is crap	The teacher analyses the collected information and selects the information necessary for further research
8. Remember about 10%, the "antidote" of the law of Sturgeon (that is, let the "crowd" choose the best)	A place for creativity, give the student a field for activity and they will give you an unpredictable result
9. The community is always right	Do not give rein to the student, strictly follow the established plan
10. Ask not what the "crowd" can do for you, but what you can do for the "crowd"	Let the student make their own conclusion

Source: prepared by the authors.

Based on practical experience in applying this model of interaction with students, the teachers of the department developed a motivational basis for the formation of entrepreneurial competencies in the youth environment (Figure 3).

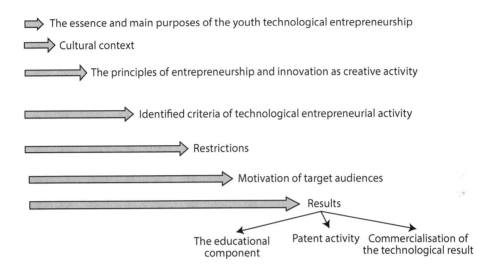

Figure 3. The motivational basis of a young entrepreneur: intellectual protest of the inventor, insight of the scientist or commercial drive of the entrepreneur?

Source: prepared by the authors.

Technological entrepreneurship: specific features of the Russian context

The existing authors' definitions of technological entrepreneurship were taken into account when determining the essence and the main idea of the youth's technological entrepreneurship, we will cite some of them:
1. Technological entrepreneurship is a style of business leadership, which identifies promising, with advanced technical equipment, possibilities of manufacturing products for their subsequent sale; accumulation of resources, for example, capital and talent; as well as managing the growth of the company and the emerging risks while applying the skills of making effective decisions.[6]

---

6   A. Mirchev, A. Dicheva, *Technological Entrepreneurship of Small and Medium Business in the Republic of Bulgaria as a Factor for Sustainable Development*, proceedings of the CBU International Conference on Integration and Innovation in Science and Education, 2013.

2. Technological entrepreneurship was defined as the combined aspiration of science and business to discover new, more efficient technologies or to improve existing ones at industrial enterprises in order to better the quality of life and meet new emerging needs.[7]

3. The main function of technological entrepreneurship is to collect a combination of specialised physical and heterogeneous assets with the aim of creating value for the firm by carrying out joint research and experiments. In this process, there may be unique or new combinations of assets, the assets themselves or their attributes. The initial combination may change over time.

Thus, in countries with a transitional type of economy, priority is placed on the inventive component of technological entrepreneurship considering the need to make a technological breakthrough in a number of industries. From this point of view, technological entrepreneurship is regarded as the creation of a new product or service with a high probability of commercialisation / with a predictable life cycle. While commitment, passion and unrelenting desire to be successful characterise the behaviour of a technological entrepreneur.

Having analysed various approaches to the definition of technological entrepreneurship, the authors of the article formulate their own authorial definition of this category: **technological entrepreneurship is a market-oriented and risk-oriented organisational integration of science and business based on research, experimental and inventive activities in the development or testing of new technologies**.

In this context, the term "technological entrepreneurship," as a managerial and scientific category, should take into account a number of characteristics common to the Russian youth.

First, the Russian context, which is based on invention. Smartness, imagination, invention are traditionally considered to be typical features of the representatives of Russian culture, and the search for unconventional solutions is a common behavioural pattern in view of the limited resources available. Given the length of the planned economy period and the scope of the restrictions, this behaviour has manifested itself in a wide variety of social and professional groups at all levels— from the household to production and science. On the other hand, during this period entrepreneurship was banned, its traditions were abandoned. The negative connotation of this phenomenon was aggravated during Perestroika, a division of the capital, when entrepreneurial activity stepped out of the shade, but its forms and practices contradicted the values of most citizens. Since that time a stable stereotype has emerged about the negative perception of private entrepreneurship by Russian citizens, which, however, is not confirmed by recent studies. And although

---

7   *Strategy of Scientific and Technological Development of the Russian Federation*, approved by the Decree of the President of the Russian Federation of 1 December 2016, No. 642.

the attitude towards wealth remains generally negative, the attitude to business, especially small one, is becoming increasingly positive but taking into consideration the influence of socio-demographic characteristics such as age, education and social and professional status. The representatives of younger age groups with higher or incomplete higher education and higher professional status demonstrate their positive attitude more often.

However, comparative international studies of entrepreneurial activity show that the level of entrepreneurial activity is not very high contrasted with other countries. As for its social recognition, we are closer to the end of the ratings. This can also be explained by the fact that for many residents of Russia, entrepreneurship is not internally sanctioned. Its values (initiative, independence, ability to express oneself, willingness to stand out, take responsibility and others) are contrary to the existing traditional social values.

Receiving recognition from different strata and groups of society is possible just by combining acceptable and rejected values. Commercialisation of invention can receive more support than entrepreneurship in traditional spheres.

Secondly, there is the university aspect, since the space of Russian and Soviet universities has created additional permissive and resource opportunities for the development of entrepreneurial activities (including the sphere of technology). As the activities related to technological entrepreneurship begin with a research process, experimental and inventive activity, the environment of technical universities in both pre-revolutionary Russia and the Soviet Union was the most supportive. Entrepreneurial initiatives could be implemented in the post-war period in the form of cooperation between universities and industrial enterprises working on contractual theme-based projects which were carried out by laboratories and departments including for certain industry segments. Organisationally, this activity did not develop, but it was enriched with key competencies and talents of research workers. On the other hand, in pre-revolutionary Russia the researching retreat as a preparation for invention and experiment was based on the values of individual independence, constant search, scientific risk, ideological advocacy, then in the Soviet Union collective responsibility, public creativity, scientific fraternity and partnership determined the content of internal processes of technological entrepreneurship. In the universities of new Russia the above values (both individual and collective) are in the process of formation.

Thirdly, the motivation of target audiences. Motivation can be either individual or collective. In technological entrepreneurship, invention is a necessary, but insufficient, component. Gifted young people, who produce technological innovations, do not always take into account the possibilities of their commercialisation. An interest in inventing, as a process of searching for an unconventional solution, can be a strong motivator. An ability to have a vision, assess risks and take responsibility for the implementation of the application of scientific and technological knowledge complements innovative activity with the entrepreneurial component. In a university environment it is necessary to motivate individuals for both invention and formation of entrepreneurial competencies, paying special attention to the specific nature of the disciplines teaching entrepreneurship, management for engineering specialties, search for role models among practising entrepreneurs.

An ability to work in a team makes it possible to achieve a synergetic effect. An individual potential may be high, but at a young age there is not enough experience and time to acquire the necessary knowledge and form the key competencies in science, technology, business. The lack of professionalism in certain spheres can be compensated by teamwork, which gives the opportunity to share ideas, knowledge, provide support, a chance to realise and build leadership potential, form a new status, put into life the values of friendship, offer mutual assistance and support which are so important for young people. At the same time, the issue of selecting and forming of a team becomes a key one in order to avoid the effect of "social loafing," withdrawal from responsibility, etc.

Conclusion

A methodologically competent approach to the formation of competencies in the field of the technological entrepreneurship in the student environment will allow the University to become not just an educational system for the student, but a Centre understood as a starting point in realising their ambitions and obtaining worthy results in the field of creating new technologies, their patenting and commercialisation.

Bibliography

Abalkin L. I., *Economic Security of Russia*, "Bulletin of the RAS" 1997, 67, 9.

Byers T. H., Dorf T. H., Nelson A. J., *Technology Ventures: From Idea to Enterprise*, McGraw Hill, Columbus 2011.

Decree of the President of the Russian Federation of 31 December 2015, No. 683 *On the National Security Strategy of the Russian Federation*, http: //www.consultant.ru/document/cons_doc_LAW_191669/ (access: 9 February 2018).

Isenberg D., *Introducing the Entrepreneurship Ecosystem: Four Defining Characteristics*, https://www.forbes.com/sites/danisenberg/2011/05/25/introducing-the-entrepreneurship-ecosystem--four-defining-characteristics/#1cf409155fe8 (access: 9 February 2018).

Mirchev A., Dicheva A., *Technological Entrepreneurship of Small and Medium Business in the Republic of Bulgaria as a Factor for Sustainable Development*, proceedings of the CBU International Conference on Integration and Innovation in Science and Education, 2013.

Россия наращивает технологическое отставание [*Russia is increasing the technological gap*], https://news.rambler.ru/scitech/39457868-rossiya-naraschivaet-tehnologicheskoe-otstavanie (access: 4 April 2019).

Strategy of Scientific and Technological Development of the Russian Federation, approved by the Decree of the President of the Russian Federation of 1 December 2016, No. 642.

Yanik A. A., *Peculiarities of Commercialization of Results of Private Sector Research and Development for NASA: Experience of the Small Business Innovation Research Program*, "Space Exploration" 2017, 2.

The Role of Innovation Management Standards in Fostering Innovation Processes in Enterprises

Prof. Sławomir Olko, Ph.D.   ⓘD https://orcid.org/0000-0001-5284-6284
Silesian University of Technology

Prof. Krzysztof Wodarski, Ph.D.   ⓘD https://orcid.org/0000-0002-4725-1064
Silesian University of Technology

Abstract

The paper presents the essence and role of innovation management standards in fostering innovation processes in enterprises. It demonstrates the scope of the selected management standards and specifies the scope of the impact of innovation management standards CEN/TS 16555 and ISO 56000 in this context. Based on the substantive standards of innovation management, the paper elaborates on the way they may assist in implementing contemporary innovation management concepts. The paper also tries to specify practical recommendations concerning the formation of the innovation management system in an enterprise, according to the standards.

Keywords: innovation, innovation management, innovation processes, standardisation, enterprises

Introduction

Using the standards that significantly affect the operations and processes implemented within organisations is a very important issue of management practice. This standard is defined by the International Organization for Standardization (ISO) as follows: "document established by consensus and approved by a recognised body that provides, for common and repeated use, rules, guidelines or characteristics for activities or their results, aimed at the achievement of the optimum degree of order in a given context" (ISO 1996). According to the European Committee for Standardization (CEN) "standards are documents that set out specifications and other technical information with regard to various kinds of products, materials, services and processes" (CEN). The essence of the standard is its practical dimension—it should not be subject to scientific discussions and instead it should utilise recognised scientific achievements. The managers, using management standards, are expected to use a common system of terms and knowledge that rationalise and improve the processes implemented within organisations.

Within recent years, one may observe the cooperation of institutions supplying standards within the scope of developing innovation management standards. In 2013, the European Standard CEN/TS 16555 was issued, within the scope of the Technical Committee CEN/TC 389—Innovation Management, under the auspices of the European Committee for Standardization (CEN). Its further versions and parts were published in 2015. At the global level, the progress of tasks' implementation within the scope of developing innovation management standards is much smaller. In 2013, within the International Standardization Organization, a new technical committee ISO/TC 279 Innovation Management has been appointed in order to develop international innovation management standards, i.e. ISO 56000.

The development of innovation management standards is a new phenomenon and it is difficult to determine the results of dissemination of these standards in practice. From the standpoint of management sciences, one may consider the role and results of applying the standards based on a comparison with other, commonly applied standards in areas such as management or project management. It is also possible to consider how innovation management standards reflect the most important challenges and concepts of innovation management described by scientific communities. These issues are addressed in this paper.

Challenges in innovation management

Even though innovation management has become the answer to contemporary problems related to civilisation development, it faces many issues extended by the modern environment. The emerging management concepts, often inspired by practical applications, are the answer to these challenges. The most important changes paradoxically concern not innovation management itself, but the changing needs, expectations and behaviours of recipients. R. Verganti has pointed to a new area of creating value for clients related to meaning for the recipient. In the innovation concept driven by design, the designing process is not as relevant as the granted or previously noticed meaning for the recipient. The author neither excludes the functionality of a product nor the utilisation of new technologies to create products and services; the most important discriminant of design-driven innovation is meaning.[1] Another phenomenon related to

---

[1]   R. Verganti, *Design Driven Innovation*, Harvard Business Press, Boston 2009.

recipients of innovation that affects innovation processes is collaborative consumption creating a systematically growing sharing economy.[2] Companies offering services such as sharing economy (e.g. Uber, AirBnb, BlaBlaCar) are direct users of this phenomenon, however, producers operating on consumer markets (e.g. automotive) also consider the ever-growing propensity of consumers to using instead of having. In case of innovative processes, this means consideration of a product or service consumption method by users, and the engagement of marketers, who are able to cooperate with users. An increasing group of consumers of the sharing economy use calculated trust based on opinions about a product or supplier provided by Internet platforms.[3]

Another contemporary challenge concerning innovation management in enterprises regards the protection of intellectual property. Traditional (closed) and open models of innovation management (open innovation) that co-exist do not facilitate the selection of innovation strategy for entrepreneurs. Both models have different ways of cooperation with the surrounding entities at each stage of the innovation process and methods of protecting intellectual property.[4] Moreover, there are also mixed models of intellectual property management, applied by enterprises: in case of some products and projects, enterprises apply the traditional innovation management model, while the open innovation model is used only in certain cases. For example Toyota—a concern that has been using the traditional (closed) innovation management model for years, has announced the disclosure of over 5 thousand own patents related to the technology of fuel cell vehicles (FCV). This is a typical symptom of the open innovation model by opening the access to complementary products suppliers (e.g. hydrogen refuelling stations), without any negotiation needs.

The field of knowledge management, including creating new knowledge, i.e. creativity management, is one closely related to the innovation management sector. This represents another challenge for enterprises facing many barriers related to creating, transferring, storing and making knowledge available. The challenges of creativity management are related to the method of engaging employees into creative processes—transfer from individual creativity to collective creativity and methods for assessing new ideas.[5] Despite underlining the meaning of creativity, creative workers (creative class defined by R. Florida)[6] there is still not enough knowledge and practical instruments to use creativity within innovation management processes.

---

[2]   R. Botsman, R. Rogers, *What's Mine Is Yours: The Rise of Collaborative Consumption*, Harper Collins Publishers, New York 2010.

[3]   Ch. Mittendorf, *Collaborative Consumption: The Role of Familiarity and Trust among Millennials*, "Journal of Consumer Marketing" 2018, 35, 4.

[4]   H. Chesbrough, W. Vanhaveberke, J. West, *Open Innovation. Researching a New Paradigm*, Oxford University Press, New York 2006.

[5]   P. Gloor, *Swarm Creativity. Competitive Advantage through Collaborative Innovation Networks*, Oxford University Press, Oxford 2006.

[6]   R. Florida, *Cities and the Creative Class*, Routlege, New York 2005.

Probably the ethical field is the most underestimated one within innovation management. Despite frequently asked questions about the level of novelty, progress, ground-breaking events, no one ever asks whether this solution is correct. Does it serve the society? Theoreticians try to answer these challenges by pointing to the meaning of social architecture of an enterprise within innovative processes,[7] the meaning of the ethical code within creative networks[8] or the introduction of the dimension of wisdom into the knowledge management model.[9] Surowiecki concludes that rational and ethical decisions are made with the engagement of various social partners providing the so-called phenomenon of crowd wisdom. Methods based on using crowd wisdom will be developed in the future and the author believes that the key to gain reliable and accurate prognoses is not only the improvement of methods, but also the satisfaction of specified conditions by the group: variety, independence and decentralisation.[10]

The previously described challenges of open innovation, knowledge management as well as creative and ethical challenges are focused on the issues of the network approach to management. Contemporary innovation, especially ground-breaking innovations comprise the effectiveness of the operation inter-organisational and social networks. Within the network, new ideas are generated, developed, accepted and implemented. The network significantly affects not only innovation management but also the contemporary organisation theory.[11]

To a certain degree, the presented challenges are being solved, and will be in the future, by the standards of innovation management. The very initiation of a dialogue concerning innovation management standards with the participation of corporate, scientific and administrative communities is a very beneficial phenomenon.

Standards in management

The essence of such a standard is its voluntary application. In particular, the European Standards published by the European Committee for Standardization (CEN) are developed by experts, established by consensus and adopted by the Members of CEN. It is important to note that the use of standards is voluntary, hence there is no legal obligation to apply them.

---

[7]   C. K. Prahalad, M. S. Krishnan, *The New Age of Innovation. Driving Co-Created Value through Global Networks*, McGraw Hill, New York 2008.

[8]   P. Gloor, *Swarm Creativity...*

[9]   J. Rowley, *The Wisdom Hierarchy: Representations of the DIKW Hierarchy*, "Journal of Information Science" 2007, 33, 2.

[10]   J. Surowiecki, *The Wisdom of Crowds*, Anchor Books, New York 2005.

[11]   J. Stachowicz, *Zmiany w zarządzaniu wobec sieciowego podejścia w teorii organizacji* [in:] *Zarządzanie organizacją. Koncepcje, wyzwania, perspektywy*, ed. by M. Grabowska, B. Ślusarczyk, Wydawnictwo Wydziału Zarządzania Politechniki Częstochowskiej, Częstochowa 2017.

Initially, the standards were used first and foremost in operational management, in case of repeatable and systematic processes (production, logistics, services). Now, management of the process considers activities within the field of research and development representing the essence of innovative processes.[12] Theoretical resources related to these phenomena may be found in the concept of the ambidextrous organisation already developed in the seventies of the twentieth century by R. Duncan. He specified organisational ambidexterity as an ability of the organisation to equal treatment of functions related to the current implementation of needs and functions, which allow for adaptation of the changing surroundings.[13] Within the first aspect, we deal with operational activity (production, services) that is naturally subjected to standardisation. The second aspect deals with strategic management, research and development, innovations, improvements, rationalisation. In this case, standardisation is more difficult because these activities require more flexibility and they are repeatable to a lesser extent.

Table 1 presents a list of the most important standards affecting organisation management. The list shows standards concerning quality management, environment management, project management, social responsibility of business and the newest—innovation management. The scope of present standards affecting organisation management could be much broader and cover, e.g. energy management, safety at work management, information safety management, risk management. In the future, the list of standards having a practical application for organisation management can be even longer.

The introduction of quality management standards influenced the practical and theoretical aspects of management. ISO 9000 standards also considered some areas of innovation management that were most clearly manifested in the standard series ISO 9004:2009. The preamble to this standard reads that success can be achieved by the introduction of improvements and innovations. The self-assessment model of this standard series is presented as an important tool identifying the areas for improvement and introduction of innovations.

---

[12]   J. Jetson, *Business Process Management. Proactical Guidelines to Succesful Implementation*, Routledge, London–New York 2018.

[13]   R. Duncan, *The Ambidextrous Organization: Designing Dual Structures for Innovation* [in:] *The Management of Organization*, ed. by R. H. Killman, L. R. Pondy, D. Sleven, North Holland, New York 1976.

Table 1. The main standards in management

Management area	Standards	Present specific fields	Years of establishment
Quality management	ISO 9000	Quality management system Organisation and its context Needs and expectations of relevant interested parties Leadership Planning Support Operation Performance evaluation	1987–2015
Environmental management	ISO 14000	Environmental policy Environmental plan Plan implementation Monitoring and corrective actions Management review	1996–2015
Project management	ISO 21500	Process groups: Initiating, Implementing, Controlling, Closing Subject groups: Integration, Stakeholder, Scope, Resource, Time, Cost, Risk, Quality, Procurement, Communication	2007–2012
Corporate social responsibility	ISO 26000	Organisational governance Human rights Labour practices The environment Fair operating practices Consumer issues Community involvement and development	2010
Innovation management	CEN/TS 16555	Innovation management system Strategic intelligence management Innovation thinking Intellectual property management Collaboration management Creativity management	2013–2015
	ISO 56000	Innovation management system Tools and methods for innovation partnership Assessment Intellectual property management Strategic intelligence management Idea management	2019–2021 (TBC)

Source: prepared by the author.

In Chapter 9 *Improvement, innovations and learning*, the subject of innovation appears in the form of recommendations as to what activities the organisation should undertake within the area of innovation, i.e.:
- identify the need for innovation,
- set and maintain an effective and efficient innovation process,
- provide proper resources which will be necessary to implement innovations on selected or all levels of management (ISO 9000:2009).

Project management is another important area of organisation management that has its own standards and is connected with the field of innovation management. The basic standard in this sector is ISO 21500, which to a high extent is based on the development of principles and is described in the Guide to the project management Body of Knowledge (PMBOK). These sources describe the project management system within organisations together with their environment and considerations. Small and medium enterprises apply projects management methods for the development of new products, even if they do not have a project management system or implemented project management standards.[14] One of key areas in project management is that of risk management covering the analysis of the existing risk sources in projects and the identification of preventive activities for limitation of their results.[15]

Innovation management standards

The European standards published in 2015 by the Technical Committee CEN/TC 389—Innovation Management, cover part of the areas having a status of technical specifications:
1. CEN/TS 16555-1 Innovation management, Part 1: Innovation management system,
2. CEN/TS 16555-2 Innovation management, Part 2: Strategic intelligence management,
3. CEN/TS 16555-3 Innovation management, Part 3: Innovation thinking,
4. CEN/TS 16555-4 Innovation management, Part 4: Intellectual Property Management,
5. CEN/TS 16555-5 Innovation management, Part 5: Collaboration management,
6. CEN/TS 16555-6 Innovation management, Part 6: Creativity management.

Figure 1 presents the main elements described in standard CEN/TS 16555. Each element is described by Clauses 4 to 11. The surroundings of the whole system are

---

[14] J. Bijańska, K. Wodarski, J. Wójcik, *Preparing the Production of a New Product in Small and Medium-Sized Enterprises by Using the Method of Projects Management*, "Management Systems in Production Engineering" 2016, 6, 2.

[15] A. Ober, K. Wodarski, *Identyfikacja i ocena ryzyka projektu badawczego w uczelni na etapie jego przygotowania*, "Zeszyty Naukowe Politechniki Śląskiej" 2014, 70; J. Bijańska, K. Wodarski, *Risk Management in the Planning of Development Projects in the Industrial Enterprises*, "Metalurgija" 2014, 53, 2.

described in Clause 4 *Context of the organization*. Clause 5 specifies the requirements concerning *Leadership for innovation* as well as *Innovation Strategy*—a formalised document defining the Organisation's objectives within the area of innovativeness. The innovation process takes place with *Enabling factors* (Clause 5) and using *Innovation Management Techniques* (Clause 11). The core for the complex approach is the innovative process (Clause 8) starting from the idea resource and ending at the results: implemented innovations and revenues gained upon them. The innovative process and its results should be subjected to assessment (Clause 9) which is the basis for *Improvement* (Clause 10) and *Planning* (Clause 6). The complex system has a series of recommendations within each of its elements described in the Clauses, however, it does not detail, e.g. specific innovation management techniques or planning instruments.

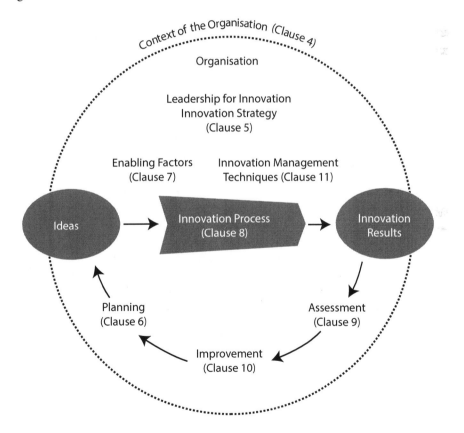

Figure 1. Key elements of the Innovation Management System described in CEN/TS 16555-1:2013 standards

Source: CEN/TS 16555-1:2013 Innovation management.

At the global level, under auspices of the International Organization for Standardization (ISO) and in cooperation with the European Committee for Standardization (CEN) there are works being performed concerning the creation of international innovation management standards. The Technical Committee ISO TC 279 has been established for that purpose, in order to create and publish a series of standards ISO/DIS 56000. According to information of the ISO for mid-2018, the standards were to be published by the end of 2018, and we know that two standards were published in mid-2019, whereas five standards are under development.[16] At the moment, 43 countries (participating members) participate in the works of the Committee ISO TC 279, while 15 countries have the status of Observing Members.[17]

Within the scope of the committee, there are four working groups operating within the following substantive areas:

1. The Innovation Management System covers seven key elements of the management system and provides more detailed guidance under each area. The group is working under the convenorship of Argentina and the main deliverable will be ISO 56002.

2. The terminology covers the fundamentals of innovation management, the Innovation Management Principles and a comprehensive list of terms and definitions. The group is led by a convener from Norway and the main publication will be ISO 56000.

3. Tools and methods covers several areas under the overall convenorship of Canada and will publish document ISO 56003. Current work is focued on guidance for Innovation Partnerships, Intellectual Property Rights (led by China) and Strategic Intelligence (led by Spain).

4. The Innovation Management Assessment will provide guidance for assessing the innovation management system of a company or organisation. The group is led by a German convener and the document number will be ISO 56004.

Recommendations for business management

The innovation management standards form general premises related to the construction of the innovation management system and innovation process management in enterprises. Due to a significant number of the surrounding considerations and context considerations (size of enterprise, discipline), the standards themselves do not provide answers. This area belongs to decision makers, or leaders responsible for creating strategies and managers responsible for the implementation of innovative processes at operational level. Considering the premises included in the basic literature concerning

---

[16]   ISO/TC 279 Innovation management, https://www.iso.org/standard/69315.html (access: 15 July 2019).

[17]   ISO/TC 279 Participation, https://www.iso.org/committee/4587737.html?view=participation (access: 15 July 2019).

innovation management[18] that summarise the years of practical experience, one may form the elements of innovation management presented in Table 2.

The strategy within the area of innovation may be included in the main organisation strategy or present a separate document. A substantive scope of the strategy may be differentiated, however, it should specify the strategic objectives within the area of innovation management, which are described using measures and indexes. Even though the standards do not specify which management instruments to apply, the balanced scorecard (BSC) is a perfect tool for the proposed conditions. According to the concept of BSC, the strategy results from the possessed vision and objectives which are specified in four perspectives: financial, internal processes, organisational capacity and client. Both the objectives and measures as well as the innovative process within the area of innovation management are assigned to the perspective of internal processes. As underlined by Norton and Kaplan, based on their experience with enterprises, innovations constitute a critical internal process responsible for creating value within a longer perspective and the opportunity to enter new markets.[19]

Table 2. Elements of innovation management in organisations compliant with standards

Element	Area of application	Characteristic
Innovation strategy	Organisation' strategy Innovation strategy as a separate document	Analysis Vision Strategic objectives
Innovation process	Maps of processes Innovation strategy Balanced scorecard	Key stages of innovation process: Search, Select, Implement, Capture[20] or Idea generation, Evaluation, Realisation[21] corresponding with organisational units and other organisational processes
Measure/indicators	Innovation strategy Innovation performance Balanced scorecard	• number of new products implemented, • revenue from new products, • number of R&D projects, • new product lead time, • number of verified ideas (proof of concept), • number of granted patents, • . . .

Source: prepared by the author.

---

[18]   P. Trott, *Innovation Management and New Product Development*, Prentice Hall 2008; J. Tidd, J. Bessant, K. Pavitt, *Managing Innovation: Integrating Technological, Market and Organizational Change*, John Wiley & Sons Ltd 2005; J. Tidd, J. Bessant, *Strategic Innovation Management*, Wiley, New York 2014.

[19]   R. S. Kaplan, D. P. Norton, *The Balanced Scorecard: Translating Strategy into Action*, Harvard Business School Press, Boston 1996.

[20]   J. Tidd, J. Bessant, K. Pavitt, *Managing Innovation...*

[21]   P. Trott, *Innovation Management...*

Table 2 also proposes a few of the most important measures of companies' innovative operations, considering the fact that the progress in innovation management and the pursuit of the innovation management system for maturity can be analysed and simulated based on the comprehensiveness and variety of the applied measures. In the practice of innovation management, one may use measures related to the final effects (e.g. income from innovation, number of introduced products) and to the stability of the internal innovative environment (e.g. the number of organisational innovations, the number of innovative projects). A. Shapiro proposes the application of a percentage of revenue from new platforms instead of a share in the sale of innovative products. By "platform" the author means dynamic interaction of a new product and its application on the market.[22]

Based on the Balanced Scorecard approach, the role of strategic initiatives must be considered when creating the innovation management system. Strategic Initiatives are action projects necessary to help the organisation be successful with its strategy. As an example, a strategic initiative may be a project related to creating an innovation management system, mapping the innovative process, creating the system of generating and evaluating ideas, etc. A system organised this way allows for creating a business model within an enterprise that is empowered by innovations.[23]

The summarising element is the assessment of enterprises' operation within innovations that enable the creation og preventive actions. Complex assessment of innovative operations in enterprises is the subject of innovation audits, the substantive scope of which is presented by the author of this paper.[24]

Conclusions

The presented process for the development of innovation management standards invites to formulate the following conclusions:
1. The scope of partners' engagement in creating standards within administrative, corporate and scientific, communities shows that innovation management standards will be very important in the future.
2. The development of a common language for theoreticians and practitioners within innovation management is especially important. Creating a common communication platform within an organisation that includes designers, R&D employees, managers, technological specialists, financial officers, operative staff and representatives of

---

[22] A. R. Shapiro, *Measuring Innovation: Beyond Revenue from New Products*, "Research-Technology Management" 2006, 49, 6.
[23] J. Brzóska, *Innowacje jako czynnik dynamizujący modele biznesowe*, Wydawnictwo Politechniki Śląskiej, Gliwice 2014.
[24] S. Olko, *Audyt innowacyjności przedsiębiorstwa – zakres merytoryczny wybranych podejść praktycznych*, "Przegląd Organizacji" 2017, 7.

external entities participating in innovative processes may be the most important result of implementing innovation management standards in enterprises.

3. The improvement of efficiency and effectiveness of the innovative processes in companies may be an important positive result of the introduction of innovation management standards. This may be achieved by creating elements of innovative strategy based on measures or indexes according to the Balanced Scorecard approach or development of the Innovation Management System (IMS), the centre of which would be represented by the developed innovation management process together with its stages, responsible units and interrelation with other processes on the map of the organisation's processes.

4. Among the expected positive elements of implementing innovation management standards, we may also indicate a better formation of organisational structures due to precise determination of innovative processes, assignment of departments to organisational cells and shaping their competences.

5. Skilful utilisation of innovation management standards may be not only a factor supporting innovation standards within large companies, but also a set of good practices for the SME sector (e.g. for selected elements described in the standards). It may also be an important element supporting the national and regional innovation system.

6. The most important contemporary challenges in innovation management such as open innovation, sharing economy, creativity management, knowledge management, intellectual property management, are discussed in innovation management standards. Innovation management standards are the least related to ethical challenges—leaving judgement as to the fairness of the implemented innovation strategy to the entrepreneurs themselves. This gap is filled to a high extent by the standards of social responsibility of the business ISO 26000.

Bibliography

Ahlemann F., Teuteberg F., Vogelsang K., *Project Management Standards: Diffusion and Application in Germany and Switzerland*, "International Journal of Project Management" 2009.

Bijańska J., Wodarski K., *Risk Management in the Planning of Development Projects in the Industrial Enterprises*, "Metalurgija" 2014, 53, 2.

Bijańska J., Wodarski K., Wójcik J., *Preparing the Production of a New Product in Small and Medium--Sized Enterprises by Using the Method of Projects Management*, "Management Systems in Production Engineering" 2016, 6, 2.

Botsman R., Rogers R., *What's Mine Is Yours: The Rise of Collaborative Consumption*, Harper Collins Publishers, New York 2010.

Brzóska J., *Innowacje jako czynnik dynamizujący modele biznesowe*, Wydawnictwo Politechniki Śląskiej, Gliwice 2014.

Burgelman R., Christensen C., Wheelwright S., *Strategic Management of Technology and Innovation. 5ᵗʰ Edition*, McGraw Hill 2009.

CEN European Committee for Standarization, https://www.cen.eu/you/EuropeanStandardization/Pages/default.aspx (access: 15 July 2019).

Chesbrough H., Vanhaveberke W., West J., *Open Innovation. Researching a New Paradigm*, Oxford University Press, New York 2006.

Delmas M. A., *The Diffusion of Environmental Management Standards in Europe and in the United States: An Institutional Perspective*, "Policy Sciences" 2002, 35.

Duncan R., *The Ambidextrous Organization: Designing Dual Structures for Innovation* [in:] *The Management of Organization*, ed. by R. H. Killman, L. R. Pondy, D. Sleven, North Holland, New York 1976.

Ferreira J. M., Fernandes C. I., Alves H., Raposo M. L., *Drivers of Innovation Strategies: Testing the Tidd and Bessant (2009) Model*, "Journal of Business Research" 2015, 68.

Florida R., *Cities and the Creative Class*, Routlege, New York 2005.

Gloor P., *Swarm Creativity. Competitive Advantage through Collaborative Innovation Networks*, Oxford University Press, Oxford 2006.

Grau N., *Standards and Excellence in Project Management—In Who Do We Trust?*, "Procedia—Social and Behavioral Sciences" 2013, 74.

International Organization for Standardization, International Electrotechnical Commission (ISO/IEC) guide 2, ISO Press, Geneva 1996.

ISO 9000:2009 Quality management (Polish version: PN-EN ISO 9001:2009), http://sklep.pkn.pl/pn-en-iso-9001-2009p.html (access: 10 June 2020).

ISO 9000:2015 Quality management systems Requirements, Quality management systems Fundamentals and vocabulary, https://www.iso.org/news/2015/09/Ref2002.html (access: 10 June 2020).

ISO/TC 279 Innovation management, https://www.iso.org/standard/69315.html (access: 15 July 2019).

ISO/TC 279 Participation, https://www.iso.org/committee/4587737.html?view=participation (access: 15 July 2019).

Jetson J., *Business Process Management. Proactical Guidelines to Succesful Implementation*, Routledge, London – New York 2018.

Kaplan R. S., Norton D. P., *The Balanced Scorecard: Translating Strategy into Action*, Harvard Business School Press, Boston 1996.

Kristinsdóttir L. K., Möller E., *ISO 21500: The Benefits of Structure, Processes and Communication*, "International Journal of Managerial Studies and Research" 2015, 3, 8.

Mittendorf Ch., *Collaborative Consumption: The Role of Familiarity and Trust among Millennials*, "Journal of Consumer Marketing" 2018, 35, 4.

Ober A., Wodarski K., *Identyfikacja i ocena ryzyka projektu badawczego w uczelni na etapie jego przygotowania*, "Zeszyty Naukowe Politechniki Śląskiej" 2014, 70.

Olko S., *Audyt innowacyjności przedsiębiorstwa – zakres merytoryczny wybranych podejść praktycznych*, "Przegląd Organizacji" 2017, 7.

Prahalad C. K., Krishnan M. S., *The New Age of Innovation. Driving Co-created Value through Global Networks*, McGraw Hill, New York 2008.

Rowley J., *The Wisdom Hierarchy: Representations of the DIKW Hierarchy*, "Journal of Information Science" 2007, 33, 2.

Shapiro A. R., *Measuring Innovation: Beyond Revenue from New Products*, "Research-Technology Management" 2006, 49, 6.

Stachowicz J., *Zmiany w zarządzaniu wobec sieciowego podejścia w teorii organizacji* [in:] *Zarządzanie organizacją. Koncepcje, wyzwania, perspektywy*, ed. by M. Grabowska, B. Ślusarczyk, Wydawnictwo Wydziału Zarządzania Politechniki Częstochowskiej, Częstochowa 2017.

Surowiecki J., *The Wisdom of Crowds*, Anchor Books, New York 2005.

Tidd J., Bessant J., Pavitt K., *Managing Innovation: Integrating Technological, Market and Organizational Change*, John Wiley & Sons Ltd 2005.

Tidd J., Bessant J., *Strategic Innovation Management*, Wiley, New York 2014.

Trott P., *Innovation Management and New Product Development*, Prentice Hall 2008.

Verganti R., *Design Driven Innovation*, Harvard Business Press, Boston 2009.

Wyroba A., *System zarządzania innowacjami w normach ISO i CEN*, IV Konferencja „Dobre praktyki zarządzania" 2015, https://wiedza.pkn.pl (access: 15 July 2019).

Organisational Innovations in the e-Business Model Maturity Assessment

Prof. Bogdan Nogalski, Ph.D. ⓘ https://orcid.org/0000-0003-0262-8355
WSB University in Gdańsk

Prof. Przemysław Niewiadomski, Ph.D. ⓘ https://orcid.org/0000-0002-2805-4671
University of Zielona Góra

Abstract

The main purpose of this paper is an attempt to create a catalogue of organisational innovations that determine the maturity of the e-commerce business model. The conduct of a conceptual study will be preceded by an extensive analysis and systematisation of the current achievements in the field of management and quality sciences. This will be reflected in a set of organisational innovations identified in the subject literature that can constitute the basis for assessing maturity of the e-commerce model (theoretical level). The reconstruction and interpretation of the subject literature will be supported by practical experience of the authors, participant observation and creative discussion among deliberately chosen experts. This will allow to create a catalogue of organisational innovations relevant from the perspective of the e-commerce model maturity assessment (design level). The preparatory study determines the development of a form (model of organisational innovations) that will be a tool enabling reconnaissance in the practice of companies (proper study). It is about recognising which of the organisational innovations listed in the catalogue are crucial from the perspective of the e-commerce model maturity assessment (empirical level).

Keywords: innovation, organisational innovations, e-business, e-commerce, innovativeness

Introduction

The generation, adaptation and effective implementation of innovations constitute an essential component of strategic development of companies serving the construction of competitive advantages. Therefore, it is justified to show the activity in the field of searching for and recognising innovative solutions coming from the (internal and external) environment, in which organisations participate. It provides the opportunity to better deal with the occurring threats and, at the same time, to participate in the ongoing changes. The organisation's success is determined, in an increasing extent, by the ability of continuous work on improving the level of efficiency in connection with the development of human capital, the creation of a pro-innovative organisational culture and adjusting to the environment as part of putting focus on the most important objectives.

The issues of innovativeness, its connections and impact on the competitiveness of companies have been the object of intense deliberations of many researchers for decades. Nevertheless, in the Polish economy, the barriers limiting the openness of entrepreneurs to this aspect are still visible. The lack of practical instruments supporting innovative processes is noticeable. An attempt to overcome these fears by changing the perception of organisational innovativeness and an indication of potential business benefits from their use constitute an important premise of the subject matter. The study comprises a response to the partially shown needs of Polish companies in the field of implementing innovative organisational solutions.

The main subject of research includes organisational innovations. The essence of the undertaken research efforts consists in an attempt to identify the key organisational innovations determining the e-commerce model maturity.[1] In this process, it is important to capture a credible research perspective, therefore, the taken issues were implemented with a focus on the selected sector.

The conduct of a conceptual study will be preceded by an extensive analysis and systematisation of the current achievements in the field of management and quality sciences. This will be reflected in a set of organisational innovations identified in the subject literature that can constitute the basis for assessing the e-commerce model maturity (theoretical level). The reconstruction and interpretation of the subject literature will be supported by practical experience of the authors, participant observation and a creative discussion among deliberately chosen experts. This will allow to create a catalogue of organisational innovations relevant from the perspective of the e-commerce model maturity assessment (design level). The preparatory study determines the development of a form (model of organisational innovations) that will comprise a tool enabling reconnaissance in the practice of companies (proper study). It is about recognising which of the organisational innovations listed in the catalogue are crucial from the perspective of the e-commerce model maturity assessment (empirical level).[2]

The paper includes not only academic postulates of innovativeness or maturity, but also practical tips for constructing guidelines for decision-makers and managers of

---

[1]   In the study, it is adopted that the maturity is defined as "a state of being complete, perfect and ready." See G. Lahrmann, F. Marx, R. Winter, F. Wortmann, *Business Intelligence Maturity Models: An Overview* [in:] *Information Technology and Innovation Trends in Organizations. Italian Chapter of AIS*, ed. by A. D'Atri, M. Ferrara, J. George, P. Spagnoletti, Springer Verlag, Naples 2010.

[2]   The concepts of e-commerce and e-business are used interchangeably in the paper.

the agricultural machinery sector. The study carries a charge of the theoretical and empirical study. It takes into account knowledge and expert experience. It can support competitive activities of creators and innovation adapters, especially that: "…in turbulent times, managers cannot assume that tomorrow will be an extension of today. On the contrary, when managing they need to keep in mind that any change can be both an opportunity and a threat…"[3]

E-business model: assumptions and recommendations

We live in a period of continuous technical revolution that turns into the phase of social relevance.[4] By observing changes on the basis of global processes, it is possible to assume the generalised statement that the present world has entered the period where efficiently acquired, analysed, processed and skilfully used information is the most valuable asset. The current society is one based on information, data and effective techniques of its processing. It is also based on the methods of their organisation, distribution and storage, and as a consequence, creating the resources of knowledge and business "wisdom." The creation and development of modern electronic communication forms with the use of ICT (*Information and Communication Technologies*)[5] technology solutions, in particular, the global Internet network, is a clear factor in the modulation of the global nature of today.

Great attention is paid to the e-commerce model, which is a relatively new form of conducting entrepreneurial activity that has become a virtual space of economic relations and particularly strong social relationships.[6] In the simplest terms, it involves conducting business activity in the Internet (network). Electronic business (e-business) consists in the use of the Internet to connect (link) and facilitate the conduct (performance) of business ventures, e-commerce, communication and cooperation inside the company and with the entire external environment.[7] E-commerce includes transactions that are carried out through IP protocol-based networks. Goods and services are ordered directly (on-line), while delivery and payment can take place on-line

---

[3]   P. F. Drucker, *Zarządzanie w czasach burzliwych* [*Management in turbulent times*], transl. J. Kajdy, Wydawnictwo Akademii Ekonomicznej w Krakowie, Kraków 1995, p. 47.

[4]   S. Lachowski, *Pracuj ciężko – baw się – zmieniaj świat* [*Work hard—have fun—change the world*], Studio EMKA, Warszawa 2010, p. 23.

[5]   ICT technologies used in IT and telecommunications are closely related to the development and progress of the semiconductor sector in the scope of miniaturisation of electronic devices. See M. A. Weresa, *Systemy innowacyjne we współczesnej gospodarce światowej* [*Innovative systems in the modern world economy*], Wydawnictwo Naukowe PWN, Warszawa 2012, p. 190.

[6]   In Poland, serious e-commerce development dates back to 2000 and later. The term "e-commerce" itself came into general use in 1997, and it was created by the IBM company.

[7]   C. Combe, *Introduction to e-Business, Management and Strategy*, Routledge, Amsterdam et al. 2006, p. 22.

or off-line.[8] Thus, in such a course of reasoning, the most universal interpretation of the meaning of "e-commerce" will be to understand it as transactions of any content, related to business activity, which are implemented with the use of ICT media. The development of technology and tools focused on ensuring a high level of interaction with users, freedom and convenience in use while taking into account a non-overload of terminal equipment proves to be particularly important.

The electronic business model eliminates unnecessary, costly and time-consuming chains of intermediaries allowing for direct access with an offer to target recipients. It eliminates time and space barriers and allows for real-time operation. E-business is a new, innovative way of the organisation's functioning. Therefore, it is more flexible, faster, cheaper, and prone to necessary modulation and more practical.[9] Innovative methods for conducting business activity on the electronic market have become a source of new ways to achieve efficiency and create values. They have contributed to a mental change in the approach to organising market activities and a shift in the current management rules, methods and processes. E-business has revolutionised business models and strategies, as well as it has changed the entire business both on the timescale and on the scale of technology.[10]

Activity of the e-business indisputably has a commercial dimension, i.e. such aimed at generating commercial processes leading to obtaining profitability (viability, lucrativeness, gainfulness). Commercialisation is basically the process of subordinating some part of social or economic life to commercial and trading rules occurring in a given place and time. It is the adjustment of a given economic entity to the market economy requirements.

In the context of the above, attention should be paid to certain symptoms of following not only the acquisition of relevant information or skills of dealing with them, but also striving for being an "efficient operator" of IT systems. There are more and more SaaS (system at service) solutions based on a cloud computing model, which leads to the need to have practical skills in their interface operation. Comprehensive analytical BI (Business Intelligence) modules seem to outstrip the ERP (Enterprise Resource Planning) class solutions that are known in practice and commonly used, MRP (Material Requirements Planning), and CRM (Customer Relationship Management). They certainly complement them in the scope of transforming data into information, and information into useful business knowledge.

---

[8] E-commerce (e-business) activity sometimes excludes orders placed by phone, fax or via e-mail. It is difficult for the authors to agree with such a perception, in the context of, for example, a strongly developing direction of e-mail marketing or e-mail automation.

[9] A. Grandys, *E-commerce* [in:] *Business Management*, ed. by A. Pomykalski, Wydawnictwo Politechniki Łódzkiej, Łódź 2008, p. 10.

[10] A. Olczak, *E-biznes – główne obszary innowacji* [*E-business—main areas of innovation*] [in:] *Innowacje w rozwijaniu konkurencyjności firm* [*Innovations in the development of the competitiveness of companies*], ed. by J. Perenc, J. Hołub-Iwan, C.H. Beck, Warszawa 2011, p. 304.

The following dynamic development of instruments of electronic exchange of data includes a number of new technologies, such as, e.g. the Internet of Things,[11] cloud computing,[12] Big Data analysis,[13] artificial intelligence, and also incremental print,[14] augmented reality[15] or cobots.[16]

The market advantage is determined not so much by the strength of resources, but by the resource in the form of key knowledge and skills of its practical application. Therefore, it is crucial to implement the processes of customising systems that take care of the coherence of many dimensions of collected and processed information.

Material and method

By using the method for reconstruction and interpretation of the subject literature[17] supported by the authors' own experience and participant observation, a number of organisational innovations that could be the foundations in the assessment process

---

[11]   L. Atzori, A. Iera, G. Morabito, *The Internet of Things: A Survey,* "Computer Networks" 2010, 54, 15; D. Zuehlkea, *SmartFactory: Towards a Factory-of-Things,* "Annual Reviews in Control" 2010, 34, 1.

[12]   X. Xu, *From Cloud Computing to Cloud Manufacturing,* "Robotics and Computer Integrated Manufacturing" 2012, 28, 1; S. Subashini, V. Kavitha, *A Survey on Security Issues in Service Delivery Models of Cloud Computing,* "Journal of Network and Computer Applications" 2011, 34, 1; O. F. Valilai, M. Houshmand, *A Collaborative and Integrated Platform to Support Distributed Manufacturing System Using a Service-Oriented Approach Based on Cloud Computing Paradigm,* "Robotics and Computer Integrated Manufacturing" 2013, 29, 1; X. V. Wang, X. W. Xu, *An Interoperable Solution for Cloud Manufacturing,* "Robotics and Computer Integrated Manufacturing" 2013, 29, 4.

[13]   J. Lee, H. A. Kao, S. Yang, *Service Innovation and Smart Analytics for Industry 4.0 and Big Data Environment,* "Procedia CIRP" 2014, 16.

[14]   J. Sęp, G. Budzik, *Możliwości aplikacyjne technologii Rapid Manufacturing w przemyśle lotniczym [Application possibilities of Rapid Manufaturing technology in the aviation industry],* "Mechanik" 2015, 12.

[15]   D. Stadnicka, D. Antonelli, *Implementation of Augmented Reality in Welding Processes,* "Technologia i Automatyzacja Montażu" 2014, 4; P. Szulewski, *Koncepcje automatyki przemysłowej w środowisku Industry 4.0 [Industrial automation concepts in the Industry 4.0 environment],* "Mechanik" 2016, 7.

[16]   D. Stadnicka, D. Antonelli, Discussion on lean approach implementation in a collaborative man-robot workstation, 6th International Conference on Business Sustainability 2016: "Management, Technology and Learning for Individuals, Organisations and Society in Turbulent Environment", Póvoa de Varzim, Portugal.

[17]   Among others: J. Cieślik, *Iluzje innowacyjnej przedsiębiorczości [Illusions of innovative entrepreneurship],* "Kwartalnik Nauk o Przedsiębiorstwie" 2014, 3; Ch. Freeman, *The Economics of Industrial Innovation,* F. Printer, London 1982; J. Huebner, *A Possible Declining Trend for Worldwide Innovation,* "Technological Forecasting & Social Change" 2005, 72, 8; T. Baczko, *Raport o innowacyjności gospodarki Polski w 2009 roku [Report on the innovativeness of the Polish economy in 2009],* Instytut Nauk Ekonomicznych Polskiej Akademii Nauk, Warszawa 2010; G. Barnett, *Innovation the Basis of Cultural Change,* McGraw Hill, New York 1953; H. Jasiński, *Innowacje i transfer technologii w procesie transformacji [Innovations and technology transfer within a transformation process],* Difin, Warszawa 2006; K. Krzakiewicz, S. Cyfert, *Imitacja w epoce innowacji – dylemat i paradoks współczesnego zarządzania [Imitation in the age of innovation—dilemma and paradox of contemporary management],* "Prace Naukowe Uniwersytetu Ekonomicznego we Wrocławiu" 2016, 420; L. J. Jasiński, *Nowe wymiary gospodarki [New dimensions of economy]* [in:] *Raport o innowacyjności gospodarki Polski w 2010 roku [Report on the innovativeness of the Polish economy in 2010],* ed. by T. Baczko, Instytut Nauk Ekonomicznych Polskiej Akademii Nauk,

of the e-commerce business model maturity was chosen. The query of literature (A) supported by brainstorming among deliberately selected experts (B)—at the design level—has allowed to compile a research tool in the form of an assessment sheet. In three four-person teams, there was a session for generating original ideas (factory of ideas). The session was conducted among 12 deliberately selected experts (Table 1); professionally active people directly or indirectly connected with the activity implemented with the use of ICT media (electronic dimension of conducted business activities).[18]

Table 1. Characteristics of experts

Position	Number	Specialisation	[%]
Business owners	4	Owner supervision	33.33
IT Director—E-commerce	1	SEO (positioning), PPC (Internet advertising), social media, copywriting, Web developers, link building	66.67
Ecommerce Director	1	Content marketing, conversion factor optimisation, lead generation	
Social Media Specialist	1	Facebook	
E-marketing Specialist	1	Designing and conducting of advertising campaigns in the Internet that generate leads and sales.	
Creative Director	1	Social media and e-marketing	
Consultant	1	Google Analytics	
Advisor	1	E-mail marketing	
Digital Marketing Consultant	1	Building of marketing teams, personal and employer branding, performance assessment, digitalisation of services and service design.	

Source: prepared by the author.

Within the framework of the session of generating ideas, the participants wrote down the organisational innovations selected by them, which, in their opinion, may be important from the perspective of the e-business model maturity assessment. The carried-out studies allowed to determine a tool for the next research, including the formulation of

Warszawa 2011; S. Marciniak, *Innowacyjność i konkurencyjność gospodarki* [*Economic innovativeness and competitiveness*], C.H. Beck, Warszawa 2010; E. Mansfield, *Industrial Research and Technological Innovation*, W. W. Norton, New York 1968; M. Pichlak, *Uwarunkowania innowacyjności organizacji. Studium teoretyczne i wyniki badań empirycznych* [*Organisational innovation determinants. Theoretical study and empirical research results*], Difin, Warszawa 2012.

[18] At this point, the authors would like to thank the Poznań company operating in the SEO/SEM industry for making it possible to carry out the survey among a team of experienced experts; company employees.

problems and key issues. They provided interesting information on the language used by "industry experts" to describe phenomena being the subject of the researchers' interest. The authors believe that it has allowed to avoid mistakes at the level of constructing questions and to adapt the language to the potential respondents.

By grouping all the mentioned ideas, and confronting them with proposals of selected researchers, formulated was a catalogue of organisational innovations (research tool in the form of a survey), which was verified (C) in the further part of the paper (and is important from the perspective of the e-commerce model maturity). The proposed survey concept included 33 closed questions referring to five spaces of the e-commerce model (Figure 1).

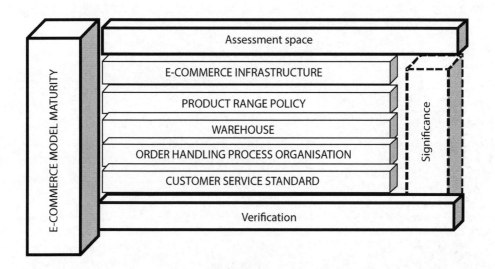

Figure 1. E-commerce model space–research areas

Source: prepared by the author.

In order to carry out the assessment, a five-point scale describing the level of significance of organisational innovation in the context of the e-commerce model maturity assessment was adopted.

The primary stage of the research was implemented in the period from February to April 2019. The research was conducted in two ways, i.e. during direct meetings organised as part of cooperation between the "Fortschritt" company and its selected business partners (19 questionnaires, 32.20% of all respondents) and during visits carried out within the 25th International Fair Of Agricultural Techniques AGROTECH held on 15–17 March 2019 (survey among 40 companies, 67.80% of all respondents). In total, the research covered 59 companies. The use of targeted selection techniques and the possibility of conducting the study during business meetings undoubtedly influenced the high effectiveness and reliability of responses during the study implementation. By taking a decision on the choice of the company and its representing respondent, an important criterion was its direct acquaintance with the authors of the study supported by many years of cooperation with the "Fortschritt" company. This made it possible to determine whether a respondent will be interested in expressing his/her views and if he/she has sufficient knowledge and experience in the scope of the taken issue.

The originally developed catalogue of innovations was assessed among 59 industry experts from micro (10.17%), small (30.51%), medium (54.24%) and large companies (5.08%)

The population of the studied entities were manufacturing companies (69.49%) and trading companies (30.51%) operating in the agricultural machinery sector carrying out the business activity in Poland. Taking into account the distribution due to the prevailing nature of production, the producers declared mass or bulk production (51.22%), short-run production (39.02%) or unit production (9.76%). In case of 21.95% of companies, the production mainly involving the assembly of components, purchased from external suppliers, to finished products, was declared, while 78.05% of companies showed the production process including several phases, within the framework of which components and finished products are consecutively produced. In case of the studied commercial companies, most of them put themselves as an intermediary between the producer and the importer on the one hand, and retail trade on the other hand (90%). The respondents declare purchases of a large quantity of goods from producers (77.78%) or importers (22.22%) and the sale of a smaller quantity of a wide range of products to retail companies.

Having regard to the sample distribution in terms of age, 27.12% constituted the surveyed in the age range to 40 years, 37.29% in the age range of 41–50, 25.42% in the range of 51–60 years, while 10.17% of the surveyed were over 60 years of age (Table 2).

Table 2. Characteristics of the studied population by age (N = 59)

Range	Age	
	Number of participants	[%]
to 30 years	N = 4	6.78
from 31 to 40 years	N = 12	20.34
from 41 to 50 years	N = 22	37.29
from 51 to 60 years	N = 15	25.42
over 60	N = 6	10.17
In total	N = 59	100.00

Source: own work.

Among the surveyed, a group of persons with high school and higher education was the biggest: (90%), 67.80% of which had higher education, 22.03%—high school education, and 10.17%—vocational education. Detailed characteristics are shown in Table 3.

Table 3. Characteristics of the studied population by education (N = 59)

Range	Education	
	Number of participants	[%]
Primary education	N = 0	0.00
Vocational education	N = 6	10.17
High school education	N = 13	22.03
Higher education	N = 40	67.80
In total	N = 59	100.00

Source: own work.

In the course of the carried-out studies, an attempt was made to interpret the results and conduct a more thorough analysis based on the respondents' declarations. The analysis proceeded in accordance with the previously assumed stages. The first of them was correct preparation of the obtained primary data and its proper arrangement. Such a data processing method made it possible to sort the material, arrange innovations together in appropriate groups and reject such data which, from the perspective of the tested issue, occurred to be unreliable or at least questionable. The next stage was a description of the obtained data and its interpretation as shown in the further part of this study.

Innovations in the e-commerce maturity assessment—research model creation

The proposed concept of assessment included 33 descriptions specified in the form of organisational innovations. According to the expert assessment, the indicated levels were considered significant and decisive for the e-commerce model maturity. Therefore, they were considered to be fundamental within the framework of the conducted assessment. The assessment of significance of the organisational innovations from the perspective of the business model maturity is quite difficult, however, an attempt to conduct it was taken in the study. The research results are shown in individual tables.

The opinion on the model maturity in the field of e-commerce infrastructure was prepared with the use of seven selected organisational innovations (Table 4).

Table 4. E-commerce infrastructure in the business model maturity assessment

Assessment descriptions	Implementation level (% of indications)					$\bar{X}$
	Feature value					
	1	2	3	4	5	
Software and license	–	2.0	8.0	20.0	29.0	4.29
	–	3.4	13.6	33.9	49.2	
Sales platforms	–	2.0	6.0	25.0	26.0	4.27
	–	3.4	10.2	42.4	44.1	
Internal integration of the on-line store platform	1.0	2.0	7.0	27.0	22.0	4.14
	1.7	3.4	11.9	45.8	37.3	
External integration of the on-line store platform	–	2.0	6.0	28.0	23.0	4.22
	–	3.4	10.2	47.5	39.0	
Integration with electronic marketing activities	–	2.0	5.0	24.0	28.0	4.32
	–	3.4	8.5	40.7	47.5	
Product architecture management	–	3.0	5.0	26.0	25.0	4.24
	–	5.1	8.5	44.1	42.4	
Introduction of contracting tools	1.0	3.0	6.0	27.0	22.0	4.12
	1.7	5.1	10.2	45.8	37.3	

Source: own work.

In the course of the implemented research—within the framework of the organisational innovations classified within the "e-commerce infrastructure" group—attention was paid to the sales platform engine (average rating of 4.29; 49.2% of indications for the assessment of five points). Attention was paid to the "Open Source" solution selection of the sales platform that is editable and possible to be individually developed. The implementation of comprehensive sales platforms open to integration was considered as a key activity[19] (an average rating of 4.27; 44.1% of indications for the assessment of five points). Desirable action—significantly defining the e-commerce model maturity—was declared as an increase in the level of internal integration of the on-line store platform with other internal systems, such as: CRM (Customer Relationship Management), WMS (Warehouse Management Systems), ERP (Enterprise Resource Planning), accounting programmes and others (average rating of 4.14; 37.3% of indications for the assessment

---

[19] The following panels were defined within the expert research: order panel, customer panel, product panel, marketing panel, content management panel CMS (Content Management System) content management panel, customer and customer relationship management panel CRM (Customer Relationship Management), statistics/analytics panels, and control panels.

of five points). Similarly, the external integration of the on-line store platform with systems of logistics service providers, external partners, advertisers, agents or clients does not remain without significance (average rating of 4.22; 39.0% of indications for the assessment of five points). In the opinion of respondents, maturity is significantly defined by the ability to implement solutions which, within the framework of the sales platform, will enable full integration with the electronic marketing activities (average rating of 4.32; 47.5% of indications for the assessment of five points).[20]

A big challenge for modern e-commerce—in the opinion of respondents—is the introduction of solutions within the sales platform allowing for generating and managing the product architecture (average rating of 4.24; 42.4 % of indications for the assessment of five points) and the introduction of contracting tools (average rating of 4.12; 37.3% of indications for the assessment of five points).

The conducted assessment was an excellent opportunity to exchange views and experience on issues within the e-commerce infrastructure. The research results strengthened the authors' belief that modern companies are characterised by a high level of knowledge and awareness as to the direction of desirable activities in the mentioned scope.

The opinion on the level of the e-commerce model maturity in terms of the product range policy was prepared with the use of four variables, or research questions (Table 5).

Table 5. Product range policy in the e-commerce model maturity assessment

Assessment descriptions	Implementation level (% of indications)					$\bar{X}$
	Feature value					
	1	2	3	4	5	
Cross sourcing	1.0	3.0	9.0	27.0	19.0	4.02
	1.7	5.1	15.3	45.8	32.2	
Standard for qualifying business partners	1.0	1.0	11.0	28.0	18.0	4.03
	1.7	1.7	18.6	47.5	30.5	
Delivery management procedures	1.0	1.0	8.0	29.0	20.0	4.12
	1.7	1.7	13.6	49.2	33.9	
Product rotation management	1.0	1.0	7.0	28.0	22.0	4.17
	1.7	1.7	11.9	47.5	37.3	

Source: own work.

---

[20] As part of the expert research, attention was paid to general and personalised advertising, remarketing, retargeting or Google AdWords, tracking links, analytics, marketing automation or e-mail automation.

Along with the development of the so-called global market, the attitude to providing the delivery resources, as an element of constructing competitive advantage, is changing. In today's market realities, it is difficult to imagine companies that adopt the Single or Multiple Sourcing model and consistently stick to it. It is sometimes worth taking a risk and betting on a cooperation with one innovative supplier which will allow us to strengthen our position and give preference to the market in a given field. On the other hand, it is worth looking for new opportunities, verifying quality and striving for the competition development. Depending on the size and business objectives, the studied companies approach the management of supply sources flexibly. Since both Single and Multiple Sourcing have their advantages and disadvantages, maybe it is worth colliding them and going in the direction of Cross Sourcing, which is a combination of the two above strategies; especially in the context of the e-commerce model (average rating of 4.02, 32.2% of indications for the assessment of five points). It is important from the perspective of the e-commerce model to strengthen high standards of honesty both inside the organisation and in business relationships with business partners. Suppliers play an important role in the above processes. They are expected to comply with certain standards as well as the provisions of generally applicable law. The requirements of cooperation with suppliers are considered to be the basis for successful business relationships, hence they are a criterion in the e-commerce model maturity assessment process (average rating of 4.03; 30.5% of indications for the assessment of five points). Modern management of a supply chain is one of the most important tasks requiring implementation in the e-commerce model. The growing demand for products and growing customer expectations require changes in the traditionally understood supply chain—through the introduction of innovative technologies, changes in processes, procedures and rules or the development of current systems (average rating of 4.12; 33.9% of indications for the assessment of five points).[21] The challenge faced by people responsible for logistics and operations in the e-commerce model are fluctuations in the level of orders. Changes in the level of orders are usually related to fluctuations in the stock level, which results in the product rotation management. This strategy is most often used so that products from the "long tail," i.e. less rotating, but constituting a full range of offers, are available in the dropshipping[22] or just-in-time model, while the popular items are sold from the warehouse.

This strategy allows companies to flexibly adapt to the prevailing market conditions, hence—in the opinion of respondents, it constitutes an important criterion for assessing the e-business model maturity (average rating of 4.17; 37.3% of indications for the assessment of five points).

---

[21] They make the company gain, in individual areas of the supply chain, the opportunity to increase throughput while reducing the cost of stock maintenance and operational costs.

[22] Dropshipping is a form of logistic outsourcing. Such a model of cooperation is most often preferred by large importers or companies selling products with specific storage conditions (large dimensions, perishable goods, etc.).

E-business is becoming an increasingly popular activity that requires appropriate solutions, including a dedicated e-commerce warehouse. Most importantly, the warehouse system applied in the facility needs to be flexible and allow for easy modifications and expansion depending on the changing trends and preferences of customers and company growth. The innovations that should efficiently support the performance of all warehouse operations, with particular emphasis on flawless and effective completion and logistics of return, are highly important. Therefore, the opinion on the e-commerce model maturity level—prepared with the use of eight variables—was referred to the management level (Table 6).

Table 6. Warehouse management in the e-commerce model maturity assessment

Assessment descriptions	Implementation level (% of indications) Feature value					X̄
	1	2	3	4	5	
Introduction of management system/s	–	1.0	3.0	28.0	27.0	4.37
	–	1.7	5.1	47.5	45.8	
Implementation of service standards	–	2.0	5.0	26.0	26.0	4.29
	–	3.4	8.5	44.1	44.1	
Dynamic management of the product database	–	2.0	5.0	30.0	22.0	4.22
	–	3.4	8.5	50.8	37.3	
External data export from the on-line store platform	1.0	2.0	5.0	26.0	25.0	4.22
	1.7	3.4	8.5	44.1	42.4	
Dynamic management of warehouse inventory updates	1.0	2.0	5.0	27.0	24.0	4.20
	1.7	3.4	8.5	45.8	40.7	
Standards for dealing with product defects	1.0	2.0	6.0	27.0	23.0	4.17
	1.7	3.4	10.2	45.8	39.0	
Multidirectional data processing	1.0	2.0	5.0	30.0	21.0	4.15
	1.7	3.4	8.5	50.8	35.6	
Intra-warehouse logistics system	1.0	4.0	9.0	25.0	20.0	4.00
	1.7	6.8	15.3	42.4	33.9	

Source: own work.

Advanced computer programmes that support managers in difficult decision-making situations allow to improve operational supply management. In view of the above, the innovative system supporting the implementation of all warehouse operations related to the trade of goods within the warehouse and production cycle, as well as receiving and sending products, increasing the control degree optimising work and allowing for the elimination of paper-based service constitute an important criterion in the e-commerce model maturity assessment (average rating of 4.37; 45.8% of indications for the assessment of 5 points). Their implementation indirectly determines an increase in the value offered to buyers, i.e. improvement of the customer service quality. Establishing and maintaining an appropriate level of customer service is one of the most important strategic decisions of the company. There is no doubt that the implementation of service standards is a key element of customer service management and, therefore, it should be taken into account in the e-commerce model maturity assessment (average rating of 4.29; 44.1% of indications for the assessment of five points).[23]

Over the last few years, great emphasis has been put on introducing the functionality of the dynamic product database management (list of goods, groups and product lines) with the possibility of integration with the sales platform. It determines the possibility of perception of a wider perspective of the product group. This is probably the reason why, in the opinion of respondents, the indicated innovation should determine the e-commerce model maturity (average rating of 4.22; 37.3% of indications for the assessment of five points) and should, as such, constitute an indicator of the carried-out assessment. Similarly, attention is paid to the possibility of external data export from the on-line store platform (average rating of 4.22; 42.4% of indications for the assessment of five points). Such integration enables, among others, the export of an extended XML file, which allows for an even richer presentation of the product offer.

In the context of the carried-out research, attention was indeed paid to the comprehensive management of warehouse inventories of products (average rating of 4.20; 40.7% of indications for the assessment of five points) and standards of dealing with product defects (average rating of 4.17; 39.0% of indications for the assessment of five points). From the perspective of the taken issue, it occurred to be important to optimise the warehouse costs and activities carried out inside such a facility; attention was paid to the smoothly and efficiently operating intra-warehouse logistics system (average rating of 4.00; 33.9% of indications for the assessment of five points) requiring the proper balancing between human aspects, the implementation of technologies and automation of processes, and striving for the achievement of often very ambitious objectives set in the warehousing logistics area. The priority in the warehouse logistics is to create a system that facilitates the fastest possible access to information about the place of storage of goods, minimisation of operational costs, that is efficiency and productivity, while maintaining the safety of employees. In the context of the above, it is

---

[23] With regard to customer service, standardisation will mean the implementation of uniform standards of dealing with clients in the entire organisation; whereby standardisation must include both interpersonal service and logistic service elements.

recommended to implement profiled warehouse solutions that create the possibility of multi-directional data processing; the above combine to create the e-commerce model maturity (average rating of 4.15, 35.6% of indications for the assessment of five points).

In order to optimise long-term benefits, it is crucial to introduce a "customer--oriented" philosophy and business culture that ensure effective marketing, sales and service processes. Therefore, the level of e-commerce model maturity was also referred to the order handling process organisation with the use of seven variables (Table 7).

Table 7. Organisation of the order handling process– maturity determinant

Assessment descriptions	Implementation level (% of indications) Feature value					X̄
	1	2	3	4	5	
Implementation of dynamic order flow management tools	1.0	2.0	5.0	26.0	25.0	4.22
	1.7	3.4	8.5	44.1	42.4	
Implementation of customer service standards	1.0	1.0	5.0	26.0	26.0	4.27
	1.7	1.7	8.5	44.1	44.1	
Implementation of integration with external systems of forwarding companies	1.0	1.0	4.0	26.0	27.0	4.31
	1.7	1.7	6.8	44.1	45.8	
Electronic payment platforms	1.0	1.0	3.0	26.0	28.0	4.34
	1.7	1.7	5.1	44.1	47.5	
Customer path	1.0	2.0	4.0	26.0	26.0	4.25
	1.7	3.4	6.8	44.1	44.1	
Introduction of standards for handling exchanges, returns and complaints	1.0	1.0	6.0	23.0	28.0	4.29
	1.7	1.7	10.2	39.0	47.5	
Implementation of dynamic progress path management tools with the customer's order	1.0	2.0	7.0	22.0	27.0	4.22
	1.7	3.4	11.9	37.3	45.8	

Source: own work.

The management of a modern supply chain forces the company to have an efficient tool that will allow to synchronise all the "links" of the chain affecting its performance. From this perspective, it is recommended to implement tools of dynamic order flow management.[24] As it allows to develop high standards in supply management, and it provides a basis for increasing the market advantage of the company, in the opinion

[24] The effective "supply chain" functioning is supported by B2B platforms that facilitate the exchange of information and improve sales by automation of the process of placing and completing orders.

of respondents it significantly determines the e-commerce model maturity (average rating of 4.22; 42.4% of indications for the assessment of five points). These standards should result, on the one hand, from the company strategy, while on the other, from knowledge and experience of employees based on modelling activities that lead to success. It is worth standardising those areas that have the greatest impact on sales but also on the customer's experience. Service standards in the e-commerce model maturity assessment are quite important (average rating of 4.27; 44.1% of indication for the assessment of five points), but they should not be confused with procedures.[25]

In the e-commerce model, it is crucial that the order is carried out quickly, efficiently and effectively. This requires an appropriate system with costly work automation as well as integration with external systems (electronic payment platforms, systems of forwarding companies, etc.). With regard to the above, e-commerce model maturity is conditioned by full integration with courier companies (average rating of 4.31; 45.8% of indications for the assessment of five points). It allows for great automation and acceleration of the process of shipping goods to customers. As part of the assessment, attention was also paid to the unification of electronic payment services (average rating of 4.34; 47.5% of indications for the assessment of five points). In this case, the e-commerce model maturity is expressed by a degree of integration of the IT system with payment platforms (e.g. PayU, PayPal). It is emphasised that it is necessary to implement binding mechanisms of the received payments with completed orders.

In the e-commerce model, a resource of information on where to locate information about the stage of the decision, at which the suppliers should engage in a dialogue with the customer, is very valuable. Currently, popularity is gained by a "customer journey map," that is a graphic presentation of this process with marked points of the supplier's commitment. With the right tools (e.g. Marketing Automation) for analysis of the customer behaviours in the network, it is possible to develop more effective marketing strategies. The most important source of knowledge necessary to build the customer's path are, of course, the customers themselves. Information obtained from them is the most valuable, hence the methods which combine to create the tool enabling their acquisition are so crucial in the e-commerce model (average rating of 4.25; 44.1% of indications for the assessment of five points). In the context of the above, attention is also paid to the implementation of tools for management of the dynamic progress path with the customer's order (average rating of 4.22; 45.8% of indications for the assessment of five points) and the introduction of standards for handling exchanges, returns and complaints (average rating of 4.29; 47.5% for the assessment of five points).

Referring to the relationships with the client, it should be assumed that a client satisfied with cooperation will come back, and, furthermore, they will provide appropriate references. Owing to such an orientation, the company's portfolio will include

---

[25] In the opinion of the authors, standards improve sales processes, while procedures kill sales and make it artificial and devoid of an individual approach.

fewer short-term clients and more long-lasting relationships. However, it requires appropriate customer service standards (Table 8).

Table 8. Customer service standards—model maturity descripts

| Assessment descriptions | Implementation level (% of indications) | | | | | X̄ |
| | Feature value | | | | | |
	1	2	3	4	5	
Tools supporting electronic customer service	1.0	2.0	5.0	25.0	26.0	4.24
	1.7	3.4	8.5	42.4	44.1	
Tools supporting communication with the client	–	–	5.0	25.0	29.0	4.41
	–	–	8.5	42.4	49.2	
Brand refreshing	1.0	2.0	4.0	29.0	23.0	4.20
	1.7	3.4	6.8	49.2	39.0	
Implementation of loyalty programmes	–	2.0	6.0	26.0	25.0	4.25
	–	3.4	10.2	44.1	42.4	
Dynamic mailing management	–	1.0	6.0	25.0	27.0	4.32
	–	1.7	10.2	42.4	45.8	
Electronic advertising	–	2.0	5.0	26.0	26.0	4.29
	–	3.4	8.5	44.1	44.1	
Use of social media	–	1.0	6.0	26.0	26.0	4.31
	–	1.7	10.2	44.1	44.1	

Source: own work.

The concern for the professionalism of made transactions is one of the most important factors determining high-quality customer service in the e-commerce model. The key factors that build customer loyalty, and at the same time make the e-commerce model maturity—in the opinion of the studied companies—are service quality, service functionality and response speed conditioned by the implementation of tools supporting electronic customer service (average rating of 4.24; 44/1% of indications for the assessment of five points). In the "mature" e-commerce model, it is important to precisely define the way of communication with the market and to choose the appropriate information exchange tools (average rating of 4.41; 49.2% of indications for the assessment of five points). From this perspective, it becomes significant to introduce brand-refreshing solutions (average rating of 4.20; 39.0% of indications for the assessment of five points) and to implement affiliate or loyalty programmes (average rating of 4.25; 42.4% of indications for the assessment of five points).

The "mature" e-commerce model consists in providing a potential customer with an attractive offer through such tools as a website, on-line store, auctions or social media. Contextual advertising, creating brand information, brand PR, as well as building loyalty and commitment also play a great role (average rating of 4.29; 44.1% of indications for the assessment of five points).

E-commerce is a concept that permanently changes the model of functioning of companies in the studied sector. The production and sales management processes in the current shape will be significantly changed. The entire transformation of the industry to e-business will be a significant change from the perspective of the organisation and processes. In the paper, it was adopted that the e-commerce model constitutes a paradigm around which it is crucial to build an advantage for the upcoming 4.0 industry era.[26]

The e-commerce model maturity in the area of effective implementation of organisational innovations by the studied companies is relatively high. It is expressed by the ability to effectively choose the selected lean management tools so that their implementation supports the organisation's objectives and strategies.

The paper proposes a procedure and a tool that allow to identify key innovations of the e-commerce model, which, according to the authors, will contribute to fragmentary completion of the shortages in knowledge in this scope.

The method of maturity assessment presented in the article can be used to indicate the strengths and weaknesses and to identify the areas for improvement. The studied companies declare a high level of maturity in the implementation of individual innovations, which, as the authors think, shows their transformation in accordance with the concept of Industry 4.0.

Summary

Shaping of the competitiveness level of modern companies is and will be undoubtedly based on innovative activity. The shortening market life cycle of most products (services, ideas, concepts, etc.) implies the need of permanent adaptation of modern companies to new environmental conditions, and thus, the design and implementation of business models, adequately to market needs. Therefore, it is necessary to systematically explore the emerging market opportunities in every area of market activity.

In the paper, it was crucial to make an attempt to capture an important role of organisational innovations and the key premise for further exploration of the research

---

[26]   Cf. B. Nogalski, P. Niewiadomski, A. Szpitter, *Przemysł czwartej generacji a strategiczne działania dostosowawcze polskich wytwórców sektora maszyn rolniczych* [*4th generation industry versus strategic adjustment activities of the Polish manfuacturers of the agricultural machinery sector*], "Przegląd Organizacji" 2018, 11.

problem raised in the paper is undoubtedly confirmation of the occurrence of strong links and interrelations between organisational innovations and the e-commerce model maturity. In practice, it means that the companies implementing innovative activity in the area of e-business are characterised by vulnerability and the potential to achieve a higher level of competitiveness in the studied sector.

The mentioned premises present a certain image of the proposal to increase the level of organisational innovativeness in the e-commerce model. They should be treated as basic elements for further discussions on finding ways to stimulate innovative attitudes giving an excuse to build innovative business models. Not only the susceptibility to changes of the management and executive personnel, but also an increase in the innovative potential awareness, which should be considered together, seem to be necessary. It is not enough to respond to the environment, the participation in generating changes is crucial.

The continuation of research should also include the verification of enhanced innovations of the e-commerce model in case of entities from other sectors because there is certainly a number of differences that should be recognised and taken into account in the course of further searching.

Bibliography

Atzori L., Iera A., Morabito G., *The Internet of Things: A Survey*, "Computer Networks" 2010, 54, 15.

Baczko T., *Raport o innowacyjności gospodarki Polski w 2009 roku [Report on the innovativeness of the Polish economy in 2009]*, Instytut Nauk Ekonomicznych Polskiej Akademii Nauk, Warszawa 2010.

Barnett G., *Innovation the Basis of Cultural Change*, McGraw Hill, New York 1953.

Cieślik J., *Iluzje innowacyjnej przedsiębiorczości [Illusions of innovative entrepreneurship]*, "Kwartalnik Nauk o Przedsiębiorstwie" 2014, 3.

Combe C., *Introduction to e-Business, Management and Strategy*, Routledge, Amsterdam et al. 2006.

Drucker P. F., *Zarządzanie w czasach burzliwych [Management in turbulent times]*, transl. J. Kajdy, Wydawnictwo Akademii Ekonomicznej w Krakowie, Kraków 1995.

Freeman Ch., *The Economics of Industrial Innovation*, F. Printer, London 1982.

Grandys A., *E-commerce* [in:] *Business Management*, ed. by A. Pomykalski, Wydawnictwo Politechniki Łódzkiej, Łódź 2008.

Handel elektroniczny, https://pl.wikipedia.org/wiki/Handel_elektroniczny (access: 28 May 2019).

Huebner J., *A Possible Declining Trend for Worldwide Innovation*, "Technological Forecasting & Social Change" 2005, 72, 8.

Jasiński H., *Innowacje i transfer technologii w procesie transformacji [Innovations and technology transfer within a transformation process]*, Difin, Warszawa 2006.

Jasiński L. J., *Nowe wymiary gospodarki [New dimensions of economy]* [in:] *Raport o innowacyjności gospodarki Polski w 2010 roku [Report on the innovativeness of the Polish economy in 2010]*, ed. by T. Baczko, Instytut Nauk Ekonomicznych Polskiej Akademii Nauk, Warszawa 2011.

Krzakiewicz K., Cyfert S., *Imitacja w epoce innowacji – dylemat i paradoks współczesnego zarządzania* [*Imitation in the age of innovation—dilemma and paradox of contemporary management*], "Prace Naukowe Uniwersytetu Ekonomicznego we Wrocławiu" 2016, 420.

Lachowski S., *Pracuj ciężko – baw się – zmieniaj świat* [*Work hard—have fun—change the world*], Studio EMKA, Warszawa 2010.

Lahrmann G., Marx F., Winter R., Wortmann F., *Business Intelligence Maturity Models: An Overview* [in:] *Information Technology and Innovation Trends in Organizations. Italian Chapter of AIS*, ed. by A. D'Atri, M. Ferrara, J. George, P. Spagnoletti, Springer Verlag, Naples 2010.

Lee J., Kao H. A., Yang S., *Service Innovation and Smart Analytics for Industry 4.0 and Big Data Environment*, "Procedia CIRP" 2014, 16.

Mansfield E., *Industrial Research and Technological Innovation*, W. W. Norton, New York 1968.

Marciniak S., *Innowacyjność i konkurencyjność gospodarki* [*Economic innovativeness and competitiveness*], C.H. Beck, Warszawa 2010.

Nogalski B., Niewiadomski P., Szpitter A., *Przemysł czwartej generacji a strategiczne działania dostosowawcze polskich wytwórców sektora maszyn rolniczych* [*4th generation industry versus strategic adjustment activities of the Polish manfuacturers of the agricultural machinery sector*], "Przegląd Organizacji" 2018, 11.

Olczak A., *E-biznes – główne obszary innowacji* [*E-business—main areas of innovation*] [in:] *Innowacje w rozwijaniu konkurencyjności firm* [*Innovations in the development of the competitiveness of companies*], ed. by J. Perenc, J. Hołub-Iwan, C.H. Beck, Warszawa 2011.

Pichlak M., *Uwarunkowania innowacyjności organizacji. Studium teoretyczne i wyniki badań empirycznych* [*Organisational innovation determinants. Theoretical study and empirical research results*], Difin, Warszawa 2012.

Sęp J., Budzik G., *Możliwości aplikacyjne technologii Rapid Manufacturing w przemyśle lotniczym* [*Application possibilities of Rapid Manufaturing technology in the aviation industry*], "Mechanik" 2015, 12.

Stadnicka D., Antonelli D., Discussion on lean approach implementation in a collaborative man-robot workstation, 6th International Conference on Business Sustainability 2016: "Management, Technology and Learning for Individuals, Organisations and Society in Turbulent Environment", Póvoa de Varzim, Portugal.

Stadnicka D., Antonelli D., *Implementation of Augmented Reality in Welding Processes*, "Technologia i Automatyzacja Montażu" 2014, 4.

Subashini S., Kavitha V., *A Survey on Security Issues in Service Delivery Models of Cloud Computing*, "Journal of Network and Computer Applications" 2011, 34, 1.

Szulewski P., *Koncepcje automatyki przemysłowej w środowisku Industry 4.0* [*Industrial automation concepts in the Industry 4.0 environment*], "Mechanik" 2016, 7.

Valilai O. F., Houshmand M., *A Collaborative and Integrated Platform to Support Distributed Manufacturing System Using a Service-Oriented Approach Based on Cloud Computing Paradigm*, "Robotics and Computer Integrated Manufacturing" 2013, 29, 1.

Wang X. V., Xu X. W., *An Interoperable Solution for Cloud Manufacturing*, "Robotics and Computer Integrated Manufacturing" 2013, 29, 4.

Weresa M. A., *Systemy innowacyjne we współczesnej gospodarce światowej* [*Innovative systems in the modern world economy*], Wydawnictwo Naukowe PWN, Warszawa 2012.

Xu X., *From Cloud Computing to Cloud Manufacturing*, "Robotics and Computer Integrated Manufacturing" 2012, 28, 1.

Zuehlkea D., *SmartFactory: Towards a Factory-of-Things*, "Annual Reviews in Control" 2010, 34, 1.

Born Global Organisations in the Contemporary Networks of Relations

Michał Teczke, Ph.D.   https://orcid.org/0000-0001-9617-1936

Cracow University of Economics

Abstract

The formation of enterprises that have been focused on functioning on the global market since their incorporation is one of the phenomena currently observed within Industry 4.0. Globalisation and internationalisation are nowadays characteristics of the modern world economy, based on the rapid flow of goods, services and information. This directly affects the increase in the number and degree of the intensity of economic ties between individual countries, their regional groupings and enterprises.[1] Enterprises operating mainly in the modern technologies industry (software producers are particularly noteworthy; they operate on the market that is very favourable to the formation of born global organisations) are trying to make use of the effect in an innovative way. They quickly define the global market as the market of their activities. The use of global distribution networks enables almost immediate engagement of newly established organisations in competitive struggles on global markets. Such activities have a huge impact on competition in the sector. No security and stability resulting from constant pressure from competitors is becoming an everyday reality for more and more enterprises, regardless of their size and experience. Such a situation enforces continuous development and innovation. Stagnation is perceived as one of the most dangerous symptoms that can lead to the removal of any organisation from the market in a short time.

Keywords: born global organisations, internationalisation, globalisation, innovation, global networks

Sources of internationalisation

The born global concept has its source in the internationalisation processes of national economies and individual areas of the functioning of enterprises. Internationalisation is often seen as an expansion aimed at increasing the volume of

---

[1]   J. Rymarczyk, *Internacjonalizacja i globalizacja przedsiębiorstwa*, PWE, Warszawa 2004, p. 11.

production and thus obtaining the possibility of faster depreciation of expenditure on research and development, implemented through either increasing export development or direct investment. They are very important factors, but bringing the essence of internationalisation to nothing other than concerns is too narrow of an understanding.[2] Enterprises operating outside their country of origin decide to make use of different competition strategies and choose different business models. The new phenomena in the international expansion of enterprises started to include the so-called early internationalisation of enterprises, which is a consequence of new market conditions, changes in the technology of production, transport, communication, as well as higher qualifications of people, in particular, broadly understood competencies of managers.[3] Professional managerial skills are of great significance in a rapidly globalising world. Sales of goods and services through the use of global distribution channels provides every company that is a member of the network with access to all markets within its reach. Some behaviours (for example, the company vision, mission or the values presented by employees of the organisation), and even products or services are perceived completely differently in different cultural circles (for example, for political reasons, it was forbidden to wear yellow shirts in Malaysia, and to sell jasmine flowers in China).

The literature on the subject contains many definitions of internationalisation. Some authors believe that any economic activity that is undertaken outside the organisation's country of origin can be regarded as internationalisation.[4] To say that the internationalisation of a company is expressed in its large involvement in operations on world markets is another approach. It consists in intensive and multilateral international connections.[5] Internationalisation is one of the reasons for the volatility of international relations, causing, inter alia, the transfer and transnationalisation processes (understood as the degree of relations between a given economy and the global economy, mainly through the activities of transnational corporations). Such a process is carried out through the flow and allocation of resources, such as: the flow of management personnel, technology, organisational methods and others, from one economy to another. At the same time, it favours the development of international relations, causing the creation and dissemination of material and psychosocial values. The process of internationalisation differs from globalisation in that international ties do not have to be of a global nature and can only concern a selected territory or field. Globalisation is, therefore, the

---

[2]   J. Brillman, *Nowoczesne koncepcje i metody zarządzania*, transl. K. Bolesta-Kukułka, PWE, Warszawa 2002, p. 30.

[3]   R. Oczkowska, „*Urodzeni globaliści*" jako nowoczesna koncepcja internacjonalizacji przedsiębiorstw, "Przegląd Organizacji" 2013, 4, p. 3.

[4]   R. Helm, *Internationale Markteintrittsstrategien*, Josef EulVerlag, Köln 1997, p. 12.

[5]   Z. Pierścionek, *Strategie konkurencji i rozwoju przedsiębiorstwa*, Wydawnictwo Naukowe PWN, Warszawa 2003, p. 454.

highest level of internationalisation.[6] Embedding the concept of entrepreneurship in a group of international phenomena (international entrepreneurship) was an important moment. It has been defined as a combination of innovation, pro-activity and openness to taking risks that are not affected by national barriers. The aim is to build and develop a chain of value creation in an organisation.[7] Born global enterprises constitute a great example of the presented concept. Especially in the first phase of their development due to the small size and relatively low risk associated with possible failures, they are willing to take more risky decisions than large enterprises. Innovation and pro-activity are also characteristic features of this type of enterprises. This is even consistent with the classic concepts, such as the life cycle of the Greiner organisation, where it is pointed out that growth through innovation is the basis for development and gaining competitive advantage for small and young organisations. All of the elements are additionally strengthened by the impact of the network. It is a catalyst for rapid organisation development and intensive sales growth that would not be possible with the use of traditional distribution networks. The start-up of international companies, even global ones, from the moment they were founded is one of the modern concepts. The growing tendency of this trend is the result of: new market conditions, changes in the production technology, transport, communication, as well as higher qualifications of people, in particular, the broadly understood competencies of managers. Enterprises are most often associated with high-technology innovative industries and produce unique products.[8]

Only those companies that have already gone through the entire internationalisation process were taken into account while conducting initial research on international enterprises. The following question was asked: "What optimal strategies and tactics should be used, being present in many markets?" However, not much time has been devoted to the issues concerning the acquisition of markets. It can be seen that from today's perspective, the second question is just as important, or perhaps even more important considering the potential for business development. The contemporary view of this issue is dominated by the conviction that, if possible, we should turn to many markets to minimise the losses associated with a collapse including only one sales market. In the classic internationalisation approach, companies that have achieved the status of a global player have gone a long way that began on the local market. Such companies were often established as small family enterprises. Examples, among other global brands, can be such brands as Adidas and Puma (both originate from the firm

---

[6] U. Krystek, E. Zur, *Handbuch Internationalisierung—Globalisierung—eine Herausforderung für die Unternehmensführung*, Führung Springer Verlag, Berlin–Heidelberg 2002, p. 5.

[7] M. Gabrielsson, V. H. Kirpalani, P. Dimitratos, C. A. Solberg, A. Zucchella, *Born Global: Propositions to Help Advance the Theory*, "International Business Review" 2008, 17, p. 386.

[8] S. Hollensen, *Global Marketing*, Pearson Education Limited, Harlow 2001, p. 65.

Gebrüder Dassler Schuhfabrik founded by the brothers Rudolf and Adolf Dassler in 1924), or the Aldi discount (a company founded in 1946 by the brothers Karl and Theo Albrecht—the very name related to its family character, ALDI comes from the name Albrecht Diskont).

Two of the best-known models describing internationalisation processes are those from the Nordic school, the POM and Uppsala models. The Uppsala model goes back to the behavioural theory of the company, in which R. H. Cyret and J. G. March, were among the first who defined the learning process of an organisation as its continuous adaptive behaviour.[9] In the discussed model, the internationalisation process is understood as a process of the enterprise's continuous learning. Assuming that enterprises undertake adaptation activities, one can conclude that they are gradually gaining more and more complete knowledge about the market in which they operate and are able to make decisions that are the most advantageous from the point of view of the organisation. Enterprises, gaining new experiences, gradually increase the degree of internationalisation, going from a domestic company, through a multinational (international) enterprise to global firms. It can be observed that the transition through new forms of expansion into foreign markets takes the form of a sequence and starts from export, through a joint venture to direct investments and enterprise development from a national enterprise through an international and multinational enterprise to a global enterprise. According to the concept of the discussed model, the internationalisation process is sequential, which indicates the development of engagement in foreign markets over time.[10] The Uppsala model assumes that the first interactions between a local company and foreign markets are occasional and often accidental exports.

Analysing the assumptions from the perspective of the emergence and functioning of born global enterprises, it can be concluded that the internationalisation process is quite different. In the first place, the learning process of enterprises of this type is focused on the development of professional skills of the company's employees. The indicated adaptation process is focused not on adapting to local conditions but on the requirements of global clients and locating potential outlets. The degree of internationalisation has been high since its establishment. According to a study conducted by K. Przybylska, nearly 1/3 of the surveyed 53 exporters achieved at least 30% of sales revenues on foreign markets during the first three years of operation,[11] which proves that the interaction between these companies and foreign markets is not occasional and accidental, but permanent and conscious. The companies selected in the study corresponded to the assumptions presented by B. M. Oviatt: "small and medium-sized

---

[9] B. Mikuła, *Organizacje oparte na wiedzy*, Wydawnictwo Akademii Ekonomicznej w Krakowie, Kraków 2006, p. 44.

[10] R. Oczkowska, „*Urodzeni globaliści*"..., p. 4.

[11] K. Przybylska, *Bornglobal – nowa generacja małych polskich przedsiębiorstw*, "Gospodarka Narodowa" 2010, 7–8, p. 72.

enterprises employing up to 500 employees, usually operating in high-tech industries, which achieved a significant share in sales in foreign markets in a few years from the start of their operations are considered to be born global."[12]

The POM (Product—Operation—Market) model assumes that the first contacts start with regular exports. This model also assumes that the internationalisation process is faster when the markets are homogeneous and that there can be gradual internationalisation (the method of frog jumps) resulting from the legal regulations functioning in the given country.[13] In the classic approach, internationalisation is a specific sequence of actions, being the result of restrictions imposed on companies that start operating in markets other than those previously known. Determinants of the process include: lack of sufficient knowledge about foreign markets, lack of resources allowing expansion into foreign markets, risk related to entering the foreign market, the psychological and geographical distance between the home country and the expansion market, costs, tariff barriers or non-tariff barriers.[14]

Some of the basic assumptions of the above-mentioned classic concepts of internationalisation are not confirmed in the case of born global companies. For them, homogeneity or heterogeneity of the market is of secondary importance. It is of greater significance from the company's point of view to find a market gap and using an innovative approach to gain a competitive advantage, based on professional skills. The pace and effectiveness of decisions made will be the key to achieving success in the confrontation with big global competitors who have achieved their position in a classic manner. When conducting considerations regarding internationalisation, it is impossible to miss issues related to the transfer of intellectual capital. In the countries in which production is located, one can note a relatively fast increase in the level of knowledge of the hired employees who not only master, but also perfect the models of the established tycoons. In the countries being the subject of internationalisation activities, new, dynamically developing enterprises emerge to flexibly adapt to the changes in the environment, while being deprived of the burden of their predecessors, from whom they obtained the necessary intellectual resources. As a result, countries that were originally only providers of labour force are transforming into economies in which knowledge begins to play an increasingly important role. Internationalisation, therefore, does not affect only enterprises. They are only a prelude to the process of internationalisation, and the later stage is the globalisation of national economies.

The organisations that spread into international markets, according to classic models, exert pressure on newly acquired markets, stimulating potential, current and future

[12] B. M. Oviatt, P. P. McDougall, *Towards a Theory of International New Ventures*, "Journal of International Business Studies" 1994, 25, 1, p. 48.

[13] A. Blomstermo, D. Sharma, *Learning in the Internatiolisation Process of Firms*, Edward Elgar Publishing Ltd., Massachusetts 2003, p. 261.

[14] M. Gorynia, *Strategie zagranicznej ekspansji przedsiębiorstw*, PWE, Warszawa 2007, p. 64.

employees to increase their professional competence. Due to the increased interest in acquiring appropriate qualifications and the development of scientific centres, there is an increasing number of people who are willing to bear the risk related to setting up new, innovative ventures for which the born global model seems to be definitely more attractive than the classic path. Therefore, it seems reasonable to assume that "classical" international organisations are largely responsible for the increasingly intensive development of born global enterprises, which in turn are perceived as a significant threat to their own position in global markets. It can be seen that thanks to their flexibility, the companies are able to offer highly competitive products at a relatively low price. The intellectual capital possessed is one of the basic factors determining the pace of the internationalisation process. The greater is the knowledge about foreign markets, the faster the internationalisation process takes place. This is due to the fact that having a large amount of knowledge clearly reduces the risk of undertaking activities outside the well-known operating framework, which in turn results in increasing resources invested outside the company's country of origin. Activities of enterprises on the global market clearly show that in practice it is not necessary to go through all stages of internationalisation. Depending on the situation prevailing within the enterprise as well as in its environment, internationalisation can take place in various ways. The support which companies can obtain in the form of distribution networks is also important.

Internationalisation of distribution

The concept of born global becomes a huge opportunity for small- and medium-sized companies that offer products to a relatively narrow group of consumers, or those that, producing products targeted at a wide group of recipients, immediately gain access to them. In the first case, limiting the enterprise only to the local market results in a shortage of consumers of the final product, and thus problems in the functioning of the enterprise. A quick transition to the global market clearly increases the number of potential recipients, and thus significantly improves the perspective of the company's operation. In the second case, it should be emphasised that enterprises operating in a new technologies sector, offering products and services of a virtual nature, have a decisive advantage in the area of technology transfer, when compared to firms which produce real goods. Looking for the answer to the question of "what factors favor the international expansion of born global companies," we may first mention:[15]

---

[15]   M. Codogni, J. Duda, M. Kudełko, R. Kusa, A. Peszko, M. Teczke, Ł. Wacławik, J. Wąchol, *Wybrane aspekty innowacyjności przedsiębiorstw w warunkach gospodarki globalnej*, Wydawnictwo AGH, Kraków 2013, p. 65.

- The dynamic development of communication technologies, accelerating international information flows and reducing their costs (e.g. e-mail, mobile telephony). It enables the interactions of even small enterprises with suppliers and customers around the world, including the relatively fast acquisition of knowledge about foreign markets, efficient implementation of international operations. The Internet (websites, e-commerce) and the possibilities of virtual activities are particularly conducive to the creation and development of born globals.
- Globalisation of technologies through joint activities in the field of research and development, international technology transfers, unification of education in the field of technical sciences and business (e.g. within e-learning) enables the access of small enterprises to innovations, technologies and knowledge.
- The growing importance of niche markets with international and global reach, especially in highly developed countries. This means an increase in the demand for specialised goods and services that are often standardised.
- Innovative technological processes (e.g. with the use of microprocessors) enable the production of complex, atypical components and non-standard finished products in small batches, and their individual adaptation to the diverse requirements of consumers. Specialised small enterprises can thus achieve a high level of international competitiveness.
- The flexibility of small enterprises in their operations in foreign markets. Shortening the life cycles of products, rapid changes in the needs of buyers require short response time, efficient adaptation to international expectations and tendencies. Flexibility connected to innovativeness is favoured by born globals in the implementation of market strategies, often aggressive ones.
- The functioning of global networks of relations between domestic and international distributors, suppliers and sub-suppliers, final buyers, etc. Entering a network—an enterprise has the opportunity to create beneficial long-term relations with partners, even when it is small and has no international experience.

In the literature on the subject, there are no clear criteria to define precisely which enterprises can be considered born global. Some general assumptions appear, such as those presented in the previous part of the deliberations, indicated by B. M. Oviatt, but there are no explicit economic models and definitions indicating when a company can be included in the born global group, and when it is a phenomenon of very accelerated internationalisation. However, it can be noticed that the majority of born global companies are enterprises operating in hi-tech segments, based on knowledge and specialised technology (e.g. biotechnology, IT, nanotechnology, telecommunications and others). In the period of the dynamic changes taking place on global markets at a time when a large part of innovative behaviours is created outside global leaders, small and medium enterprises should pay close attention to the opportunities offered by the rapid internationalisation of business activities. Financial constraints are among the most common problems faced by the entrepreneurs planning international expansion. It is natural that small enterprises do not have financial stocks allowing their aggressive expansion into international markets. They often do not even have enough resources to start production. The public collection of funds on crowdfunding platforms is one of the more frequently used solutions. Such platforms enable manufacturers' presentations of ideas and convincing potential customers to financially support their planned projects. Platform building companies, therefore, build a network by connecting potential founders and companies or individuals who need financial support. The key to achieving the expected results is the number of potential founders associated in the crowdfunding network. Kickstarter is one of the first and most popular sites. Based on the statistics,[16] there are almost 16.5 million users in the network who have successfully helped to complete more than 165,000 projects supporting creators with an amount of more than USD 4.3 billion. The record project supported on Kickstarter is the Star Citizen game. It has collected more than USD 250 million from 2012 to 2019. Huge financial resources are collected by blockchain solutions (i.e. decentralised transaction platforms in a distributed infrastructure network). Bitcoin and Ethereum are, among others, based on blockchain systems. The top 10 collections in 2 years (2016/2017) totalled more than USD 1 billion. Crowdfunding is more and more often matched, in terms of the value of financing, to the venture capital market. According to the World Bank, by 2025, the value of transactions concluded by various types of social media platforms can amount to approx. USD 100 billion.[17]

Consumer-business type networks can have a huge impact on the potential of organisational development, generating the necessary funds to start operations or transfer activities from local to international and global centres. Crowdfunding also has its obvious drawbacks. The first and probably the most important one is the necessity of arousing interest in a product or service of a sufficiently large number of people, so that their support covers the costs of developing the given business. As far as it is probable in the case of organisations operating in industries addressed to a wide audience (e.g. film, games, music, etc.), it can be extremely difficult to obtain financing through crowdfunding for companies operating in market niches, manufacturing products or services addressed to a very narrow audience. Such companies very often start their businesses as start-ups, looking for a business model that enables rapid development. A report published by Startup Poland indicates that the creation of specialised software for other business entities (B2B) is the main area of interest for Polish start-ups (76% of all respondents). The sources of capital that start-up representatives mainly point to include: their own funds (68%), Venture Capital (40%) and funds granted by PARP or NCBiR (38%). Crowdfunding networks occupy one of the last places with a 2% share.

---

[16]   Provided by the website: https://www.kickstarter.com/help/stats (access: 25 May 2019).
[17]   *Crowdfunding's Potential for the Developing World*, Information for Development Program (infoDev), infoDev/The World Bank, Washington 2013.

However, when asked: "What external sources of financing do you intend to acquire within the next 6 months?" 11% of respondents indicated crowdfunding. It can be seen that start-ups are trying to internationalise very quickly. When asked: "What part of sales do you execute outside Poland?," it turns out that more than half of respondents execute 50% or more of their sales abroad. Foreign markets are entered the earliest by big data products and tools for programmers and developers (every fifth start-up in the area started operations abroad already at the very beginning). The largest percentage of exporting companies includes start-ups offering products related to technology for marketing and tools for programmers and developers. Those who manufacture products based on big data, analytics/business intelligence, IoT (Internet of Things), electronics/robotics, games/entertainment, design and education are highly-appreciated among exporting companies. The rank of natural sciences/health sector is the lowest on the list.

Born Global in modern distribution networks

The e-commerce market is growing very dynamically year by year, increasing turnover, attracting potential producers and customers from around the world. In addition to the increasingly popular trade in goods, which is done via electronic media, including through Amazon, Ebay or the native Allegro, such virtual sales networks as Steam, Origin, Xbox Live PSN and GOG are becoming more popular. Such networks are used by IT companies, on the one hand, to integrate the communities that create them and, on the other, to sell products and services created by both large and small enterprises. The number of potential clients associated in the network is a magnet attracting producers. PSN has approx. 94 million users who can potentially be interested in purchasing the software offered on the platform. Steam—90 million active users, Xbox live—approx. 64 million, Origin—39 million. It should be noted that there can be the same users on different platforms, i.e. user can have an account on each platform, nevertheless the number of users on each of them is large enough to attract the interest of both large and small developers. It is also worth emphasising that this market is not fully saturated. Platform owners compete with each other offering software producers various benefits, resulting in temporary product exclusivity, i.e. a period in which the product is available only on one of the platforms for a specified period of time. As an example we may indicate Epic Store which gathered 85 million users during 4 months of its existence (December 2018—March 2019), all of whom are potential customers of the distribution network. Some networks use solutions somewhat reminiscent of crowdfunding. For example, the Steam Greenlights programme was offered on the Steam platform (Steam Direct replaced it in 2018). It was a proposal mainly for small companies that could propose their ideas to interested users and thus gain additional funds. Within the same network, it was possible to obtain funds for financing production and afterwards to start digital sales. At present, there is the "Early Access" programme where users can buy and use unfinished products. This is another way thanks to which companies can obtain additional financial resources to complete their production. This form of sale is another method available only for virtual products, since the users buying within the "Early Access" programme are fully aware of the imperfections of the purchased product. They know, however, that through their financial involvement they support further development of the programme and can expect "patches" and modifications aimed at improving functionality until the end of the development process, when they become owners of fully functional products. This solution is, of course, unfeasible in the case of physical products.

Internationalisation, or globalisation in a broader sense, is not only a domain of enterprises. Globalisation processes also apply to people who often feel citizens of virtual communities.[18] The processes should be used to build relations between consumers and the business that could become one of the elements improving the quality of the offered products.

Operating on the e-commerce market, the place where we are residing physically is of little importance. Nothing prevents us from shopping outside the country where we are located. Approx. 1.79 billion people have made online purchases in 2018, it is estimated that by 2021 this number will increase to at least 2.14 billion.[19] Statistically, the greatest number of online purchases (from the FCMG sector—fast moving goods) will be purchased by residents of South Korea (19.7%), Great Britain (7.5%) and Japan (7.5%). On-line sales are a fast growing sector, as confirmed by data on the number of users of such sites as the American Amazon or Chinese AliExpress/Alibaba. According to the data presented on statista.com, there are over 300 million registered users of Amazon, while the Alibaba group (which includes Alibaba.com, Guangzhou EvergrandeTaobao FC, Taobao, Tmall, UCWeb, AliExpress, Juhuasuan.com, 1688.com, Alimama.com, Ant Financial, Cainiao, Lazada, YoukuTudou, AlibabaCloud) has more than 529 million registered accounts, against which our native leader—Allegro, with over 20 million registered users, seems small, however, the difference of the markets on which these companies operate is to be taken into account. Table 1 presents the number of users of the largest enterprises operating in the e-commerce industry.

Table 1. Number of users of the largest companies in the e-commerce industry in 2018

Platform	Number of users
Alibaba	515,000,000
Amazon.com	304,000,000
Groupon	260,000,000

---

[18]   M. Codogni, J. Duda, M. Kudełko, R. Kusa, A. Peszko, M. Teczke, Ł. Wacławik, J. Wąchol, *Wybrane aspekty...*, p. 105.

[19]   Cf. statista.com (access: 1 June 2019).

Platform	Number of users
JF.com	258,300,000
Amazon App Store	240,000,000
Ebay	170,000,000
Flipkart	100,000,000
Rakuten	90,000,000
Amazon Prime	80,000,000
Etsy	54,000,000
Wal-Mart Mobile	22,000,000
Allegro	20,000,000
Zalando	19,000,000

Source: own study based on: *User Totals for close to 1,100 of the World's Top Social Networks, Apps and Services*, https://expandedramblings.com (access: 7 March 2019).

Those portals can also be considered a kind of decentralised, distributed network around the world. The number of users means that not only retailers but also manufacturers are more willing to offer their products using global sales networks. An important question that is hard to be answered unequivocally at the moment is whether such sales networks as Amazon are a stimulus for the development of born global organisations. Consumers are increasingly going beyond the narrow understanding of the term "buy," whereby the notion of "I have" or "I am" is becoming more and more important. This phenomenon is particularly noticeable in the modern / high-tech sector. Consumers merge into groups with common preferences, creating specific requirements and expectations networks. The relations established between members become an important factor determining purchase preferences and an indication for the producers with respect to what recipients expect from their products. Manufacturers create a space in which customers can express themselves freely by providing feedback in the form of expectations formulated with respect to products. The value of e-information is becoming a key issue affecting the effectiveness of the organisation. Enterprises are looking for opportunities to diversify groups of customers so that they can easily select incoming information. For one group of recipients, the possession of the latest model of a mobile phone will be a distinguishing feature of their social status or possession. For others, the same object will mean extravagance or snobbery. Even negative information can be used by producers to draw conclusions about how to more effectively reach unconverted groups of recipients, how to change their beliefs or clearly define the reasons for their dissatisfaction. Consumers can be very strongly attached to objects of certain brands, such as cars, phones, computers, cosmetics. The search for added value in the form of having a prestigious product is often the result of the pressure exerted on the entity by other consumers. It is natural for consumers to improve their businesses so that they can be adapted to their needs. More and more people are aware that while the voice of a single consumer remains unnoticed, people who connect online have a real impact on corporate policy. We can, therefore, observe a reversal of a well-known dependency. Not only companies change consumer preferences, but consumers themselves demand changes in the functioning of their products. Companies are beginning to understand that the consumers' voice cannot be ignored. Basing potential improvements only on employed specialists can be less efficient than an organised group of users using the product on a daily basis and sharing their insights with the company.

Conclusions

As a result of the fourth industrial revolution observed every day, more and more recipients become "on-line" buyers and their preferences are a reaction to the impulses from the network, e.g. coming via social media (such as Facebook, Instagram or Twitter). Due to the increasing use of electronic media, we are observing a rate of information flow unknown so far, and thus dynamic changes in consumer behaviour around the world. It can also be seen that enterprises have a smaller, than it seems, influence on the directions of information flow. This is due to the fact that the virtual world allows consumers to participate in the creation and spread of new products. It should be strongly emphasised that today's managers cannot afford to ignore the needs and opinions of their customers. Customers must be considered an integral part of their business. Using widespread and cheaper access to information, customers look for information about the offered good or service. The number of offers is the problem with which conscious consumers struggle every day. It takes too much time to look at all possible offers, and their complexity and the risk of making a mistake confuses and distresses customers. Customers look at the business model in which the company is placed in the centre with less and less enthusiasm, and they "revolve" around the brand—passively awaiting a signal generated by the company. As a result, the role of a customer is constantly changing. A customer, often isolated as a passive recipient in the past, is now being increasingly involved in the information flow and its activity is not only expected by producers, but also stimulated by them. Enterprises are forced to adapt to changes taking place on the market or to accept the loss of market share. Well-informed consumers with full access to information are capable of making informed consumer decisions. For many companies that use the policy of obstructing the flow of information to consumers, this is a total novelty that they have to face today. People have a natural inclination to connect according to their interests, needs and experiences. The fast growth rate in access to the Internet, as well as easier mobile communication (telephony and applications) facilitate the process of consumer consolidation.

The created consumer networks whose members share certain views and feelings, are not limited by geographical or social barriers; they revolutionise new markets and transform the ones formed long time ago. It can be noticed that the natural tendency to build a community, which is one of the foundations of human functioning, finds its new expression in virtual communities.

To sum up, particular attention should be paid to the increased development of born global enterprises. It is a direct response to the changes taking place in the market. On the one hand, a global network of connections brings consumers closer to producers, makes products readily available and information about them reach almost every corner of the world and causes that the most popular products become a determinant of the social status or belong to a specific social group. On the other, it has a great impact on increasing competition. Slow internalisation processes (POM and Uppsala models) are replaced by rapid internationalisation through the appearance of companies that have perceived the global market as their own from the very beginning. Enterprises, using modern distribution systems, take over new markets, becoming more and more present in such emerging sectors as entertainment, computer and telephone applications and modern services (in particular in the IT sector). Born global is increasingly becoming a noteworthy option for startups looking for an appropriate business model that enables dynamic development and fast capitalisation of innovation. Born global features allow companies of this type to quickly penetrate the global market in search of market gaps that are possible to develop. The pace and dynamics of the business are the key to success, giving such companies real opportunities to establish a competitive fight in the sector of modern technologies. Each new activity carries a risk of failure, but in this case, the costs incurred upon a failed investment are lower than in the case of slow internationalisation, which causes increased pressure on the use of this model of operation. A global network of connections between customers, large and small producers of companies creating virtual distribution chains enable the creation and continuous evolution of solutions that provide a chance of running a global business regardless of the size of the enterprise and the country of origin.

Bibliography

Blomstermo A., Sharma D., *Learning in the Internatiolisation Process of Firms*, Edward Elgar Publishing Ltd., Massachusetts 2003.

Brilman J., *Nowoczesne koncepcje i metody zarządzania*, transl. K. Bolesta-Kukułka, PWE, Warszawa 2002.

Codogni M., Duda J., Kudełko M., Kusa R., Peszko A., Teczke M., Wacławik Ł., Wąchol J., *Wybrane aspekty innowacyjności przedsiębiorstw w warunkach gospodarki globalnej*, Wydawnictwo AGH, Kraków 2013.

Crowdfunding's Potential for the Developing World, Information for Development Program (infoDev), infoDev/The World Bank, Washington 2013.

Gabrielsson M., Kirpalani V. H., Dimitratos P., Solberg C. A., Zucchella A., *Born Global: Propositions to Help Advance the Theory*, "International Business Review" 2008, 17.

Gorynia M., *Strategie zagranicznej ekspansji przedsiębiorstw*, PWE, Warszawa 2007.

Helm R., *Internationale Markteintrittsstrategien*, Josef EulVerlag, Köln 1997.

Hollensen S., *Global Marketing*, Pearson Education Limited, Harlow 2001.

Johannson J., Wiedersheim-Paul F., *The Internationalisation of the Firm—Fourswedishcases*, "Journal of Management Studies" 1975, 12, 3.

Krystek U., Zur E., *Handbuch Internationalisierung—Globalisierung—eine Herausforderung für die Unternehmensführung*, Führung Springer Verlag, Berlin–Heidelberg 2002.

Mikuła B., *Organizacje oparte na wiedzy*, Wydawnictwo Akademii Ekonomicznej w Krakowie, Kraków 2006.

Oczkowska R., *„Urodzeni globaliści" jako nowoczesna koncepcja internacjonalizacji przedsiębiorstw*, "Przegląd Organizacji" 2013, 4.

Oviatt B. M., McDougall P. P., *Towards a Theory of International New Ventures*, "Journal of International Business Studies" 1994, 25, 1.

Pierścionek Z., *Strategie konkurencji i rozwoju przedsiębiorstwa*, Wydawnictwo Naukowe PWN, Warszawa 2003.

Przybylska K., *Bornglobal – nowa generacja małych polskich przedsiębiorstw*, "Gospodarka Narodowa" 2010, 7–8.

Rymarczyk J., *Internacjonalizacja i globalizacja przedsiębiorstwa*, PWE, Warszawa 2004.

Web sources

https://www.businessinsider.com/epic-games-store-total-users-2019-3?IR=T (access: 21 May 2019).

https://www.kickstarter.com/help/stats (access: 25 May 2019).

https://www.statista.com/statistics/251666/number-of-digital-buyers-worldwide/ (access: 21 May 2019).

User Totals for close to 1,100 of the World's Top Social Networks, Apps and Services, https://expandedramblings.com (access: 7 March 2019).

Motives for Creating Open Innovation in Enterprises Operating in Poland

Prof. Agnieszka Sopińska, Ph.D.   https://orcid.org/0000-0002-8421-3227

Patryk Dziurski, Ph.D.   https://orcid.org/0000-0003-2132-8657
Warsaw School of Economics

Abstract

The paper discusses results of research carried out to identify the main motives/drivers for creating open innovation in enterprises operating in the Polish market. As there is no list of potential motives for creating open innovation that would be universally or generally approved by researchers, the authors propose their original classification which they have empirically validated on a group of 122 innovative companies operating in the Polish market. The obtained results have confirmed the four earlier formulated research assumptions. Firstly, internal motives more strongly encourage innovative enterprises operating in the Polish market to create open innovations than external drivers. Secondly, the industry in which a company operates does matter for the motives followed when creating open innovations. Thirdly, being part of a business group also impacts the drivers for creating open innovation. Fourthly, the size of an enterprise impacts the motives for creating open innovation.

Keywords: open innovation, innovation, innovativeness, innovation process, enterprises

Introduction

Changes that are taking place in the contemporary environment of enterprises have resulted in a situation when it is more effective to create open innovation based on cooperation with external actors rather than doing it within a closed model. The innovation process is open in the conception and commercialisation stage. The concept of open innovation is a paradigm according to which companies can and should use external as well as internal ideas in their innovation processes and internal and external paths to the market.[1]

---

[1]   H. W. Chesbrough, *Open Innovation: The New Imperative for Creating and Profiting from Technology*, Harvard Business School Press, Boston (Mass.) 2003.

There is a wide variety of reasons why enterprises decide to opt for open innovation model. In the literature those reasons are referred to as "motives" or "drivers." Since most researchers use both terms interchangeably, the authors consider them as a synonymous. This paper is aimed at identifying the main motives/drivers for creating open innovation in enterprises operating in the Polish market. Conclusions were drawn based on the results of the study carried out in 2019 on a group of 122 innovative enterprises operating in the Polish market within the framework of a research project titled "Motives and Barriers for Creating Open Innovation."[2]

Due to the absence of a universal list of potential motives for creating open innovation that could be generally approved by all researchers, the authors proposed their own classification that was empirically validated on a group of innovative enterprises in Poland.

Motives for creating Open Innovation

The authors reviewed the literature addressing the motives for creating open innovation and discovered that it lacks a universal list of potential drivers for creating open innovation that could be generally approved by all researchers. In addition, only a handful of researchers dealing with this issue are trying to systematise drivers by creating their own classifications. Others limit themselves to enumerating such motives or focus their studies on a specific group of drivers.

The group of researchers who are trying to classify motives for creating open innovation includes, inter alia: X. L. Fu, J. Z. Li, H. R. Xiong and H. W. Chesbrough.[3] They divide motives for creating open innovation into push and pull factors in creating open innovation. Among the push factors of open innovation they list all internal weaknesses of a firm, while they seek pull factors mainly in its external environment. According to them, pull factors include: fast environmental changes and pressures; availability of skilled workers, knowledge, or venture capital; more intense competition from rivals, suppliers, or new entrants; technology intensity and fusion; knowledge transfer and leveraging of spillovers.

Amongst Polish researchers, inter alia, R. Stanisławski[4] has made an attempt to categorise motives for creating open innovation by equating the reasons for opening

2   Report from statutory research no. KZiF/S/48/18 titled "Motywy i bariery tworzenia otwartych innowacji" [*Motives and barriers for creating open innovation*]; research manager: A. Sopińska; researchers: A. Sopińska, P. Dziurski, Warsaw School of Economics [Szkoła Główna Handlowa], Warsaw 2019.

3   X. L. Fu, J. Z. Li, H. R. Xiong, H. W. Chesbrough, *Open Innovation as a Response to Constraints and Risks*, "Asian Economic Papers" 2014, 13, 3, p. 32.

4   R. Stanisławski, *Open innovation a rozwój innowacyjny mikro, małych i średnich przedsiębiorstw* [*Open innovation and innovative growth in micro, small and medium-sized enterprises*], Politechnika Łódzka, Łódź 2017, pp. 80–81.

the innovation process in small and medium-sized enterprises (SMEs) with the possibility to achieve three types of benefits in the field of cooperation, commercialisation, and patents. In each of these areas he has listed several benefits that can be achieved by SMEs if they take an open approach to creating innovation.

There is also T. Kraśnicka[5] who considers a specific type of innovation: management innovation and proposes to divide the motives for creating management innovation into two categories: external and internal factors of generating and implementing management innovation. The external factors include: market competition and its intensity; technology; government operations; environmental dynamics and uncertainty; stage in the industry life cycle; length of a product life cycle; and ease or difficulty with which a product can be replaced. On the other hand, there are internal factors, such as: skills and features of managers; their management style; organisational culture, and enterprise profile.

Unfortunately, most researchers do not classify motives for creating open innovation limiting themselves to just making the lists of such motives based on research studies which they have conducted. They most frequently link them with firm-specific characteristics, industry of the firm's operations or type of innovation. As a result, we get sets of drivers for creating open innovation which are incomparable due to differences in their sizes and content. For instance, the list of motives for creating open innovation proposed by M. McPhillips[6] includes as many as ten drivers: meeting customer requirements; acquiring new knowledge; reducing time to market; better use of internal creativity; reducing operational risk; expanding a social network; reducing costs; setting up industrial standards and fostering technological position of a company; strengthening learning effects; and ensuring the autonomy by agreeing on cross-licensing with other entities. J. K. Loren,[7] in turn, proposes a list of motives for engaging external partners in an innovation process consisting of just three drivers: reducing cost and risk; achieving economies of scale; and taking advantage of technological convergence and resource synergy.

An expanded list of eighteen factors—motives for creating innovations in services—has been proposed by U. Kłosiewicz-Górecka.[8] She enumerates the following motives: reducing the environment damage; reducing consumption of materials and energy; increasing employment; increasing service capacity; improving health and safety

5 T. Kraśnicka, *Innowacje w zarządzaniu. Nowe ujęcie* [*Management innovation: New approach*], C.H. Beck, Warszawa 2018, p. 51.

6 M. McPhillips, *Rola innowacji otwartych w klastrach* [*Role of open innovation in clusters*], Ph.D. thesis, Politechnika Gdańska, Gdańsk 2018, pp. 50–51.

7 J. K. Loren, *What Is Open Innovation?* [in:] *A Guide to Open Innovation and Crowdsourcing. Advice from Leading Experts*, ed. by P. Sloane, Kogan Page Limited, London 2011, pp. 5–14.

8 U. Kłosiewicz-Górecka, *Innowacje w sektorze usług – motywy, bariery oraz wsparcie działalności innowacyjnej* [*Innovation in the service sector: Motives, barriers, and support to innovation*], "Handel Wewnętrzny" 2016, 5, 364, pp. 115–127.

standards; reducing labor cost; lowering the cost of a service; entering new markets; enhancing flexibility services provision; increasing the market share; replacing outdated ways of providing services with new ones; enhancing productivity; offering a new service; expanding the range of services; increasing sales turnover; improving quality of service; and attracting new clients.

When examining the innovation processes in the Podkarpackie Voivodeship, the team of researchers composed of L. Woźniak, A. Lewandowska, R. Pater, M. Stopa, and M. Chrzanowski[9] identified the following motives for implementing innovation: entering new markets; complying with regulations or standards; reducing operational costs; innovation forced by customers; reducing the order lead time; improving quality; and maintaining or strengthening the company's market position.

For the sake of comparison, in a monograph edited by T. Kraśnicka and T. Ingram[10] we can come across a proposal suggesting eight sources of impulse and motivations for innovation. These are: improving quality; entering a new market; increasing income; increasing productivity; seeking competitive advantage; improving product/service safety; client expectations; and reducing costs.

As the heart of open innovation lies in the cooperation of various market players, motives identified by T. Gołębiowski and M. S. Lewandowska[11] for the cooperation of enterprises can also be viewed as motives for creating open innovation. The two researchers identified the following motives for cooperation between enterprises: improving product quality; broadening the range of products; enhancing research and development operations; improving production processes; strengthening marketing performance; improving purchases and sales logistics; strengthening financial performance; decreasing demand on the market; having better access to markets; the wish to internationalise; unused production capacity; economies of scale; protection against competition, and informal relationships between managers.

The absence of a universal list of motives for creating open innovation that could be approved by all researchers has encouraged the authors to propose their own list. The list of motives (drivers) for creating open innovation composes of fifteen items broken down into two sets of internal and external motives. Internal motives are effects of internal situation of a given company and its shape and innovative potential.

---

[9] L. Woźniak, A. Lewandowska, R. Pater, M. Stopa, M. Chrzanowski, *Po co nam innowacyjność? Problem innowacyjności w regionie peryferyjnym na przykładzie województwa podkarpackiego* [*Why do we need innovation? Innovation in peripheral region: The case of Podkarpackie region*], Oficyna Wydawnicza Politechniki Rzeszowskiej, Rzeszów 2015.

[10] *Innowacyjność przedsiębiorstw – koncepcje, uwarunkowania i pomiar* [*Enterprise innovativeness: Ideas, conditions, and measurement*], ed. by T. Kraśnicka, T. Ingram, Wydawnictwo Uniwersytetu Ekonomicznego w Katowicach, Katowice 2014.

[11] T. Gołębiowski, M. Lewandowska, *Kooperacja a sprawność marketingowa przedsiębiorstw na przykładzie polskich przedsiębiorstw przemysłu elektromaszynowego* [*Cooperation and marketing performance on the example of Polish electromechanical industry*], "International Journal of Management and Economics" 2010, 27, pp. 202–224.

External motives come from the external environment. Next, the authors further divided internal motives into two categories: motives linked with the innovation process and those linked with the market. Innovation-centric motives aim at improving the effectiveness of the innovation process, while market-centric ones are geared towards the improvement of the overall market position of an enterprise. The classification of potential motives for creating open innovation is presented in Table 1.

Table 1. Classification of potential motives (drivers) for creating open innovation

Type of motive (driver)		Motives (drivers)
Internal motives	Innovation-centric motives	Shortening the innovation process
		Reducing the costs of innovation
		Increasing the number of innovations
		Reducing the risk of innovation
		Improving the use of own research potential
		Earning from own unused inventions
		Acquiring new knowledge and technology
	Market-centric motives	Possibilities to gain new clients
		Improving the competitiveness of an enterprise
		Improving the loyalty of existing clients
		Increasing revenue from innovations
External motives		Highly turbulent external environment
		Competitive pressure
		Pressure exerted by business partners
		Possibility to receive financial support for open innovation (e.g. EU programs)

Source: authors' own research.

The proposed classification of potential motives for creating open innovation was empirically validated for innovative enterprises in the Polish market.

Research method

Identification of the main motives for creating open innovation by enterprises in the Polish market was one of the four research tasks delivered under a wider research project titled "Motives and Barriers for Creating Open Innovation."[12] Other research tasks in this project addressed: identification of the scale of open innovation in the Polish market; identification of barriers for creating open innovation; and measurement of external knowledge search breadth and depth in open innovations. It needs to be stressed that the project was conceived as a natural complement of three research projects that had been previously successfully accomplished under the management of A. Sopińska and focused on open innovation in the Polish market.[13] They resulted in two monographs devoted to this very subject.[14]

The study was carried out between January 12 and 30 of 2019 using the computer--assisted telephone interviewing method (CATI method). The questionnaire included close-ended single and multiple-choice questions. As innovation is a process, the authors had to take account of the time that normally lapses between the moment when innovation is conceived and its implementation and commercialisation. In the research, a 3-year time perspective (2016–2018) was adopted.

The research targeted innovative enterprises in the Polish market. They were drawn from databases of the most innovative companies in Poland according to "Gazeta Prawna" and "Kamerton." The research sample was validated with information obtained from the Bisnode Polska database of contact and the financial data of companies operating in the Polish market.

Random sampling was the technique followed in selecting the sample for the study. However, the enterprise to be included in the sample had to have a proven track record of at least one open innovation (generated in cooperation with external actors) created within three years (2016–2018). The response rate in the study reached 69%.

---

[12]   Report from statutory research no. KZiF/S/48/18...

[13]   In 2015: Research project no. KZiF/S/03/15 titled *Konfiguracja zasobów w modelach otwartych innowacji*, etap 1: *Innowacje produktowe* [*Resource configuration in open innovation model*, stage 1: *Product innovation*]; research manager: A. Sopińska; researchers: A. Sopińska, P. Wachowiak, W. Mierzejewska; in 2016: Research project no. KZiF/S/36/16 titled *Konfiguracja zasobów w modelach otwartych innowacji*, etap 2: *Innowacje procesowe* [*Resource configuration in open innovation model*, stage 2: *Process innovation*]; research manager: A. Sopińska; researchers: A. Sopińska, W. Mierzejewska; in 2017: Research project no. KZiF/S/17/50 titled *Otwarte innowacje. Modele współpracy w otwartych innowacjach. Zarządzanie wiedzą w otwartych innowacjach* [*Open innovation. cooperation models in open innovation. Knowledge management in open innovation*]; research manager: A. Sopińska; researchers: A. Sopińska, P. Dziurski.

[14]   A. Sopińska, W. Mierzejewska, *Otwarte innowacje produktowe realizowane przez przedsiębiorstwa działające w Polsce. Podejście zasobowe* [*Open product innovation implemented in enterprises operating in Poland. Resource approach*], Wydawnictwo SGH, Warszawa 2017; A. Sopińska, P. Dziurski, *Otwarte innowacje. Perspektywa współpracy i zarządzania wiedzą* [*Open innovation. Cooperation and knowledge management perspective*], Oficyna Wydawnicza SGH, Warszawa 2018.

The minimum size of the sample for the population covered by the study was 115 enterprises. In the study the authors conducted N = 122 interviews which ensured the statistical significance of results at the level 0.05.

Enterprises included in the research were moderately differentiated. When it comes to their size measured with employment, the sample was dominated by large- (40.2%) and medium-sized entities (32.8%). In the sample, high-tech service companies (37.7%) prevailed slightly over enterprises from other, non-high-tech industries (36.9%). A clear majority of studied enterprises were not parts of business groups (77%). The characteristics of enterprises examined against selected parameters are given in Table 2.

Table 2. Characteristics of enterprises examined against selected parameters

Parameter		No. of enterprises	Share %
Enterprise size by employment	Micro (0–9 people)	3	2.5
	Small (10–49 people)	30	24.6
	Medium (50–249 people)	40	32.8
	Large (250 and more)	49	40.2
Industry	High-tech manufacturing industry acc. to OECD	31	25.4
	High-tech service industry acc. to OECD	46	37.7
	Other industries	45	36.9
Being part of a business group	Yes	28	23.0
	No	94	77.0

Source: authors' own research: N = 122.

Based on earlier studies focused on open innovations in the Polish market and a literature review, the authors formulated four research assumptions concerning the motives for creating open innovation in the Polish market:
1. Internal motives rather than external encourage innovative enterprises in the Polish market to create open innovation.
2. The industry, in which an enterprise operates, impacts the drivers for creating open innovation.
3. Being a part of a business group impacts the types of motives for creating open innovation.
4. The size of an enterprise impacts the drivers for creating open innovation.

The above assumptions were empirically validated by the authors in research studies, the results of which are presented below.

Results of the study on motives for creating open innovation in innovative enterprises in the Polish market

The motives given most often by 122 innovative enterprises operating in the Polish market as incentives for creating open innovation include: improving competitiveness of an enterprise (18.1%); increasing revenue from innovations (15.4%); possibility to gain new clients (14.1%); and improving loyalty of existing clients (13.3%). In contrast, drivers for open innovation given the least frequently are: pressure exerted by business partners (0.8%); earning from own unused inventions (1.1%); improving the use of own research potential (1.1%); competitive pressure (1.3%); highly turbulent external environment (1.3%); and the possibility to receive financial support for open innovation, e.g. from EU programs (1.7%).

Following the authors' classification of motives, it can be concluded that internal drivers for creating open innovation clearly prevailed over external motives. The sum of the number of indications for internal motives was far greater (in total 94.9% of all indications) than for external ones (in total 5.1% of all indications). In addition, the set of internal motives was clearly dominated by market-centric motives (60.9% of all indications) rather than innovation-centric motives (34.1% of all indications). Each of the four internal market-centric motives scored over a dozen of indications (from 13.3% to 18.1% of all indications). Among internal motives relating to innovation generation the following were relatively the most important: reducing the cost of innovation (10.3%); increasing the number of innovations (6.9%); and shortening the innovation process (6.7%). Examination of the distribution of indications for internal drivers connected with the innovation process has allowed us to conclude that enterprises included in the study were much more oriented at inbound open innovation rather than at outbound open innovation. This is confirmed by a negligible share of indications in two categories of drivers inherently linked with outbound open innovation, such as: improving the use of own research potential (1.1%) and earning from own unused inventions (1.1%). For the sake of comparison, a motive clearly linked with inbound open innovation, i.e., acquiring new knowledge and technology received 4.4% of indications.

The detailed distribution of scores for individual motives for creating open innovation in companies operating in the Polish market is presented in Figure 1.

The researchers wanted to find out whether enterprises from different industries select different motives for creating open innovation. For the purpose of the research, the authors applied a division of industries into three categories according to the OECD classification: high-technology manufacturing industries; high-technology service industries; and other industries. The analysis of distribution of answers revealed clear differences in the frequency with which individual drivers were selected depending on the industry from which a given enterprise originates. The biggest differences in the frequency of indications were observed for the following five motives:

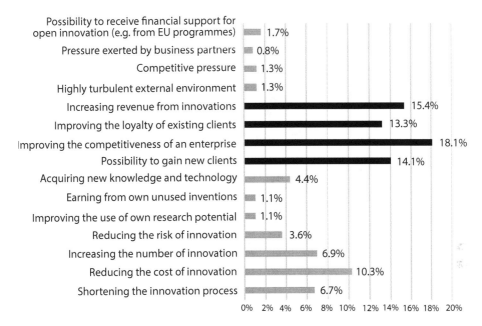

Figure 1. The motives for creating open innovation by innovative enterprises in the Polish market

Source: authors' own research; N = 475 (multiple answer questions).

- increasing revenue from innovations—the motive indicated the most frequently by enterprises from other industries and more rarely indicated by high-tech manufacturing enterprises;
- shortening the innovation process—the motive the most often indicated by enterprises from high-tech services and more rarely by high-tech manufacturing enterprises;
- competitive pressure—the driver the most often indicated by high-tech manufacturing enterprises and disregarded by enterprises from other industries;
- reducing the cost of innovation—the most often indicated motive by enterprises form other industries and more rarely by enterprises from high-tech service industries;
- acquiring new knowledge and technologies—the most often indicated driver by enterprises from other industries and more rarely by enterprises from high-tech manufacturing industries.

The smallest differences in motives for creating open innovation were observed for two categories of drivers: improving the competitiveness of a company (a motive considered relevant independently of the industry) and earning from own unused inventions (a motive considered of little significance independently of the industry).

We need to stress that some categories of external motives were not indicated at all by specific categories of enterprises. Thus, enterprises from other industries ignored two motives: competitive pressure and pressure exerted by business partners. High-tech manufacturing enterprises did not consider the possibility to receive financial support for open innovation as a motive for creating open innovation. However, they indicated external motives (except for possibility to receive financial support) much more frequently than enterprises from high-tech service industries and other industries.

Researchers also wanted to provide an answer to the question concerning differences in drivers for creating open innovation between companies that are part (or not) of a business group. The authors analyzed the distribution of answers indicating motives for creating open innovation in two subsets: a subset of enterprises operating within a business group and separately in a subset of enterprises that do not belong to any business group. The comparative analysis of data for both subsets confirmed that there are differences as to the drivers for creating open innovation. The biggest differences were reported for five motives:

- increasing the number of innovations—a motive clearly more often indicated by enterprises that do not belong to any business group;
- increasing revenue from innovations—a motive more frequently indicated by enterprises which were members of business groups;
- possibility to receive financial support for creating open innovation—a motive more often indicated by enterprises that form part of a business group;
- shortening the innovation process—a motive more often indicated by enterprises not belonging to a business group;
- reducing the cost of innovation—a motive more often indicated by enterprises not belonging to a business group.

The smallest differences in the frequency of indications were reported for three categories of motives: pressure exerted by business partners, improving the use of own research potential (motives of little relevance to all respondents), and acquiring new knowledge and technology (a motive of medium relevance to all respondents). We also need to note that external innovation-centric motives were more often indicated by independent enterprises than by those, which belong to a business group.

The final aspect of the analysis of drivers for creating open innovation in companies operating in the Polish market empirically validated in the research aimed at finding out if the size of an enterprise impacts the types of motives they have indicated. The examination of responses has led authors to a positive answer to this question. Firstly, the authors revealed substantial differences in the frequency with which individual motives were indicated depending on the size of an enterprise. The biggest differences were found in most internal motives linked with innovation and partly with market-centric motives. Secondly, a substantial portion of motives were not indicated at all by micro-enterprises. That was true of most external motives (with the exception of a highly turbulent external environment) and two internal motives: earning from own unused inventions and an increasing number of innovations.

Conclusion

Quantitative research conducted on a sample of 122 innovative enterprises in the Polish market has helped the authors of the paper to positively validate all four research assumptions.

Firstly, in enterprises covered by the study internal motives for creating open innovation prevailed over external motives. Amongst internal drivers, market-centric motives dominated over the innovation-centric ones. In addition, the detailed analysis of motives linked with the innovation process demonstrated that the examined enterprises were much more inbound than outbound open innovation oriented.

Secondly, clear differences were observed in the frequency with which individual motives for creating open innovation were indicated by enterprises from different industries. Interestingly, competitive pressure and pressure exerted by business partners were not indicated at all by enterprises from outside of the high-tech sector while the possibility of receiving financial support for creating open innovation was not given as a motive for creating open innovation by enterprises from high-tech manufacturing enterprises.

Thirdly, the research confirmed differences as to the types of drivers for creating open innovation indicated by companies within business groups and by independent enterprises. Innovation-centric internal motives were more frequently indicated by enterprises that do not belong to business groups while the possibility to acquire funding for creating open innovation was clearly more often indicated by companies within business groups. The latter enterprises selected more frequently increasing revenue from innovations as a motive for creating open innovation.

Fourthly, the size of the examined enterprises mattered for the types of motives for creating open innovation. Substantial differences could be observed in the frequency of indications of motives depending on the size of an enterprise. A big portion of motives was not indicated by micro-enterprises at all.

The authors are aware of some limitations of the study and its conclusions resulting from the adopted research method and the size of the research sample. Conclusions in the study have been drawn based on respondents' opinions (representatives of innovative enterprises operating in the Polish market), and not on objective measures. Also, the size of the research sample—which, however, was representative—is not very great (122 enterprises). In the authors' opinion, the above quantitative studies can be viewed as a starting point for more in-depth qualitative studies to be conducted in the future.

Bibliography

Chesbrough H. W., *Open Innovation: The New Imperative for Creating and Profiting from Technology*, Harvard Business School Press, Boston (Mass.) 2003.

Fu X. L., Li J. Z., Xiong H. R., Chesbrough H. W., *Open Innovation as a Response to Constraints and Risks*, "Asian Economic Papers" 2014, 13, 3.

Gołębiowski T., Lewandowska M., *Kooperacja a sprawność marketingowa przedsiębiorstw na przykładzie polskich przedsiębiorstw przemysłu elektromaszynowego* [*Cooperation and marketing performance on the example of Polish electromechanical industry*], "International Journal of Management and Economics" 2010, 27.

Innowacyjność przedsiębiorstw – koncepcje, uwarunkowania i pomiar [*Enterprise innovativeness: Ideas, conditions, and measurement*], ed. by T. Kraśnicka, T. Ingram, Wydawnictwo Uniwersytetu Ekonomicznego w Katowicach, Katowice 2014.

Kłosiewicz-Górecka U., *Innowacje w sektorze usług – motywy, bariery oraz wsparcie działalności innowacyjnej* [*Innovation in the service sector: Motives, barriers, and support to innovation*], "Handel Wewnętrzny" 2016, 5, 364.

Kraśnicka T., *Innowacje w zarządzaniu. Nowe ujęcie* [*Management innovation: New approach*], C.H. Beck, Warszawa 2018.

Loren J. K., *What Is Open Innovation?* [in:] *A Guide to Open Innovation and Crowdsourcing. Advice from Leading Experts*, ed. by P. Sloane, Kogan Page Limited, London 2011.

McPhillips M., *Rola innowacji otwartych w klastrach* [*Role of open innovation in clusters*], Ph.D. thesis, Politechnika Gdańska, Gdańsk 2018.

Report from statutory research no. KZiF/S/48/18 titled *Motywy i bariery tworzenia otwartych innowacji* [*Motives and barriers for creating open innovation*]; research manager: A. Sopińska; researchers: A. Sopińska, P. Dziurski, Warsaw School of Economics [Szkoła Główna Handlowa], Warsaw 2019.

Sopińska A., Dziurski P., *Otwarte innowacje. Perspektywa współpracy i zarządzania wiedzą* [*Open innovation. Cooperation and knowledge management perspective*], Oficyna Wydawnicza SGH, Warszawa 2018.

Sopińska A., Mierzejewska W., *Otwarte innowacje produktowe realizowane przez przedsiębiorstwa działające w Polsce. Podejście zasobowe* [*Open product innovation implemented in enterprises operating in Poland. Resource approach*], Wydawnistwo SGH, Warszawa 2017.

Stanisławski R., *Open innovation a rozwój innowacyjny mikro, małych i średnich przedsiębiorstw* [*Open innovation and innovative growth in micro, small and medium-sized enterprises*], Politechnika Łódzka, Łódź 2017.

Woźniak L., Lewandowska A., Pater R., Stopa M., Chrzanowski M., *Po co nam innowacyjność? Problem innowacyjności w regionie peryferyjnym na przykładzie województwa podkarpackiego* [*Why do we need innovation? Innovation in peripheral region: The case of Podkarpackie region*], Oficyna Wydawnicza Politechniki Rzeszowskiej, Rzeszów 2015.

The Entrepreneurial Context of Nonprofit Manager Assessment: Comparative Case Study

Tomasz Kusio, Ph.D. (iD) https://orcid.org/0000-0003-0508-6520
Cracow University of Economics

Abstract

There has been a strong debate in the last years about entrepreneurship and the competencies that each person should demonstrate in order to be a successful entrepreneur, successful and effective employee as well as successful manager. The new economic reality, which among others can be described as remaining under the influencing power of globalisation, makes the management processes more global-oriented. This is also the reason of more internationally-oriented organisations, which do not necessarily operate in a for-profit way, but also not-for-profit. Therefore, it becomes increasingly important to discuss the role of a manager in such international organisations and especially non-profit ones. Still, it also becomes important to discover the personal characteristics of such managers, especially taking into account the entrepreneurial dimension. The text presents an introductory analysis of two case studies which describe two European student organisations. Special attention is put on the concept of work assessment of managers of such specific entities.

Keywords: manager assessment, managerial competences, student organisations, AIESEC, AEGEE

Introduction

Several theories and approaches were used to explain the entrepreneurial phenomenon. These theories and approaches are related to personal characteristics, attitudes, environmental and economic factors and also relate to the degree of entrepreneurial culture that a society promotes as well as to the personal cognitive state during the decision-making process. Certainly most of the supported theories converge to the opinion that an entrepreneur should demonstrate several qualifications,[1] which according to European Qualification Framework should be described in terms of three types of learning outcomes such as a) knowledge, b) skills and c) wider competencies.

Knowledge is the facts, feelings or experiences known by a person and means the outcome of the assimilation of information through learning and is the body of facts, principles, theories and practices that is related to a field of study or work such as entrepreneurship. Concerning skills in the European Qualification Framework working document that are defined as the knowledge and experience needed to perform a specific task or job and the personal ability to apply knowledge, to use know-how to complete tasks and solve problems. Additionally, it is supported[2] that the definition of skills is used for a specific level of performance, while Proctor and Dutta[3] define skills as the targeted and well-organised behaviour and the required knowledge and experience for the execution of a specific task or project. Finally, skills usually refer to "a level of performance, in the sense of accuracy and speed in performing particular tasks (skilled performance)."[4]

Trying to define competencies, the majority of researchers and practitioners conclude that these are the knowledge, skills and know-how in a specific task. Competencies also refer to the ability to use knowledge, skills and personal, social and/or methodological skills, in work or study situations and in professional and/or personal development including: i) cognitive competence; ii) functional competence; iii) personal competence; and iv) ethical competence.[5] Fulfilling a competence level, an individual is able to use his/her knowledge, skills and wider competencies according to the requirements posed by a particular context, situation or problem and is able to deal with complexity his/her level of competence.[6] The sense of initiative and entrepreneurship refers to an individual's ability to turn ideas into entrepreneurial action. This includes creativity, innovation and risk-taking, as well as the personal ability to plan and manage tasks in order to achieve these objectives.

Although the definition of an entrepreneur may in many cases be strongly connected with a successful manufacturer or company owner, it does not necessarily refer only

---

[1]   A. Vasiliadis, C. Vitsilaki, H. Efthimiou, *Entrepreneurship and Entrepreneurial Intentions: The Education Effect*, Proceedings of International Conference for Entrepreneurship, Innovation and Regional Development (24–25 April), Thessaloniki 2009.

[2]   J. Winterton, F. Delamare-Le Deist, E. Stringfellow, *Typology of Knowledge, Skills and Competences: Clarification of the Concept and Prototype* (Panorama Series, No. 1397), Office for Official Publications of the European Communities, Luxembourg 2005.

[3]   R. W. Proctor, A. Dutta, *Skill Acquisition and Human Performance. Thousand Oaks*, Sage, California 1995.

[4]   CEDEFOP, *Typology of Knowledge, Skills and Competences*, CEDEFOP Reference Series; 64, Brussels 2009.

[5]   European Commission, *Towards a European Qualification Framework for Lifelong Learning*, Sec (2005) 957, Brussels 2005.

[6]   EKEPIS, *Guide for Professional Profiles Development*, Gsee, Seb, Gsevee, Esee, Athens 2007.

to businesses. Entrepreneurship is not reduced simply to actions such as setting up a company. Still a greater accent is put on such definitions of entrepreneurship where it results in human activeness and does not exclusively refer to business-oriented activities, but also public- or society-oriented innovations. Therefore, entrepreneurial attitudes and behaviours are connected not just with for-profit entities but also with not-for-profit and for-society or for-public entities. The term that describes this kind of entrepreneurship is called social entrepreneurship and there are even to still more and more important extent visible and recognisable as "valuable" and "needed" such entities as social enterprises.

The dynamics of innovative processes are to an increasing extent influenced by the socio-economic reality. This applies to both innovations in business and social innovations. The topics of socially-oriented entrepreneurship which lead directly to the emergence of social innovations are gaining importance. Examples of such situation are theories of stakeholder as well as social responsibility. It is particularly important, therefore, to pay attention to entrepreneurship in the sense of people's features, especially those who are responsible for managing organisations. The issue of entrepreneurial attitudes in the perspective of globalisation is rising alongside with the increasing level of globalisation which forces a fundamental change of the national socio-economic reality. Permanent change, which is accelerated by the globalisation processes refers to the need of proper human resources management in organisations. Organisational operations should allow for the best use of human potential which could be achieved by the implementation of management concepts and methods of practical nature.[7]

Change in the process of human resources management refers to both the external environment of the organisation and the internal environment—including employees. In the theory of stakeholders in the structure of the internal environment, different groups of managers responsible for the implementation of changes can be distinguished. Such changes are now the necessary effects of an organisation's entrepreneurial activities which results from managerial decisions. Entrepreneurship, apart from being recognised as one of the basic factors determining the success of an organisation on the market, is also identified with the risk-taking of an economic undertaking. Entrepreneurialism is a risk-taking ability in the aforementioned definition. Innovation results from entrepreneurship and social innovations, and the way in which they are perceived results from economic changes focused on the need to solve social problems. The essence of social innovations is the priority of recognising solutions in the field of social interests towards other types of benefits resulting from the implementation of a given innovation.

---

[7] *Współczesne wyzwania w obszarze zarządzania zasobami ludzkimi*, ed. by E. Mazur-Wierzbicka, Volumina, Szczecin 2017, p. 5.

The globalisation context

The current global economic reality is defined, inter alia, as a new economy, or knowledge economy. The *network economy* is also present in the literature and is a new perception of economics. The origins of the globalisation process can be dated back to the beginning of the previous century, where the share of world trade in global GDP was between 20 and 30%. The first wave of globalisation lasted until the First World War, the second wave refers to the early 90s of the last decade, until the end of the Cold War, while the current period falls on a part of the third wave of globalisation. The ground-breaking moments of this process include 1957—the creation of the EEC, 2002—Eurozone and the 2006 European Cohesion Fund. Currently, over 244 million people live outside their country of origin, and the number of trips in 2016 amounted to 1.2 billion. The share of world trade in global GDP is already around 50%.

The expansive nature of globalisation, which is determined by the opening of markets, means free movement of human resources between countries and continents, cultural diversity, as well as the tightening of competitiveness and changing conditions of wage expectations. The structure of working time is also changed, divided into private life and professional life as well as more and more frequent possibilities of performing remote work. The content of the work, methods and tools for its implementation are changed.[8] Changes in the globalisation process planned in the perspective of 2025 mean, among other things:

- in the field of transport—unmanned aerial vehicles connected to the Internet, cars, aircraft, as well as common use of cars,
- in the field of telecommunications—virtual reality and a virtual workspace,
- in distribution—even more role of retail trade,
- in the field of financial services—virtual banks and insurance, as well as crowd-funding,
- in the field of factory production—even more automation,
- in the field of health care—online diagnosis, increased cross-border mobility of healthcare professionals.

The impact of globalisation on human resources management, and what is related to the assessment of employees, to a large extent refers to the deepening of digitisation, virtualisation and automation, which will directly lead towards the design and use of employee evaluation systems. Globalisation, in the future, may influence remote work and the importance of skills related to the design and operation of technologically advanced tools.

Evolving economic systems determine the dynamics of changes in the environment of business organisations. New management paradigms, of which one descriptor is

---

[8]   I. Warwas, A. Rogozińska-Pawełczyk, *Zarządzanie zasobami ludzkimi w nowoczesnej organizacji: Aspekty organizacyjne i psychologiczne*, Wydawnictwo Uniwersytetu Łódzkiego, Łódź 2016, pp. 24–25.

the use of management methods and techniques available so far for business, also in public administration or in the third sector, draw the background of human resource management, unheard of so far in the perspective of the role of the human factor in the functioning of the organisation.

The context of new management paradigms

The evolution of economic systems concerns both globalisation processes, internationalisation of organising and economic activities, as well as the growing role and importance of technical and information progress. The sequential nature of an organisation's internationalisation impacts changes in the field of human resources management.[9]

The impact of new management paradigms on personnel management will, in the perspective of years, mean an even greater share of business management methods and techniques in public administration units, as well as the third sector, non-governmental organisations, foundations and associations. The decreasing level of differentiation in management methods between managing different organisations which was the reason behind the purpose of functioning should in the future also affect the employee evaluation criteria. Such a situation should become more effective for those organisations which are oriented not-for-profit. In turn, in profit-oriented organisations, the issues of social responsibility, as well as socially-oriented innovation, will become even more important. This is because the assessment should meet the employer's as well as employee's goals. At the same time, the assessment process takes place in an organisation that is a formal institution, which is also a social institution created by the people and for the people.[10]

The stakeholder-oriented approach should set a direction for managing the organisation in such a way so that they all get satisfaction in practice. The achievement of an adequate level of satisfaction for all parties interacting with the organisation means fulfilling the goal of stakeholder-oriented management.[11] The occurrence of subject matter of stakeholders in the literature is also related to the creation of values of their management, as well as relations and dependencies that occur in the relations between the organisation and the environment. The value of an organisation is created when it meets the expectations and needs of stakeholders.[12] From the perspective of

---

[9]   R. Oczkowska, *Przedsiębiorstwo w warunkach globalnego otoczenia* [in:] *Zarządzanie zasobami ludzkimi w warunkach globalizacji*, ed. by R. Oczkowska, Uniwersytet Ekonomiczny w Krakowie, Kraków 2012, pp. 9–26.

[10] K. Radzik, *Ocena pracowników. Nowa generacja narzędzi do oceny pracowników w nowym ujęciu klasycznego modelu kompetencji*, Wolters Kluwer Business, Warszawa 2013.

[11] I. Kozłowska, *Interesariusze jako zmiana w badaniach zarządzania strategicznego*, "Organizacja i Kierowanie" 2015, 1(166), pp. 73–90.

[12] Ibidem.

the manager's work assessment, the greater value that the organisation offers for the stakeholders, the better the manager's work is assessed. That is why the factors creating value for stakeholders become important. Honesty and ethical behaviour are the considered qualities. Creating value for stakeholders translates into financial efficiency at a later stage. Customers that are satisfied and loyal to the company are a fundamental factor in its development.

In a time of growing globalisation, in which the domestic labour market is subject to ongoing changes, it seems necessary to confront the HRM processes with the perspective of changes that seem unavoidable.

The aim of the paper is to examine how current students involved in the activities of international non-profit organisations perceive the assessment areas of the person managing such an organisation in the local context. For the purpose of obtaining knowledge in the areas of assessment of persons involved in the operation of local offices of international student organisations, an analysis of two case studies was conducted.

Methodology

In order to obtain information on the personal characteristics of persons whose task is directed at today's organisations, two case studies: of AIESEC and of AEGEE were analysed. The functioning of these units has an international dimension, and the formula of their organisation consists in creating local offices that operate based on a global brand. Both organisations are widely known and appreciated and it is difficult to question the lack of both a subject of entrepreneurship in their operation, an element of social benefit, as well as the global nature of their activities. The case studies consist of a brief description of the organisation, constituting also a confirmation of the occurrence of the listed characteristics in the analysed organisations, and in the second part, an indication of criteria based on which the managers of local offices of these organisations should be assessed. The persons associated in the said organisations were asked to identify such criteria. Before preparing the materials, the participants were equipped with basic knowledge in the field of human resources management. A discussion was held with them on the methods of conducting employee assessment as well as the general assessment criteria. During the discussion, among others, the following information, relevant from the point of view of taking up the subject of non-profit manager's assessment were raised:

1. Qualification criterion, which from the point of view of an NGO manager should cover all knowledge and skills acquired at the university. As a senior manager, higher education should be required, all courses on human resource management would be desirable, knowledge of legal provisions related to the functioning of non-profit organisations should be of a value as well. Computer skills, that is, all packages useful for creating plans, flow charts, etc. are also required.

2. Efficiency criterion includes the results of work in terms of material and value achieved by the manager, i.e. first of all the effects of the actions undertaken, the funds obtained to support the statutory objectives pursued by the non-profit organisation. The time of project implementation should also be taken into account and verification whether it is possible to achieve similar results in a shorter time.
3. Behavioural criteria are used to assess the employee's behaviour. An important aspect may be an involvement in the activities of the organisation. This is an important point, because the manager should, through his/her attitude, motivate the rest of the staff to act and should be a role model for the rest of the team. Professionalism is an important point, because the organisation should pursue its goals in a clear, defined way. An important element is also the attitude towards people with whom the manager cooperates, due to the specificity of these organisations, loyalty, trust are extremely important.
4. Personality criteria include relatively constant features of the human psyche. The manager of a non-profit organisation should be empathetic towards people, this type of personality is incredibly influential on other people's work. Resistance to stress and dynamism of action is also important, because there is often limited time to achieve a planned goals.

Due to the specificity of non-profit organisations, often soft skills are more sought after and affect the choice of a given person for the position of NGO manager.

Results and Discussion

The subject of the analysis conducted for the purpose of identifying the evaluation criteria for the work of an international non-governmental organisation's manager is, in the first case, a member of the board of the local AEGEE branch, a Board Member responsible for Public Relations (BMPR). In the second described and analysed case it is the President of the local AIESEC branch. In the case of AEGEE, the analysis concerns a middle-level manager, at the second—senior management level.

AEGEE organisation

AEGEE is a European Students' Forum, an international student organisation with around 13,000 members across Europe. The Krakow branch of AEGEE has 80 formal members (and twice as many informal supporters, who are not always on the way with payment of the membership fee), and its supreme authority is the Board headed by the President. The Management Board must necessarily include the President directing the work of the organisation, the Treasurer and the Secretary. It is also necessary to choose the Vice-Presidents. AEGEE-Kraków Management Board consists of six members who do not perform the functions of either President or Vice-President. The Management Board has been working in an unchangeable form for several decades, because due to the size of the branch, a large number of decision-makers is needed. AEGEE-Krakow carried out 14 different projects in 2016, from local to international, gathering from a dozen to several hundred participants. Therefore, in each election (for a one-year period), the following members are chosen:

- President,
- Treasurer,
- Secretary (in the current term of office of the Vice President),
- Member of the Management Board for Fundraising,
- Board Member responsible for Public Relations,
- Board Member responsible for Human Resources.

The President is responsible for the entire functioning of the organisation, Treasurer for finance, the Secretary deals with broadly understood office matters. Members of the management board for FR, PR and HR are responsible for the overall activities of organisations associated with these plots. Control over the Board is exercised by the Board of Control, which may have from 3 to 6 members, and members of the Board may not have to be present. In practice, these are the members of former management boards. The Chairman of the Control Council is also elected.

Table 1. Selected evaluation criteria and proposed grading scale for the middle manager of AEGEE Krakow Office

Criteria	Assessment scale					
Knowledge of AEGEE-Krakow and AEGEE-Europe	1	2	3	4	5	6
Knowledge of Public Relations	1	2	3	4	5	6
Commitment to your work	1	2	3	4	5	6
Preparation of high-quality promotional materials	1	2	3	4	5	6
Coordinating work of PR team	1	2	3	4	5	6
Ability and punctuality of making promotional campaigns and operational activities	1	2	3	4	5	6
Very high communication skills	1	2	3	4	5	6
Creativity in solving problems	1	2	3	4	5	6
Sense of responsibility	1	2	3	4	5	6
Cooperating with other members of an organisation	1	2	3	4	5	6

Source: own elaboration.

Supplementary information to the proposed tabular form of the manager's self-assessment are quarterly reports on the activities submitted to the Board of Control. The reports should contain information on:

- scope of duties,
- what has been achieved amongst planned and unplanned activities,
- what could not be achieved,
- problems,
- assessment of cooperation with the Board of Control,
- casual conclusions, impressions (optional).

By submitting such reports, the Supervisory Board has a permanent insight into the work of members of the Management Board.

AIESEC organisation

The President of the local branch of AIESSEC is another example of a role subject to the proposed scope of the managerial position assessment. AIESEC is an international organisation run by young people, founded in 1948, currently operating in 122 countries. Its main goal is to develop leadership qualities among young people through the implementation of volunteering programmes and foreign internships.

The local branch in Krakow was established in 1979, and at present it is registered as an association and a non-profit organisation. There are currently 120 people engaged at the local branch who want to improve their skills, take advantage of new opportunities and support the development of others. The organisation structure consists of the President of the Local Branch, 9 Vice-Presidents, 20 leaders running their teams, 15 coordinators and 75 team members. The scope of responsibilities on a senior management level, for workers such as the president of a local branch includes, among others:

- cooperation with the national branch of AIESEC Polska,
- cooperation with Vice-Presidents responsible for different activities of the organisation,
- representation of the local branch during events (inside and outside the organisation),
- creating an annual strategy for the development and operation of a local branch,
- work control of all branch members,
- responsibility for the financial issues of the local branch,
- training of AIESEC members when introducing them to projects,
- implementation of innovative solutions.

Table 2. Selected evaluation criteria and proposed grading scale for the senior management of AIESEC Krakow-Office

Criteria	Assessment scale					
Knowledge of the vision and goals of the organisation	1	2	3	4	5	6
The ability to transfer organisation goals to other AIESEC members	1	2	3	4	5	6
Commitment to the one's responsibilities	1	2	3	4	5	6
Determining long-term goals of the organisation	1	2	3	4	5	6
Determining short-term goals of the organisation	1	2	3	4	5	6
High communication skills	1	2	3	4	5	6
Management of the team of vice-presidents	1	2	3	4	5	6
Supervision of the development of new members of the organisation	1	2	3	4	5	6
Supporting vice-presidents during difficult decisions	1	2	3	4	5	6
Selection of associates during recruitment to the organisation	1	2	3	4	5	6
Maintaining contacts with the national management	1	2	3	4	5	6
The ability to organise one's own work	1	2	3	4	5	6
High level of decision-making and responsibility	1	2	3	4	5	6
Ability to work under pressure	1	2	3	4	5	6
Timeliness of tasks	1	2	3	4	5	6
Innovative approach to problems	1	2	3	4	5	6

Source: own elaboration.

The questionnaire should be a tool to support conversations with employees, help in defining specific competences and outline further possibilities of employee development.

The proposed assessment of the work of managers in a non-governmental organisation concerned two similarly functioning organisations. These are two large international student organisations with a similar national formula, i.e. based on local national or regional offices. Apart from the fact that there is a great similarity between the characteristics of the analysed entities, there is also a large similarity in the viewed positions. In the first case it is a board member of a local organisation, in the second it is the president of a local organisation, therefore, representing a higher managerial position. In each of the analysed cases, involvement in the performed work is assessed, which should be directly related to independence and entrepreneurship. Also in each case, when analysing questionnaires, the evaluation should take into account knowledge of the organisation in which the managers are involved. Due to the thematic focus of one of the positions, i.e. the board member for PR, there is an indication of knowledge of the area of PR, which indirectly refers to the assessment of the quality of the work performed.

In both analysed cases, the assessment of communication skills is an important issue as an emphasis put on a high level of skills ("high communication skills," "very high communication skills"). The criterion similar to communication skills, which were also indicated in the evaluation sheets, was also maintaining contacts with the national (national) management, in the case of the president of the local branch of AIESEC. In both cases, there can be observed a similar approach appropriate time management skills. In one case, the criterion was defined as the ability and timeliness of creating promotional campaigns and conducting activities, while in the second case, timely execution of tasks, but also the ability to organise one's own work.

In the two proposed sheets for manager's performance evaluation, areas related to human resources management, namely, subordinate staff, were identified as "coordinating the work of the PR group" and "managing the team of vice-presidents."

Differences in the questionnaires are directly related to the scope of responsibilities, where a BMPR is assessed in the context of the quality of promotional materials prepared, which can also be understood as the control of his/her responsibility for the quality of these materials. This is the subject area of the person's responsibility. In the case of the president of the local branch of AIESEC, he/she is assessed for the level of decision-making, coping with stress, advice he/she performs for direct co-workers, but also recruitment and planning issues, which strongly emphasises the nature of the position held.

Conclusions

Performance assessment, according to the literature evidence, is based on four basic criteria:
- behavioural,
- personality,
- qualifying,
- efficiency.

Building evaluation tools for an NGO manager's work does not differ, in the eyes of the employees of these organisations, from the schemes of building assessment tools for the managers of other organisations, such as business entities. However, in each of the presented case studies, apart from the self-assessment questionnaire with the proposed criteria, an additional instrument should be found, such as an additional questionnaire or interview. Assessment in accordance with the materials presented may also consist of periodic reporting of activities carried out by the manager during the reporting period. In one of the proposed assessment methods, one of the objectives of assessment is also mentioned, which is to outline the possibilities of improving the assessed manager's work together with the training package proposed for him.

The roles of the manager in a non-governmental organisation are manifold. There are three managerial roles that a non-governmental organisation can distinguish:

- interpersonal—maintaining internal and external contacts, for example in order to obtain sponsors, among companies or enterprises, setting goals that a non-profit organisation wants to achieve,
- information—information sharing, such a person becomes a "source of knowledge" for other members of the organisation,
- decision making—as a senior manager, he/she makes important decisions in the area of planning activities and achieving goals.

A managerial position for many employees is the target point of their professional career. This position can also be indicated as desirable on the labour market. One can also talk about a manager as a profession, especially when people holding managerial positions change jobs, but they do not change the nature of employment, i.e. they continue their managerial duties in new work places. Working at management levels requires a wide range of competences and managerial skills. A manager is a person responsible for executing the activities of subordinated people and departments. A manager's objective is to increase work efficiency by applying appropriate methods of human resource management. It seems that being a leader in a non-profit organisation deviates in some aspects from a manager's work in a business environment. The manager of a non-profit institution should focus less on administrative and organisational matters with regard to the future of the organisation. He/she is obliged to seek opportunities for the development of his/her institution and development of capital. However, daily operations are unavoidable, such as contacting clients or administering documents. The basic functions of the manager in a non-profit organisation are frequent interactions with members (management, employees, volunteers), and people outside the institution, searching for partners and contacting with the media. Their task is to focus on the future, seek out new trends that will affect the later condition of the association.

Employee evaluation is very important because it is an assessment system that provides the organisation with structured information about the current situation in a given institution, and allows to focus activities on organisational development. As institutions operating in the third sector try to be increasingly professional and more and more often resemble enterprises in terms of management, the approach to human resource management should also become professional. Each NGO organisation sets its development plan, which is why it should also create a strategy for employee development, because it is thanks to them that it can fulfil its statutory goals. The importance of entrepreneurship in assessing the work of a non-governmental organisation manager is of no doubt for the assessing bodies, which could be the control boards.

Bibliography

Adamczyk M. D., *Przygotowanie do emerytury w kontekście rozwoju kapitału ludzkiego osób starszych – prezentacja wyników badania BALL BeActive through Lifelong Learning*, "Nierówności Społeczne a Wzrost Gospodarczy" 2017, 50, 2.

Adamska-Chudzińska M., *Psychospołeczne kontrowersje w zarządzaniu kompetencjami pracowników dojrzałych 65+*, "Nierowności Społeczne a Wzrost Gospodarczy" 2017, 50, 2.

Bogucka-Kisiel E., *Pokolenie seniorów jako wyzwanie dla bankowości* [in:] *Nauki ekonomiczne w XXI wieku – dylematy, wyzwania, perspektywy*, ed. by C. Zając, Wydawnictwo Uniwersytetu Ekonomicznego we Wrocławiu, Wrocław 2017.

Borowiecki R., Kusio T., *Determinanty rozwoju innowacyjności sektora MSP*, "Organizacja i Kierowanie" 2016, 3(173).

CEDEFOP, *Typology of Knowledge, Skills and Competences*, CEDEFOP Reference Series; 64, Brussels 2009.

EKEPIS, *Guide for Professional Profiles Development*, Gsee, Seb, Gsevee, Esee, Athens 2007.

Erensal Y. C., Albayrak Y. E., *Transferring Appropriate Manufacturing Technologies for Developing Countries*, "Journal of Manufacturing Technology Management" 2008, 19, 2.

European Commission, *Towards a European Qualification Framework for Lifelong Learning*, Sec (2005) 957, Brussels 2005.

Front K., *Wpływ uwarunkowań kulturowych na personel zagraniczny* [in:] *Współczesne uwarunkowania rozwoju przedsiębiorstw – wybrane aspekty*, ed. by P. Zwiech, Volumina, Szczecin 2017.

Glinka B., Kostera M., *Różnorodność kulturowa współczesnych organizacji. Nowe kierunki w organizacji i zarządzaniu. Organizacje, konteksty, procesy zarządzania*, Wolters Kluwer, Warszawa 2012.

Hunt B., *Managing Equity and Cultural Diversity in the Health Workforce*, "Journal of Clinical Nursing" 2007, 16, 12.

Janowska Z., *Zarządzanie zasobami ludzkimi*, PWE, Warszawa 2010.

Kozłowska I., *Interesariusze jako zmiana w badaniach zarządzania strategicznego*, "Organizacja i Kierowanie" 2015, 1(166).

Kubik K., *Wybrane problemy zarządzania organizacją wielokulturową – na przykładzie województwa podlaskiego* [in:] *Granice w zarządzaniu kapitałem ludzkim*, ed. by P. Wachowiak, S. Winch, Oficyna Wydawnicza SGH w Warszawie, Warszawa 2014.

Kusio T., *Human Capital Management in a Non-Profit Organisation* [in:] *Knowledge, Economy, Society: Strategies, Concepts and Instruments of Management*, Foundation of the Cracow University of Economics, ed. by R. Oczkowska, A. Jaki, B. Mikuła, Cracow 2016.

Lyles M. A., Salk J. E., *Knowledge Acquisition from Foreign Partners in International Joint Ventures: An Empirical Examination in the Hungarian Context*, "Journal of International Business Studies" 1996, 27, 5.

Nguyen T. D., Atsushi A., *The Impact of Cultural Differences on Technology Transfer. Management Practice Moderation*, "Journal of Manufacturing Technology Management" 2015, 26, 7.

Oczkowska R., *Przedsiębiorstwo w warunkach globalnego otoczenia* [in:] *Zarządzanie zasobami ludzkimi w warunkach globalizacji*, ed. by R. Oczkowska, Uniwersytet Ekonomiczny w Krakowie, Kraków 2012.

Proctor R. W., Dutta A., *Skill Acquisition and Human Performance. Thousand Oaks*, Sage, California 1995.

Radzik K., *Ocena pracowników. Nowa generacja narzędzi do oceny pracowników w nowym ujęciu klasycznego modelu kompetencji*, Wolters Kluwer Business, Warszawa 2013.

Stuss M. M., *Międzynarodowe zarządzanie zasobami ludzkimi – analiza pojęciowa i studium przypadku* [in:] *Granice w zarządzaniu kapitałem ludzkim*, ed. by P. Wachowiak, S. Winch, Oficyna Wydawnicza SGH w Warszawie, Warszawa 2014.

Teczke J., Kusio T., *Change Management in an International Partnership on the Example of EU Projects: A Case Study of Cracow University of Economics* [in:] *Management Science during Destabilization: Local Insight*, Vol. 7, ed. by J. Teczke, K. Djakeli, P. Buła, Cracow University of Economics, Cracow–Tbilisi 2015.

Teczke J., Kusio T., *Theory and Practice of Education Managers for Non-profit Organisations* [in:] *Management Sciences in Kazakhstan and in Poland at the Beginning of the 21ˢᵗ Century: Perspectives for Development and Cooperation*, ed. by P. Buła, J. Czekaj, H. Łyszczarz, B. Syzdykbayeva, Cracow School of Business, Cracow University of Economics, Cracow–Astana 2012.

Vasiliadis A., Vitsilaki C., Efthimiou H., *Entrepreneurship and Entrepreneurial Intentions: The Education Effect*, Proceedings of International Conference for Entrepreneurship, Innovation and Regional Development (24–25 April), Thessaloniki 2009.

Warwas I., Rogozińska-Pawełczyk A., *Zarządzanie zasobami ludzkimi w nowoczesnej organizacji: Aspekty organizacyjne i psychologiczne*, Wydawnictwo Uniwersytetu Łódzkiego, Łódź 2016.

Winterton J., Delamare-Le Deist F., Stringfellow E., *Typology of Knowledge, Skills and Competences: Clarification of the Concept and Prototype* (Panorama Series, No. 1397), Office for Official Publications of the European Communities, Luxembourg 2005.

Współczesne wyzwania w obszarze zarządzania zasobami ludzkimi, ed. by E. Mazur-Wierzbicka, Volumina, Szczecin 2017.

Analysis of Current Managerial Problems on the Example of a Distinctive Organisational Unit of Public Administration

Michał Teczke, Ph.D.   https://orcid.org/0000-0001-9617-1936

Cracow University of Economics

Abstract

The problem of managing public administration units has continued to increase for many years. These units often cannot offer proper conditions and lose the fight for the most valuable employees with enterprises operating in the private sector. From the point of view of the state's strategic interest, such a situation should be considered a threat to the stability of functioning of public administration entities. For the needs of the present article, the author focused on the Social Insurance Institution (*Zakład Ubezpieczeń Społecznych*, ZUS), whose employees have been threatening to go on strikes for several years, in an attempt to improve their financial situation. This paper will analyse generally accessible materials as well as results and conclusions of conversations conducted with the employees of the Institution. The purpose of the conducted study was to explore and specify the remuneration structure of the Institution and identify factors with the greatest impact on the current situation of the entity. The conducted study will allow for determining which elements of the remuneration system are the least effective and indicate the key areas requiring quick intervention.

Keywords: public administration, wages, competences, working conditions, perception of the institutions

Characteristics of the analysed entity

The Social Insurance Institution is an element of the public administration system, which is defined as fulfilment of collective and individual needs of the citizens resulting from the coexistence of people in communities, taken over by the state and performed by its dependent bodies and local government bodies. It constitutes all organisational structures in the state and people employed in these structures who fulfil public, collective and individual, regulatory and provisory, as well as organisational tasks of managerial and decision-making entities.[1] The Social Insurance Institution is a state organisational unit and has its own legal personality. The seat of the Institution is the Capital City of Warsaw (Journal of Laws OJ of 2015, item 121). The Institution provides services for approximately 16.5 million insured people, keeping accounts constituting records of individual insurance history of each person. It serves 7.7 million retirees and pensioners, as well as 2.5 million premium payers who are entrepreneurs. Until 2017, the Institution received 127.8 million documents and sent 74.4 million documents to insured people. The client service rooms handled 23.8 million Poles. The amount of all benefits paid by the Institution last year was about PLN 211.5 billion. All these tasks were completed by 46 thousand employees of the Institution (of which approx. 31 thousand are core employees). Their engagement level is directly related to the efficiency of the remuneration system functioning in the Institution, which is a part of the incentive scheme of the Institution. It is an unquestionable fact that employees motivated to work are highly efficient, more willing to undertake independent professional activity and establish positive relationships with clients more easily. It also performs functions of a competent and liaison body with regard to international coordination of social security systems, cooperating with many liaison institutions from other countries.[2]

Assessment of the actual condition in the analysed research object

The basic documents used during the study were:
- Corporate collective labour agreement for employees of the Institution;
- Agreements concerning principles of division of funds for payment of incentive bonuses to employees of the Branch;
- Resolution of the Management Board of the Institution on approval of the financial statement of the Institution;
- Circular letter of the Director of the Personnel Affairs Department on "Amounts of supplemental payments to particular types of benefits, housing loans and their interest from the Employee Benefit Fund;"
- Regulations of the Employee Benefit Fund;
- Work Regulations along with appendices.

The indicated documents determine the focus, first of all, on the area of material, particularly, financial incentive.

---

[1] *Prawo administracyjne*, ed. by J. Boć, Kolonia Limited, Wrocław 2013, p. 130.
[2] Z. Derdziuk, A. Niedzielski, *Nowa jakość zarządzania w administracji publicznej – Zakład Ubezpieczeń Społecznych*, "Controlling i Rachunkowość Zarządcza" 2010, 11.

The most important and, at the same time, most basic document subject to an analysis is an up-to-date table of job positions and basic wages of employees of the Institution, which is presented in Table 1. Due to the nature of information, the table contains only exemplary positions.

The table below provides information on minimum requirements to be met by employees on different positions (professional qualifications and work experience) and presents information about the so-called "salary brackets" determining the minimum and maximum wage that can be given to an employee on a particular position in a given classification category. The Institution has 16 specified classification categories (where category 1 contains the highest positions, e.g. Chief Physician of the Institution or General Control Inspector, while category 16 contains people on the lowest positions, such as cleaning lady, caretaker or porter). In the aforementioned 16 categories, 95 employee positions are arranged. As can be seen, in categories from 16 to 7 (inclusive), the minimum wage is identical with minimum remuneration for work published in the Regulation of the Council of Ministers of 12 September, 2017 on the amount of the minimum remuneration for work and the value of minimum hourly rate in 2018. The maximum rate grows with each category; however, increases are noticeable in the highest categories the most. Changes in the minimum and maximum wage rates in the Institution are presented in Figure 1.

Table 1. Job positions and the remuneration system of the Institution

Category	Exemplary positions	Requirements and qualifications	Years worked	Amount of remuneration	
				min	max
1	General Control Inspector	Higher education	7	5,000	16,000
	Director of the Institution's organisational unit	Higher education	5		
2	Coordinator	Higher education	5	4,000	13,000
	Deputy Director of the Branch	Higher education	5		
	Vice Director of an organisational unit of the Headquarters	Higher education	5		
	Spokesperson	Higher education	5		
	Actuary of the Institution	According to separate regulations	5		
3	Deputy Chief Accountant of the Institution	Higher education	4	3,000	10,000
	President's Counsellor	Higher education	4		
	Legal Advisor	According to separate regulations	0		
	Head Legislation Specialist	Higher education in law and legislative apprenticeship	7		

Cate-gory	Exemplary positions	Requirements and qualifications	Years worked	Amount of remuneration	
				min	max
4	Department Head	Higher education	4	2,700	9,000
	Centre Manager	Higher education	4		
	Control Inspector, managing the department	According to the regulations for a control inspector	4		
	Internal Auditor	According to separate regulations	1		
5	Deputy Department Head	Higher education	4	2,300	7,600
	Deputy Centre Manager	Higher education	4		
	Regional Spokesperson	Higher education	1		
	Department Manager in the Inspectorate	Higher education	3		
	Chief Specialist	Higher education	5		
6	Field Office Manager	Higher/secondary education	3–8	2,200	7,200
	IT Specialist	Higher/secondary education	3–8		
	Supervision Inspector	According to separate regulations	5		
7	Legislation Specialist	Higher education in law and legislative apprenticeship	2	minimum wage	6,600
	Manager of an independent division	Higher/secondary education	3–8		
	Deputy Department Manager in the Inspectorate	Higher/secondary education	3–8		
	Division Manager	Higher/secondary education	3–6		
	Control Inspector	According to separate regulations	2		
8	Senior Approving Officer	Higher/secondary education	4–8	minimum wage	6,200
	Senior Specialist	Higher/secondary education	4–8		
9	Approving Officer	Higher/secondary education	3–6	minimum wage	5,600
	Specialist	Higher/secondary education	3–6		
10	Senior Inspector	Higher/secondary education	2–4	minimum wage	4,900
	Senior Accountant	Higher/secondary education	2–4		
	Junior IT Specialist	Higher/secondary education	0–3		
11	Legal Clerk	Higher education in law	0	minimum wage	4,600

Cate-gory	Exemplary positions	Requirements and qualifications	Years worked	Amount of remuneration	
				min	max
12	Inspector	Higher/secondary education	1–2	mini-mum wage	4,300
	Accountant	Higher/secondary education	1–2		
13	Operator entering data and making corrections	Secondary education	0	mini-mum wage	3,850
	Senior Clerk	Higher/secondary education	0–1		
	Driver	According to separate regulations	0		
14	Assembler	Basic education and specialised training	0	mini-mum wage	3,450
	Bookbinder		0		
	Copyist		0		
15	Legal Clerk	Secondary education	0	mini-mum wage	3,150
	Receptionist		0		
	Secretary		0		
16	Service Employee	Primary education	0	mini-mum wage	2,950
	Porter		0		
	Caretaker		0		
	Stoker		0		
	Messenger		. 0		
	Manual Worker		0		
	Cleaner		0		

Source: prepared by the author on the basis of internal materials: http://www.zus.pl/zampub/files/116682/vpNu6h6hN3U.pdf and https://wynagrodzenia.pl/artykul/zarobki-w-zus-mozna-zarobic-maksymalnie--do-176-tys-pln (access: 20 May 2020).

As can be seen in the figure above, although growth in the minimum wage in ZUS is rather small and greater increases can be observed in categories 1–4, increases in maximum wage are higher and can be described as large, particularly in the highest categories (1–3).

The Corporate Collective Labour Agreement contains information with direct impact on the present and future motivation of employees resulting from the remuneration system. The document contains, among others, information on annual raises and conditions for getting financial bonuses. & 10 of the aforementioned document states: "A raise in the Institution is given at least once a year, no later than from 1 April of a given year, with adjustment from 1 January." Paragraph 11 point 3 "The Bonus Fund is allocated for payment of bonuses to employees at least once each quarter. Payments

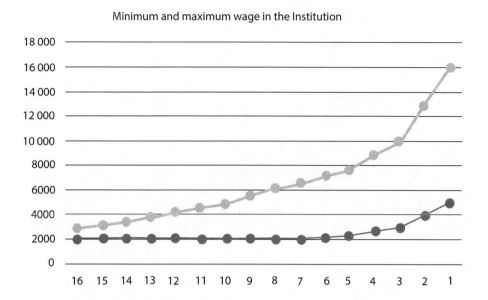

Figure 1. Minimum and maximum wage in the institution

Source: prepared by the author.

of bonuses are made until the 15th day of the month following the quarter to which the bonus applies. Payment of bonuses for the 4th quarter takes place no later than until the end of the last month of the fourth quarter." Paragraph 13 "Employees who have worked in the Institution for at least 6 months in the given calendar year shall acquire the right to a bonus from the Corporate Bonus Fund, known as 'the thirteen.'" Paragraph 14 "Employees of the Institution may be granted a special allowance amounting to 5% to 25% of the basic wage paid for the time of actual work." Paragraph 16 refers to the possibility to obtaining jubilee awards, which increases every 5 years to amount to 75% of the wage after working for 10 years to 400% of the wage after working for 45 years. The agreement also contains a provision concerning a non-payroll incentive, namely, healthcare. Paragraph 21 states that "At the expense of the Institution, employees shall be provided with medical check-ups related to mammography and the prostate gland." As it results from the financial statement of the Social Insurance Institution for 2015, in the structure of costs incurred by the Institution, presented in accordance with the income statement, remuneration had the highest share in the costs of core operational activity (constituting 95.27% of total costs) at 55.02% (PLN 225,823,800). To sum up the deliberations, it is worth noting the position of OPZZ (*Ogólnopolskie Porozumienie Związków Zawodowych*, All-Poland Alliance of Trade Unions), which was included in the letter dated July 10, 2018 to the Institution's President, Prof. Gertruda Uścińska, Ph.D. The information on the remuneration system of some employee groups show that salaries of ZUS employees look poor in comparison to the average wage in the national economy. For example, according to the data for 2017, ZUS has:

- ca. 2,931 full-time clerk positions with the average gross remuneration of PLN 2,440;
- ca. 3,862 full-time senior clerk positions with the average gross remuneration of PLN 2,699;
- ca. 6,228 full-time inspector positions with the average gross remuneration of PLN 3,003;
- ca. 9,705 full-time senior inspector positions with the average gross remuneration of PLN 3,278;
- ca. 6,665 full-time specialist positions with the average gross remuneration of PLN 3,578;
- ca. 3,484 full-time senior specialist positions with the average gross remuneration of PLN 3,946;
- ca. 1,209 full-time approving officer positions with the average gross remuneration of PLN 3,748.

So, more than 3/4 of the Institution's staff (a group of more than 34,000) of only core employees, including specialists with many years worked—does not reach the average wage in the national economy[3]. The presented accusations received a response from the Institution's spokesman, Mr. W. Andrusiewicz, who issued the following statement:

> The average basic wage presented, with some approximation, by ZZP ZUS [Trade Union of ZUS Employees] does not constitute the average remuneration in the Institution. The average remuneration, apart from the basic salary, includes any additional remuneration, such as awards, bonuses, "the thirteen," and social benefits, namely everything that is reflected in the PIT income settlement.

According to data presented by the Institution, the average wages of specialists are as follows:[4]

- Clerk: gross PLN 2,960 (1,221 full-time positions);
- Senior Clerk: gross PLN 3,138 (2,754 full-time positions);
- Inspector: gross PLN 3,625 (6,208 full-time positions);
- Senior Inspector: gross PLN 4,007 (9,817 full-time positions);
- Specialist: gross PLN 4,315 (6,773 full-time positions);
- Senior Specialist: gross PLN 4,916 (3,637 full-time positions);
- Approving Officer: gross PLN 4,753 (1,215 full-time positions).

---

[3]   http://www.opzz.org.pl/aktualnosci/kraj/w-zusie-nie-tak-kolorowo (access: 1 August 2018).
[4]   https://businessinsider.com.pl/twoje-pieniadze/praca/ile-zarabia-sie-w-zus-pensje-wynagrodzenia-lista-opzz/vvzq4vl (access: 1 August 2018).

As it can be seen, the differences in the presented data are quite substantial and apply not only to the amount of remuneration, but also to the number of full-time positions. In the same statement, the spokesman also points out that, in the last year, each employee received a special award (for the ZUS Employee Day) in the gross amount of PLN 1.5 thousand.

Although there is no doubt that, from a statistical point of view, all remuneration components listed by the spokesperson should be taken into account, from a scientific point of view, we should be aware that a one-off award paid in 2017 should not have an impact on the assessment of remuneration amounts in the previous years.

Diagnosis of the existing condition

The presented data allow for drawing important conclusions. In the first place, we should take note of problems related to wage differentials in particular categories. Information on this topic are presented in Table 2 and Figure 2.

Table 2. Wage differentials in particular categories

Classification category	Minimum wage*	Maximum wage	Wage differentials (max-min)
16	National minimum	2,950	850
15	National minimum	3,150	1,050
14	National minimum	3,450	1,350
13	National minimum	3,850	1,750
12	National minimum	4,300	2,200
11	National minimum	4,600	2,500
10	National minimum	4,900	2,800
9	National minimum	5,600	3,500
8	National minimum	6,200	4,100
7	National minimum	6,600	4,500
6	2,200	7,200	5,000
5	2,300	7,600	5,300
4	2,700	9,000	6,300
3	3,000	10,000	7,000
2	4,000	13,000	9,000
1	5,000	16,000	11,000

* minimum wage at the time of the study amounts to gross PLN 2,100.

Source: prepared by the author.

As can be seen in the table above, the wage differentials increase along with the growth in complexity of processes implemented in particular categories. The occurrence of this kind of phenomenon is nothing extraordinary, however, its scale is interesting, particularly in the lowest and the highest categories.

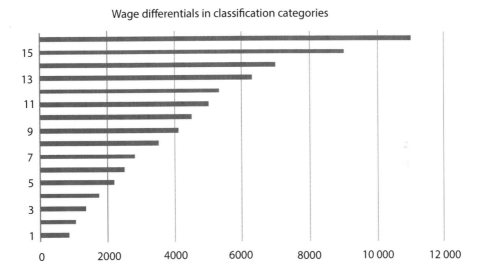

Figure 2. Wage differentials in classification categories

Source: prepared by the author.

When preparing pay spines and a pay table, it should be ensured that the wage differentials allows for flexible shaping of remunerations (the larger the differentials, the greater the flexibility) with simultaneous "strong" connection of positions with requirements and remuneration (the smaller the differentials, the stronger the connection). It should be noted that, as a result of identical minimum wage in categories from 16–7, the wage differential for 58 positions amounts to PLN 4,500. Theoretically, in accordance with the information presented in Table III.1, the Institution accepts a situation in which, e.g. a messenger (cat. 16) earns as much or more than a manager of an independent division (cat. 7). It is also puzzling whether three positions in the first category (Chief Physician of the Institution, General Control Inspector, Director of an organisational unit of the Headquarters) need to have a wage differential at the level of PLN 11 thousand. In order to present risks related to the aforementioned problems, an analysis of penetration of wage rates by particular categories should be conducted. A graphic presentation of the analysis is shown in Figure 3.

While the penetration of rates through several categories is nothing special, excessive penetration often leads to problems related to determining the remuneration, particularly for positions requiring greater competences. As can be seen in the figure above, the lower the category, the greater the penetration of the wage rate. The maximum remuneration of category 16 is practically identical to the minimum remuneration of category 3. Should the difference between the maximum remuneration of a cleaner acceptable in the Regulations and the minimum acceptable remuneration of a Deputy Branch Director amount only to PLN 50 (max. remuneration of category 16 is 2,950, minimum remuneration of category 3 is 3,000).

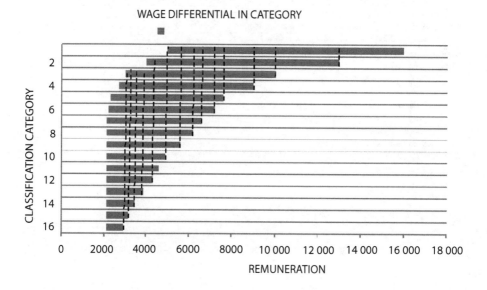

Figure 3. Penetration of rates in categories

Source: prepared by the author.

When looking at responsibility, required education, work experience, level of complexity of the decisions made, this difference seems to be much too small. If we look at the highest positions in the organisation (category 1), the penetration reaches category 9. Theoretically, it is acceptable for a fire protection specialist to earn more than the Institution's President (maximum remuneration of category 9 is PLN 5,600, and minimum remuneration of category 1 is PLN 5,000).

The literature on the subject clearly presents the fact that the labour market has become the market of the employee. Employees more and more often decide where they want to be employed by selecting from among the best offers. In order for companies to be able to look for employees ensuring the highest quality of provided services, they must have a well-built reward system, otherwise it will be very difficult to find employees and the newly employed will demonstrate high fluctuating tendencies, which is always unfavourable from the employer's point of view.

Possibilities of changes and improvement proposals

As a result of lack of access to all documents of the Institution, it is impossible to conduct a diagnostic analysis. In this situation, the researcher is forced to seek "ideal" solutions and, in the further course of research, through subsequent iterations, adapt them to the organisational capabilities of the system. In the case of prognostic modelling, it is necessary to refer to the systems theory, in particular to deliberations concerning the concept of an ideal system presented by G. Nadler, developed also by J. Trzcieniecki. This concept had a substantial impact on the development of the methodology of organisational research. When referring to the aforementioned concepts, it can be assumed that the construction of an optimising model of a prognostic nature consists of four stages:

1. Determination of a pattern, namely the ideal model.
2. Realisation of the ideal pattern that would adjust it to the actual conditions with the use of the iterative concept (subsequent approximations).
3. Formulation of conditions of changes in the existing research objects.
4. Determination of projections and implementation of the model.

In connection with methodological constraints and constraints resulting from the article form, the author will focus mainly on the first of the aforementioned stages.

One of the first problems that should be addressed is the incorrect layout of the pay spines and the pay table. Insufficient wage differentials at the simplest positions limit the possibility of regulating wages related, e.g. with efficiency or job experience. It should be also noted that the analysed internal documents of the Institution contain no information on the service premium or the functional allowance, which would have a substantial impact on the diversity of remunerations among employees. Furthermore, the remuneration policy currently implemented focuses on raising salaries by a minimum amount which, in consequence, will lead to further reduction in wage differentials. Objectively, requirements set for employees of the Institution are very high and, at the same time, the wage proposed by the employer can be considered relatively low (particularly on lower and middle positions, which cover more than 75% of all positions in the Institution). The problem was also addressed by Krzysztof Dyka—a Board Member supervising the System Operation and Exploitation Division. In the article published by money.pl, he states that, without changes to the remuneration policy, the nearby future may bring problems with retention of qualified staff and acquisition of new employees with specific specialisations[5]. To solve the indicated problem connected with the need to search for proper employees, the Institution has

---

[5]   https://www.money.pl/gospodarka/wiadomosci/artykul/zus-praca-w-zus-informatyk-w-zus-it,205,0,2408397.html (access: 10 August 2018).

begun the procedure of raising the minimum wages proposed to the newly employed. Unfortunately, the pressure put only on increasing wages of potential candidates quickly led to flattening of the wage curve in categories. Considering the rate amounts offered to potential candidates, a negative opinion of the public on the Institution and the effect of flattening the wage curve, the introduced solutions are unfortunately of no positive influence on the employees' work motivation. A similar position was presented by trade unions. The website of OPZZ states:

> the remuneration policy implemented in the Institution resulted in levelling of wages of specialists with many years worked as compared to the newly employed. Wages have also been significantly flattened. ZUS is no longer an attractive employer on the market. No wonder that employees of the Institution lack motivation to work; there is no proverbial light at the end of a tunnel, there are no prospects; furthermore, there are no clear principles of rewarding and promotion or a career path—this discourages the employees even more, which may unfortunately impact ZUS customers after some time.

The only solution to the mounting problem is an actual reassessment of jobs, determination of new wage intervals and increase of real remuneration to a level at least similar to the market conditions. The policy under which the newly employed, who do not yet have knowledge, practice and experience, receive wages lower by several or a few dozen PLN than employees with many years of experience is extremely discouraging for the presently employed. To solve this problem, it is necessary to increase employment in encumbered sections or reorganise the work of the whole Institution. Unfortunately, there is no easy solution to the indicated problem. Low remunerations are once again standing in the way.

The Institution is at a very difficult phase. The situation requires radical steps and use of available measures. The postulate of increasing remunerations is a necessary prerequisite for the Institution to be treated as an interesting employer on the labour market. Virtually all core positions require an increase in remunerations, both in terms of wages proposed to the newly employed and to employees with many years of experience. Managers of any organisation should be aware that loss of an experienced employee is irreparable. Employees should be treated as the basic capital in a knowledge-based economy. Each training, each solved issue increases professional skills of the staff. An experienced employee lost cannot be replaced by employing someone new in his or her place. Employee development is an investment and, as any investment, should yield maximum return. Employees leaving their jobs are an irreparable loss. The problem of raising remunerations of the Institution's employees is exacerbated by a negative social perception. The Institution collects contributions for many purposes (not always implemented by the Institution itself—e.g. health insurance, which is implemented by NFZ (*Narodowy Fundusz Zdrowia*, National Health Fund)) and its actions are very often received in a negative way. It is surprising that, 2 years ago along with the Institute of Public Affairs, ZUS conducted a large study concerning Knowledge about the Institution. The report on the study "Knowledge of and attitudes towards social insurance," available at the website of ZUS, confirms the presented opinions. To the question of "How do you assess the functioning of ZUS?," the average grade in the scale of 1–5 was 2.7—what is important, highly positive answers were given only by 2% of respondents. Opinions expressed during panel discussions concerning associations with the Institution were also mostly negative, e.g.:[6]

- Oh, I won't say it, because what came to my mind was very nasty. . . . Appropriation.
- We pay a lot and receive little later on.
- Something is not right with this social insurance and social profession, because I have not come across one person who would have good things to say about such an institution.
- Misery.

The society's negative perception of the Institution significantly limits the possibilities of solving problems related to the amount of remunerations. The only real possibility to improve the situation of employees is in the hands of politicians who, perhaps afraid of drops in popularity, do not respond to the mounting problem.

Conclusion

The excessively low flexibility of remunerations on the lowest positions and the excessively wide wage brackets on the highest positions constitute a clear problem, limiting the effectiveness of operation of the remuneration system. The average wages of core employees should be considered insufficient. Awarding bonuses to newly employed staff, with simultaneous lack of additional tangible incentives for the experienced staff, causes discouragement and, in consequence, the desire to change the employer, and contributes to an increase in unwanted employment fluctuation.

In the author's opinion, the Institution's situation is presently very difficult; continuous disputes between Trade Unions and the Management are destructive for social interest. An agreement between all parties is necessary, as well as the introduction of real changes that will enable improvement in the work efficiency in the Institution. It is necessary to introduce a full-scale social campaign making the citizens aware of the importance of functions implemented by the Institution. It is further necessary to increase remunerations of core employees. Even taking into account more positive data proposed by the Spokesperson of the Institution, the average remuneration in the group of more than 31 thousand core employees amounts to gross PLN 4,581 and

---

[6]   http://www.zus.pl/documents/10182/44573/Raport+wiedza+system+emerytalny/040bd2a1-094a-4d97-9d77-e0bddc19e845 (access: 20 August 2018).

is lower than the national average presented by the Central Statistical Office (*Główny Urząd Statystyczny*, GUS) for the 1st quarter of the current year. After subtracting the high one-time award received on the occasion of the ZUS Employee Day, the disproportion is further increased (average remuneration of PLN 4,456). Unfortunately, further ignoring of employee needs, caused by fear of a negative social opinion, may lead in the worst scenario even to a paralysis in the work of the whole Institution. It is necessary to stop the loss of experienced employees through gradual but regular improvement in working conditions in the Social Insurance Institution.

Bibliography

Borkowska S., *Strategie wynagrodzeń*, Oficyna Ekonomiczna, Kraków 2001.

Borkowska S., *System motywowania w przedsiębiorstwie*, PWN, Warszawa 1985.

Derdziuk Z., Niedzielski A., *Nowa jakość zarządzania w administracji publicznej – Zakład Ubezpieczeń Społecznych*, "Controlling i Rachunkowość Zarządcza" 2010, 11.

Kozioł L., Tyrańska M., *Motywowanie pracowników w teorii i praktyce*, Biblioteczka Pracownicza, Warszawa 2002.

Krupski A., *Rada Nadzorcza Zakładu Ubezpieczeń Społecznych – namiastka partycypacji czynnika społecznego w działalności ZUS*, "Ubezpieczenia Społeczne. Teoria i Praktyka" 2010, 6.

Krupski A., *Specyfika pozycji prawnej Zakładu Ubezpieczeń Społecznych*, "Ubezpieczenia Społeczne. Teoria i Praktyka" 2015, 1.

Prawo administracyjne, ed. by J. Boć, Kolonia Limited, Wrocław 2013.

Woźniak J., *Współczesne systemy motywacyjne*, Wydawnictwo Naukowe PWN, Warszawa 2012.

Zając C., *Zarządzanie zasobami ludzkimi w grupach kapitałowych*, PWE, Warszawa 2012.

Websites

http://www.opzz.org.pl/aktualnosci/kraj/w-zusie-nie-tak-kolorowo (access: 1 August 2018).

http://www.zus.pl/documents/10182/44573/Raport+wiedza+system+emerytalny/040bd2a1-094a-4d97-9d77-e0bddc19e845 (access: 20 August 2018).

https://businessinsider.com.pl/twoje-pieniadze/praca/ile-zarabia-sie-w-zus-pensje-wynagrodzenia-lista-opzz/vvzq4vl (access: 1 August 2018).

https://www.money.pl/gospodarka/wiadomosci/artykul/zus-praca-w-zus-informatyk-w-zus-it,205,0,2408397.html (access: 10 August 2018).

http://www.zus.pl/zampub/files/116682/vpNu6h6hN3U.pdf (access: 20 May 2018).

Customer Service in a Marketing and Logistics Approach

Prof. Piotr Buła, Ph.D.　⑩　https://orcid.org/0000-0001-8741-8327
Cracow University of Economics
University of Johannesburg

MSc Paulina Kozieł　⑩　https://orcid.org/0000-0003-3741-5018
The Jan Kochanowski University in Kielce

Abstract
Customer service is one of the key concepts in a modern enterprise. It occupies one of the main places in the sphere of logistics and marketing activities. Thanks to an appropriate level of service, a satisfied customer establishes long-term relationships with the company. The right level of customer service means responding to the needs and expectations of potential customers.
The article draws attention to the significant role and importance of customer service in the company in terms of marketing and logistics. The topicality of issues was also highlighted by providing an overview of recent Polish research in this area.

Keywords: customer, customer needs, customer service, marketing customer service, logistic customer service, level of customer service

Introduction

The role of the customer for modern enterprises is significant. Each enterprise operating on the market depends on the customer whose decisions related to the purchase of a given product or the use of a given service allow to profit. Enterprises should, therefore, focus their activities on the customer and his needs, in particular drawing attention to an appropriate level of customer service. Logistic customer service, due to its importance in the company and giving meaning to all logistics activities and processes is often also called customer logistics.[1]

---

[1] J. Zrobek, *Marketing w działaniach logistycznych* [in:] *Logistyka gospodarcza. Uwarunkowania, zarządzanie, tendencje*, ed. by W. Starzyńska, W. J. Rogalski, J. Zrobek, Naukowe Wydawnictwo Piotrkowskie, Piotrków Trybunalski 2013, pp. 143–144.

The purpose of this study is to present selected aspects of customer service, including its marketing and logistics approach. The source basis for the study is the available literature on the subject and reports on the level and quality of customer service in Polish enterprises. For the purposes of the article, a review of research in this area was also conducted.

The concept and essence of customer service

The issue of customer service has many dimensions and can be interpreted in different ways. It includes both logistics and marketing aspects. Customer service is related to meeting various customer needs.[2]

The main determinant for maintaining long-term relationships with customers is their degree of satisfaction with the level of customer service. To obtain and maintain the desired level of service, the company should firstly learn and objectively understand how its customers define customer service, and then redefine the concept in categories that matter to them, meet their needs and allow them to achieve their goals.[3]

Customer service includes all activities that are undertaken with the intention of developing a service strategy, order fulfilment, as well as after-sales service. This term covers all areas of customer contact, both tangible and intangible. This approach to customer service shows that it is part of both marketing and logistics.[4]

D. Kempny calls customer service a "skill or ability to meet customer requirements and expectations, mainly regarding the time and place of ordered deliveries, using all available forms of logistics activity, including: transport, storage, inventory management, information and packaging."[5]

The goal of customer service is:[6]

- ensuring the desired quality of service and maintaining an appropriate level of implementation of the basic elements of customer service,
- providing the customer with added value, perceived as benefits, in an effective manner,
- ensuring that the correct relationship between the time of placing an order and its completion is achieved,
- helping to increase customer satisfaction.

---

[2]   *Logistyka w biznesie*, ed. by M. Ciesielski, PWE, Warszawa 2006, p. 128.

[3]   M. Christopher, H. Peck, *Logistyka marketingowa*, transl. M. Ślusarczyk, PWE, Warszawa 2005, pp. 43–44.

[4]   M. Kramarz, *Elementy logistyczne obsługi klienta w sieciach dystrybucji. Pomiar, ocena, strategie*, Difin, Warszawa 2014, p. 46.

[5]   E. Gołembska, *Logistyka w gospodarce światowej*, C.H. Beck, Warszawa 2009, p. 168.

[6]   S. Kauf, A. Tłuczak, *Logistyczna obsługa klienta. Metody ilościowe*, Wydawnictwo Naukowe PWN, Warszawa 2018, p. 11.

Customer service in the traditional sense is associated only with the moment of transaction. However, it can be divided into three types of elements: pre-transaction, transactional and post-transactional. This division is the same as the process approach to service.[7]

Pre-transaction elements include, among others: formulation of customer service policy principles, availability for customers, organisational structure of the service company and system flexibility. However, transaction elements of customer service include: length of the order cycle, stock availability, order fulfilment rate, and order status information. Transactional elements, in turn, include, among others: availability of spare parts, so-called call time (technician arrival in case of call), monitoring of products at the customer, guaranteeing, complaints and consideration of customer complaints.[8]

The literature presents a five-step approach to understanding customer needs in customer service. It requires a detailed understanding of customer needs, as well as the importance they assign to each of the elements of service. These stages include.[9]

1. Defining the competition plane—getting to know the "best" competitors in a given industry or market and the standards of customer service that they provide.
2. Analysing customer service items—identifying customer service items (group interviews, thematic groups, in-depth surveys) perceived by the customers themselves.
3. Identifying key elements of customer service—getting to know the most important elements of service (according to the customers themselves) that determine the choice of a specific company by the customer.
4. Market segmentation—the division of clients into segments according to preferences and similar views on key elements of service.
5. Comparing business results with the best in a given industry/market—the purpose of the comparison is to provide a higher level of customer service.

Enterprises should identify actual customer needs and adapt customer service standards to them. It is the service standards and the degree of their implementation that determine the quality of customer service. Regarding the level of service, four key gaps in customer service are defined.

Gap 1 arises in the transactional phase of customer service; it is the difference between the established parameters of the service (customer service standards) and the quality of service expected by the customer. This gap is the result of incorrect definition of service standards through incorrectly conducted customer preferences. The lack of segmentation and disregarding the separate needs of different customer groups also contribute to its creation.

7   *Marketing usług logistycznych*, ed. by G. Rosa, M. Jedliński, U. Chrąchol-Barczyk, C.H. Beck, Warszawa 2017, p. 235.
8   M. Christopher, H. Peck, *Logistyka marketingowa...*, pp. 44–45.
9   Ibidem, pp. 46–47.

Gap 2 arises during the order delivery phase (transactional phase). Its creation results from the fact that the process actually conducted does not meet the standards set in the pre-transaction phase. The problem with the implementation of the process therefore appears at the level of logistics tasks according to the standards set out in the customer service policy. The reason for this may be improperly implemented processes (contrary to the adopted customer service policy) or unpredictable disturbances occurring at the stage of process implementation.

Gap 3 is the difference in the perception of the quality of service actually provided in relation to the service performance parameters set by the supplier. Problems arising at gap 1 and 2 may have consequences in the incorrect adoption of the satisfaction rate indicator. In particular, defining the customer's expectations incorrectly will have consequences in his real perception of the level of service.

Gap 4 involves determining the actual level of customer satisfaction with the supplier's order completion process. The level of customer satisfaction is the difference between the level of service expected by the customer and the quality of the order process actually perceived by him.[10]

Logistic and marketing aspect of customer service

Customer service in the logistics dimension focuses primarily on the area of physical distribution of goods, related to satisfying the requirements and expectations of customers, implemented according to the 7W principle, and, therefore, it is important to provide the right customer, the right product, in the right quantity, at the right time, in the right place in the right condition and at the right price. Logistics customer service implements the 7W principle using all available forms of logistics activity, including transport, storage, inventory management, information and packaging.[11]

According to E. Gołembska, logistic customer service "consists in creating product availability, measured by the ability to fulfil orders from current stocks, in the right place and time of receipt of the order."[12]

Logistic customer service can be viewed in three dimensions. The first of these concerns activities related to the execution of the order cycle, and, therefore, it relates, among others to: preparing the enterprise for the service process, accepting orders, maintaining customer relations, developing the order within the company, managing inventory, completing and issuing ordered products, shipping and transporting goods, transferring products to the recipient, invoicing and payment process, installation of individual products and training in their use, warranty and

---

[10]   M. Kramarz, *Elementy logistyczne...*, pp. 49–50.
[11]   J. Dyczkowska, *Marketing usług logistycznych*, Difin, Warszawa 2014, p. 123.
[12]   E. Gołembska, *Logistyka w gospodarce...*, p. 168.

post-warranty service, accepting any complaints or returns as well as accepting and utilising packaging.

The second level of perception of logistics customer service is the provision by the company of desired service standards (of adequate quality) or maintaining the appropriate level of performing the basic activities included in customer service. These may include, e.g. completeness of the order, specific delivery time, timeliness of delivered products or availability of products from the warehouse.

The third way of perceiving logistic customer service refers to treating it as a management philosophy and mission of a given company. It is connected with subordinating all activities of the company to the needs and goals of its customers as well as to ways of satisfying these needs and achieving goals. Treating the customer in the above manner allows to achieve customer satisfaction with the services offered to him.[13]

The above three levels of perception of logistics customer service should not be treated selectively as variants, it is necessary to analyse them as complementary elements, or as a whole.[14]

The essence of logistic customer service is that a customer purchasing a given product or using a specific service, simultaneously acquires other benefits associated with it. The value purchased by the customer is not only the value of the product, but also the values that flow from customer service standards. This means that the product in the company's warehouse and the product purchased by the customer, despite the same physical and functional characteristics, differ significantly in terms of value presented. This is due to the fact that in addition to the visual and functional features of the product, additional conditions and actions accompanying the transaction and the use of the product are important for the customer—before, during and after the transaction.[15]

Customer service from a logistics point of view is closely related to four elements:[16]

- Time—the time counted from the moment the order is placed until the customer receives the order, i.e. the sum of time needed to forward the order (preferably using the Internet), order processing by the seller, preparing the goods for shipment, sending, transport;
- Reliability—the ability of the company's logistics system to ensure delivery intact and in a timely manner, i.e. in line with customer expectations;
- Communication—the ability of an enterprise information system to exchange data with customers (e.g. order confirmation, delivery information, accepting a complaint, etc.);
- Convenience—flexibility, i.e. adjusting the company's logistics system to the various requirements of customers.

---

13   *Logistyka w biznesie*, pp. 128–129.
14   Ibidem, p. 129.
15   Ibidem, p. 130.
16   A. Szymonik, I. Nowak, *Współczesna logistyka*, Difin, Warszawa 2018, p. 95.

When exploring the scope of customer service, it is possible to separate the tasks that are part of the competences of marketers and logistics competencies. Figure 1 presents marketing and logistics activities that affect the customer service process. The sphere of marketing (marketing-mix) in this area includes product, price, distribution and promotion. Logistics activities, on the other hand, are activities related to shaping inventory, storage, packaging of products, order processing, transport and customer service (logistics-mix). These spheres interpenetrate each other, but the area of their mutual interest are the processes of distribution and customer service. Thanks to the skilful integration of logistics activities with marketing activities, an enterprise can achieve a synergy effect, thus multiplying the benefits for both the company and the customer, which will be reflected in the appropriate, desired level of customer service.

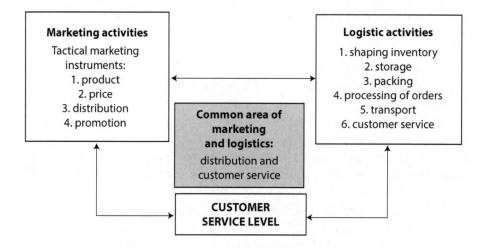

Figure 1. Marketing and logistics activities affecting the level of customer service

Source: M. Szydełko, *Logistyczna obsługa klienta jako element kształtowania przewagi konkurencyjnej przedsiębiorstwa*, "Logistyka" 2012, 5, p. 197.

Marketing is perceived as a process of learning about the client's needs, satisfying them and creating them. Logistics, on the other hand, is seen as a tool that allows meeting customer needs in terms of time, place and quality of service. The reason for such a large correlation between marketing and logistics is, therefore, their customer orientation.[17] Table 1 presents elements (features) of customer service in the area of marketing and logistics. In both logistic customer service and marketing customer service, four elements can be identified that define individual activities related to

---

[17]   *Marketing usług...*, p. 236.

the customer service process. These include: time, reliability, communication and convenience. Understanding customer needs in this area and satisfying them with the help of appropriate marketing and logistics tools is the key to achieving customer satisfaction from the transaction. Ensuring an adequate level of customer service in the area of logistics and marketing in the long term will also allow building long-term business-customer relationships.

Table 1. Elements/features of marketing and logistic customer service

Element/ Feature	Marketing	Logistics
Time	Time for receipt and consideration of complaints; the period for accepting returns; business opening hours; waiting time for service at checkout; one customer service time	Time of order placement and execution; transportation time; loading and reloading time; loading unit forming time
Reliability	Punctuality of opening the enterprise; staff competence; consideration of complaints; the ability to obtain information at a dedicated service point; inventory availability	Inventory level in a warehouse; punctuality; cargo security and storage; correct order performance; correctness of completing transport documents
Communication	Distribution of promotional brochures; product tracking; kindness of staff; information on the packaging about the shelf life	Cargo tracking; transmission of order information
Convenience	A specified number of people available to the customer; the ability to pay bills online; telephone provision of information; telephone reservation of services; payment in instalments	Placing an order by phone, internet; selection of transport branches; offering logistics services packages; logistic consulting; night deliveries

Source: I. Dembińska-Cyran, J. Hołub-Iwan, J. Perenc, *Zarządzanie relacjami z klientem*, Difin, Warszawa 2004, p. 45.

Marketing and logistics customer service in the light of Polish research

As part of the Polish Quality of Service Programme, an annual customer survey is conducted regarding the level and quality of customer service provided in 46,000 enterprises from over 200 industries. In 2018, the average level of satisfaction with customer service in Poland was 77.2% (in 2017 this result was 0.5% higher). This means that every fifth customer is not satisfied with the level of customer service in the Polish enterprises.

According to the administrative division of Poland, in 2018 the level of customer satisfaction with their service in all voivodships exceeded 70%. The highest percentage of customer service quality can be found in the Podlasie Voivodship—88.9% (73.6% in 2017, which was the lowest result) and Warmian-Masurian Voivodship—80.5%

(in 2017—75, 9%). The highest result, as in the previous year, in district capitals was recorded by Białystok—91.6% (in 2017—79.2%) of satisfied customers.

Definitely the worst level of customer service according to surveys is presented by the Łódź Voivodeship—71.0% (in 2017—77.9%). Among the cities, Rzeszów and Kielce are the worst performers, with the index not exceeding 70% of satisfied customers.

The highest rated industries in terms of satisfaction with customer service were successively tourism and hotel industries—90.8% (in 2017—82.9%), restaurants and cafes—81.9% (in 2017—81.1%) and beauty salons and perfumeries—80.9% (in 2017—83.3%). Customers are least satisfied with the service provided by offices and institutions—54.8% (in 2017—60.4%).[18]

On the other hand, according to the survey conducted by KPMG regarding the experience of customers with individual industries in Poland, the value of the indicator was calculated, allowing the assessment of the level of customer service for brands in individual industries. The highest value of this indicator was recorded by non-food retail enterprises, whereas service providers were the worst, similarly to the previous year, the lowest result was recorded by electricity and gas suppliers.[19]

The topic of customer service is also the subject of empirical research in Poland in various industries or market segments. Table 2 presents an overview of selected surveys on customer service in enterprises operating in Poland.

Table 2. Review of selected studies on customer service in Poland

Author (year of publication)	Research subject	Scope and subject of research
K. Zięba (2008)	57 randomly selected companies from the window and door manufacturers industry operating in Poland	Research on the level of customer service. Studies have shown a low degree of customer interest on the part of the surveyed enterprises. Only in 50% of enterprises the customer service was rated as good, in the case of one company—as very good.
E. Gołembska (2009)	Food business; an enterprise dealing in the distribution of metal products (64 key clients); construction sector company	Research on the assessment of the logistic quality of customer service using indicators considered appropriate for this type of enterprise. Research has identified the weaknesses in logistics customer service and the key elements of customer service in the assessment of customers.

---

[18]   *Gwiazdy Jakości Obsługi 2019 przyznane! Poznaj Laureatów oraz najnowsze wyniki badania jakości obsługi w Polsce*, https://www.jakoscobslugi.pl/artykul/gwiazdy-jakosci-obslugi-2019-przyznane-poznaj-lau-reatow-oraz-najnowsze-wyniki-badania-jakosci-obslugi-w-polsce (access: 15 June 2019); *Które firmy najbardziej dbają o klienta? Już po raz dwunasty nagrodzono najlepszych!*, https://direct.money.pl/artykuly/porady/ktore-firmy-najbardziej-dbaja-o-klienta-juz,149,0,2428309.html (access: 15 June 2019).

[19]   *[Cyfrowy] klient nasz pan. Jak marki na polskim rynku zarządzają doświadczeniami klientów*, https://assets.kpmg/content/dam/kpmg/pl/pdf/2019/02/pl-top-100-brands-2018.pdf (access: 15 June 2019).

Author (year of publication)	Research subject	Scope and subject of research
A. Strychalska--Rudzewicz, A. Rudzewicz (2011)	Managers of logistics or marketing departments of 66 manufacturing and service enterprises operating in the Warmian-Masurian Voivodeship	Research on customer service evaluation in the field of logistics and marketing carried out by the method proposed by Novich Neil. Research results indicate that the majority of surveyed companies declare that they measure the level of customer service that they offer systematically and randomly examine the more important cases of reasons for losing their customers and acquiring customers from competitors.
R. Barcik, M. Kubański (2012)	Managers of food businesses located in the Podbeskidzie region	Research showing how the implementation of selected issues related to logistic customer service looks like in practice. Research shows that the surveyed enterprises have differences in the perception of the importance of logistic customer service, which allows for the separation of two groups of enterprises. The first of them are enterprises with managerial staff that understands the essence of logistics, while the second are enterprises in which care for an appropriate level of logistic customer service is pushed to the background.
M. Daroń (2015)	Customers of food businesses on the B2B market and employees of the surveyed company	Logistics customer service research conducted bipolarly—external analysis carried out in the form of Servqual among clients of the examined company and internal analysis conducted among the employees of this company directly involved in the implementation of deliveries. The research results showed that the actual level of customer service in the studied enterprise is lower than expected by the customers. None of the examined elements of logistics customer service fully meets the needs of customers.
P. Smolnik (2015)	100 clients of the metal production and service enterprise	Research on the level and quality of logistic customer service in the studied enterprise. The respondents rated the level of customer service as good (56%) and very good (33%), which means that few customers are dissatisfied with the service. As many as 75% of respondents declare using the offer of the examined company again due to their satisfaction with cooperation with the company and the high level of service.
J. Dyczkowska (2015)	165 individual customers to whom products are delivered by logistics operators in the West Pomeranian and Pomeranian Voivodships	Research on the importance of logistics customer service for the customer himself and the measurement and assessment of the level of service, and consequently the choice of the logistics operator. According to the conducted research, individual clients, when deciding on the selection of a logistics operator, are guided by an appropriate level of logistic customer service, in particular the time criterion, as the main determinant of the service process.

Author (year of publication)	Research subject	Scope and subject of research
M. Kadłubek (2017)	147 enterprises for commercial road freight transport in the Silesian Voivodeship	Research on the perception of the idea of customer service in logistics management of the surveyed enterprises, conducted on representatives of the surveyed entities. The research made it possible to conclude that most of the respondents have little awareness of the gravity of or do not see benefits in shaping customer expectations and perception of the company and its offer by implementing components of the pre-transaction phase. As much as 35.9% of the surveyed entities admitted the lack of elements preparing the enterprise for logistic customer service.
M. Świtała, M. Cichosz, J. Trzęsiok (2018)	112 manufacturing and trading businesses in Poland	Research on customer satisfaction with logistics services. Research results indicate a connection between a higher level of customer satisfaction and long-term cooperation with the company, caused by a deeper understanding of the needs and expectations of customers and adjustment of customer service standards to them.

Source: own study based on: K. Zięba, *Poziom obsługi klienta jako źródło przewagi konkurencyjnej* [in:] *Przedsiębiorstwo i klient w gospodarce opartej na usługach*, ed. by I. Rudawska, M. Soboń, Difin, Warszawa 2009, pp. 339–341; E. Gołembska, *Logistyka w gospodarce światowej*, C. H. Beck, Warszawa 2009, pp. 172–173; A. Strychalska-Rudzewicz, A. Rudzewicz, *Obsługa klienta w koncepcji logistyczno-marketingowej*, "Logistyka" 2012, 6, pp. 946–951; R. Barcik, M. Kubański, *Logistyczna obsługa klienta w przedsiębiorstwach przemysłu spożywczego. Teoria, a praktyka*, "Logistyka" 2012, 2, pp. 396–401; M. Daroń, *Logistyczna obsługa klienta w przedsiębiorstwie branży spożywczej. Analiza zewnętrzna i wewnętrzna*, "Studia Ekonomiczne. Zeszyty naukowe Uniwersytetu Ekonomicznego w Katowicach" 2015, 249, pp. 307–310; P. Smolnik, *Jakość logistycznej obsługi klienta na przykładzie wybranego przedsiębiorstwa*, "Autobusy. Technika, eksploatacja, systemy transportowe" 2016, 6, pp. 1549–1552; J. Dyczkowska, *Zarządzanie logistyczną obsługą klienta*, "Zeszyty Naukowe Uniwersytetu Szczecińskiego. Problemy zarządzania, finansów i marketingu" 2015, 2, 41(875), pp. 454–457; M. Kadłubek, *Postrzeganie idei obsługi klienta w zarządzaniu logistyką badanych przedsiębiorstw*, "Zeszyty Naukowe Politechniki Śląskiej. Organizacja i zarządzanie" 2017, 114, pp. 196–202; M. Świtała, M. Cichosz, J. Trzęsiok, *How to Achieve Customer Satisfaction? Perspective of Logistics Outsourcing Performance*, "LogForum" 2019, 15, 1, pp. 44–48.

Summary

The issue of customer service goes beyond the area of logistics, including marketing activities. Striving to determine the right level of customer service in practice comes down to identifying his needs and preferences in order to be able to satisfy him later. Analysing the cited research, it should be concluded that the level of customer service in Polish enterprises cannot be unambiguously, positively or negatively assessed. It depends on many factors. The overview of research also presents various positions of the management in relation to customer service standards as well as various assessments of the level and quality of service that customers have encountered.

However, all the research presented shows the need to increase interest in customer service in Polish enterprises, both in marketing and logistics. The customer, having a free choice, will take advantage of the offer of the enterprise, whose level of service will satisfy him—it will meet his needs and expectations and meet his objectives.

Bibliography

Barcik R., Kubański M., *Logistyczna obsługa klienta w przedsiębiorstwach przemysłu spożywczego. Teoria, a praktyka*, "Logistyka" 2012, 2.

Christopher M., Peck H., *Logistyka marketingowa*, transl. M. Ślusarczyk, PWE, Warszawa 2005.

[Cyfrowy] klient nasz pan. Jak marki na polskim rynku zarządzają doświadczeniami klientów, https://assets.kpmg/content/dam/kpmg/pl/pdf/2019/02/pl-top-100-brands-2018.pdf (access: 15 June 2019).

Daroń M., *Logistyczna obsługa klienta w przedsiębiorstwie branży spożywczej. Analiza zewnętrzna i wewnętrzna*, "Studia Ekonomiczne. Zeszyty naukowe Uniwersytetu Ekonomicznego w Katowicach" 2015, 249.

Dembińska-Cyran I., Hołub-Iwan J., Perenc J., *Zarządzanie relacjami z klientem*, Difin, Warszawa 2004.

Dyczkowska J., *Marketing usług logistycznych*, Difin, Warszawa 2014.

Dyczkowska J., *Zarządzanie logistyczną obsługą klienta*, "Zeszyty Naukowe Uniwersytetu Szczecińskiego. Problemy zarządzania, finansów i marketingu" 2015, 2, 41(875).

Gołembska E., *Logistyka w gospodarce światowej*, C.H. Beck, Warszawa 2009.

Gwiazdy Jakości Obsługi 2019 przyznane! Poznaj Laureatów oraz najnowsze wyniki badania jakości obsługi w Polsce, https://www.jakoscobslugi.pl/artykul/gwiazdy-jakosci-obslugi-2019-przyznane-poznaj-laureatow-oraz-najnowsze-wyniki-badania-jakosci-obslugi-w-polsce (access: 15 June 2019).

Kadłubek M., *Postrzeganie idei obsługi klienta w zarządzaniu logistyką badanych przedsiębiorstw*, "Zeszyty Naukowe Politechniki Śląskiej. Organizacja i zarządzanie" 2017, 114.

Kauf S., Tłuczak A., *Logistyczna obsługa klienta. Metody ilościowe*, Wydawnictwo Naukowe PWN, Warszawa 2018.

Kramarz M., *Elementy logistyczne obsługi klienta w sieciach dystrybucji. Pomiar, ocena, strategie*, Difin, Warszawa 2014.

Które firmy najbardziej dbają o klienta? Już po raz dwunasty nagrodzono najlepszych!, https://direct.money.pl/artykuly/porady/ktore-firmy-najbardziej-dbaja-o-klienta-juz,149,0,2428309.html (access: 15 June 2019).

Logistyka w biznesie, ed. by M. Ciesielski, PWE, Warszawa 2006.

Marketing usług logistycznych, ed. by G. Rosa, M. Jedliński, U. Chrąchol-Barczyk, C.H. Beck, Warszawa 2017.

Smolnik P., *Jakość logistycznej obsługi klienta na przykładzie wybranego przedsiębiorstwa*, "Autobusy. Technika, eksploatacja, systemy transportowe" 2016, 6.

Strychalska-Rudzewicz A., Rudzewicz A., *Obsługa klienta w koncepcji logistyczno-marketingowej*, "Logistyka" 2012, 6.

Szydełko M., *Logistyczna obsługa klienta jako element kształtowania przewagi konkurencyjnej przedsiębiorstwa*, "Logistyka" 2012, 5.

Szymonik A., Nowak I., *Współczesna logistyka*, Difin, Warszawa 2018.

Świtała M., Cichosz M., Trzęsiok J., *How to Achieve Customer Satisfaction? Perspective of Logistics Outsourcing Performance*, "LogForum" 2019, 15, 1.

Zięba K., *Poziom obsługi klienta jako źródło przewagi konkurencyjnej* [in:] *Przedsiębiorstwo i klient w gospodarce opartej na usługach*, ed. by I. Rudawska, M. Soboń, Difin, Warszawa 2009.

Zrobek J., *Marketing w działaniach logistycznych* [in:] *Logistyka gospodarcza. Uwarunkowania, zarządzanie, tendencje*, ed. by W. Starzyńska, W. J. Rogalski, J. Zrobek, Naukowe Wydawnictwo Piotrkowskie, Piotrków Trybunalski 2013.

Human Resources Management in Enterprises 4.0: Opportunities, Threats and Challenges for Practice and Theory

Prof. Czesław Zając, Ph.D.   ⓘ   https://orcid.org/0000-0003-2407-7232
Wrocław University of Economics

Abstract

Human resources management in modern enterprises has been undergoing numerous transformations. This is also valid for Enterprises 4.0. The unique feature of these enterprises, shaped mainly by a wide application of advanced production technologies, IT systems and demand for employee competencies, which differ from the existing ones, poses serious challenges for their managers and HR specialists. Challenges of this kind as well as opportunities and threats that they involve are subject to discussion in this paper. It also sets the directions and perspectives for further research of this issue that is topical and important for both the theory and practice of management.

Keywords: human resources management, Generation Z, enterprises 4.0, variety, competencies, industrial revolution

Introduction

The concept of Industry 4.0, which originated in Germany, is viewed as the completion of the fourth phase of the so-called "industrial revolution"[1] initiated in the early years of the 21st century. This phase is characterised by a transition from electronic and computerised systems to processes of smart manufacturing systems of the new generation, which have been increasingly applied on an industrial scale. Industry 4.0

---

[1]   M. Olender-Skorek, *Czwarta rewolucja przemysłowa a wybrane aspekty teorii ekonomii*, "Nierówności Społeczne a Wzrost Gospodarczy" 2017, 51.

can be defined as "a new technological generation" in the field of production, which heads towards the design of manufacturing systems integrating data processing with matter processing. This direction can be called *matter digitalisation* and its assumptions are implemented in the form of smart factories controlled by Cyber-Physical Systems (CPS) in the Internet of Things environment.[2] The birth of Industry 4.0 alters the existing character and "face" of Enterprises 4.0 functioning within its area. Moreover, it generates many demanding challenges for managers operating on various levels of management in those enterprises. They also pave the way for new research approaches and new directions for exploration of diverse processes and phenomena occurring in them.

The aim of the study is to present a synthetic analysis and evaluation of opportunities, threats and challenges in terms of practice as well as to indicate new directions for research in the field of human resources management in Enterprises 4.0.

Synthetic evaluation and analysis of human resources management in Enterprises 4.0

The changing conditions and environment for the functioning of contemporary enterprises, called Enterprises 4.0, result from escalating global competition. Such competition is manifested by an tincrease in the quality of products and a decrease in the costs of their production achieved, i.a., through the growth of expenditures on implementation of industrial robots. As it has been more commonly approved, the above-mentioned types of competition become feasible owing to the transformation of modern enterprises into "smart organisations" relying on artificial intelligence, an "agile" and fully flexible manufacturing of products and providing "smart services." The conditions for such transformation of enterprises and for their core business activities are secured, among other things, by:

- integration of computer networks with unified abilities and exchange of information in real time;[3]
- increasing range in the expansion of the Internet of Things in the area of production and services provided for various groups of end users;
- application of CPS (Cyber-Physical Systems);
- increasing scale of big databases service generating the necessity of carrying out advanced analyses on them;
- rising number of robot applications on an industrial scale.

---

[2]   J. M. Moczydłowska, *Rewolucja przemysłowa 4.0 jako źródło nowych wyzwań zarządzania kompetencjami zawodowymi*, Difin, Kraków 2018.

[3]   M. Goliński, *Informacja i techniki informacyjne jako przyczyna zmiany*, "Nierówności Społeczne a Wzrost Gospodarczy" 2013, 32.

Additionally, the changing conditions of Enterprises 4.0 functioning lead directly to significant changes in resources at their disposal including human resources. They also bring about numerous challenges for enterprises in terms of practice and theory of human resources management. Those challenges include:[4]

- emphasis on an increase in the effectiveness and optimisation of labour costs through innovation in the area of HR;
- acquisition and retention of highly competent, talented and committed staff, capable of fulfilling complex tasks in technologically elaborate and socially and culturally diverse work environments;
- necessity to resolve problems stemming from generation changes (Generations Y and Z), demography and mobility on labour markets;
- development of a global mindset and related employee competencies, including competencies of human resources managers;
- architecture reconfiguration of HR function through elements connected with network development, use of information technologies, remote management and also virtualisation of this function;
- integration of social, economic and ecological aspects on the concept of sustainability.

The essence of some of these challenges will be discussed further in the following part of the paper.

Performance management and labour costs management result directly from significance attributed to the issue of effectiveness in the field of management and economics.[5] The issue of performance management, which is related to the concept and method of management by objectives, should be also directly referred to the area of human resources management in Enterprises 4.0, examined in the context of task fulfilment resulting from the objectives of an enterprise, carried out by employees. Performance effectiveness perceived in such a way involves in practice an increasingly wider use of High Performance Work Systems—HPWS, High Performance Work Practices—HPWP and also Human Performance Improvement—HPI tools. The latter should be viewed as a set of HR practices effectively allowing to shape attitudes, behaviours and individual work performance, teamwork as well as the performance of the whole organisation.[6] A comprehensive view of the discussed issue within the HRM dimension reflects accurately the idea expressed by A. Pocztowski. The author assumes that "performance management is a a formalised and integrated process of shaping attitudes, behaviours and results of human activities connected with tasks

---

4   A. Pocztowski, *Zarządzanie zasobami ludzkimi*, Państwowe Wydawnictwo Ekonomiczne, Warszawa 2018.
5   B. Ziębicki, *Efektywność organizacyjna podmiotów sektora publicznego*, Wydawnictwo Uniwersytetu Ekonomicznego w Krakowie, Kraków 2014.
6   *Systemy wysoce efektywnej pracy*, ed. by S. Borkowska, IPISS, Warszawa 2007.

fulfilment and role playing whose overall aim is to create and deliver values to end users in harmony with the objectives of an organisation".[7] In practical terms this translates into the necessity of integration of performance management on various levels of enterprise organisation and then the integration of this management with particular objectives and tasks fulfilled within human resources management, which involves, i.a.: setting individual and team goals, building commitment among employees, measuring effects for the development of their competencies, attitudes, behaviours and work performance, improving internal communication and evaluation systems. Hence, business priority within this range comes down to measurement not only of work performance but also creating organisational solutions enabling the identification and evaluation of dependencies between staff competencies and the effectiveness of their work.

From the viewpoint of effectiveness we should also discuss the next among the above mentioned challenges, i.e. the necessity to acquire and retain highly competent, talented and committed staff, capable of fulfilling complex tasks in a technologically elaborate and socially and culturally diverse work environment. It refers not only to technical competencies, enabling to fulfil roles and tasks in the modern enterprise environment operating on the basis of advanced information and telecommunication technologies, but also to social competencies allowing specialists and managers in Enterprises 4.0 to communicate and cooperate effectively and, moreover, to liaise with the world outside. In modern enterprises new requirements as to the competencies mentioned above and difficult challenges which are involved in them refer also to managers and specialists in HR. The representatives of this profession in Enterprises 4.0 are particularly accountable for creating a suitable organisational climate, appropriate in-house human relationships and devising effective staffing arrangements. Additionally, they are bound to offer support in the creation and implementation of such solutions to other managers and employees.

New competency requirements represent a major challenge for managers and specialists in HR considering the increasing number of workers from Y and, in the foreseeable future, Z generations within the recruitment structures of modern companies. It should be explicitly indicated that the workers of Generation Y have grown up in the conditions of a market economy and advanced information technologies, new travel possibilities and educational opportunities extending beyond the borders of their native country. This has led to the reinforcement, among others, of such characteristics, attitudes and behaviours detailing Generation Y like: low loyalty level towards employers, strong multiple job and career change orientation, common use of modern means of communication and social media presence.

---

[7]   A. Pocztowski, *Zarządzanie…*, op. cit.

Representatives of this generation, in contrast to the previous one, are characterised by dissimilar needs and expectations from their employers and also different value systems. This generates a directly diverse shape of psychological contracts operative in Enterprises 4.0 since "specific needs, value features and expectations of new generation representatives demand changes in overall approach towards these representatives as ordinary employees and using other than traditional ways of HR management."[8] The diagnosis and accurate understanding of the approach of Generation Y representatives towards their professional career open up a range of opportunities for enterprises. However, they also pose threats and force them to create attractive motivational incentives, design effective talent management programmes, build staff commitment and efficient ways of communication.[9]

It is my firm belief that the specific character of the Enterprise 4.0 organisational environment and a new approach to their human resources management will be conducive to the encouragement of the spread and promotion in practice of three-module personnel function models, whose structure is represented by:[10]

- shared service centres;
- HR business partnership;
- centres of expertise.

It will also encourage strategic decision-makers in these enterprises to reconfigure the architecture of this function in the cross-section of all its principal components in terms of process, structure, instruments and competence. Presumably, the possibility of evaluating the effectiveness of this architecture, carried out through efficiency, productivity and organisational behaviour could become an indicator of such reconfiguration.

Summary

Instead of final conclusions arising from the considerations, at the end, I would like to emphasise that the specific character of Enterprises 4.0, besides opportunities, threats and challenges for practices of human resources management opens up new perspectives and directions for further exploration of these issues to successive scientists and researchers. At the same time, it should be noted that although the issue in question is very complex and difficult to explore empirically, it is also very interesting in its

---

[8] S. Koper, *Zarządzanie talentami na przykładzie pracowników pokolenia Y przedsiębiorstw w Polsce i w Niemczech*, maszynopis, Wrocław 2019, p. 30.

[9] M. McQueen, *Pokolenie Y. Współistnienie czy współdziałanie. Nowe zasady komunikacji międzypokoleniowej*, Studio Emka, Warszawa 2016.

[10] D. Ulrich, *Human Resource Champions. The Next Agenda for Adding Value and Delivering Results*, Harvard Business School Press, Boston (Mass.) 1997.

cognitive aspect. I believe that new and promising directions in human resources management in enterprises discussed in this paper come down to:

- new dimensions and directions of contextual change in human resources management resulting from specific characteristics of Enterprises 4.0;
- evolution of paradigms in human resources management;
- variety and complexity management;
- sustainability as a conceptual basis for staffing processes;
- human capital management from the perspective of Generation Z;
- a new approach to competence management in the light of modern organisational requirements.

Bibliography

Goliński M., *Informacja i techniki informacyjne jako przyczyna zmiany*, "Nierówności Społeczne a Wzrost Gospodarczy" 2013, 32.

Koper S., *Zarządzanie talentami na przykładzie pracowników pokolenia Y przedsiębiorstw w Polsce i w Niemczech*, maszynopis, Wrocław 2019.

McQueen M., *Pokolenie Y. Współistnienie czy współdziałanie. Nowe zasady komunikacji międzypokoleniowej*, Studio Emka, Warszawa 2016.

Moczydłowska J. M., *Rewolucja przemysłowa 4.0 jako źródło nowych wyzwań zarządzania kompetencjami zawodowymi*, Difin, Kraków 2018.

Olender-Skorek M., *Czwarta rewolucja przemysłowa a wybrane aspekty teorii ekonomii*, "Nierówności Społeczne a Wzrost Gospodarczy" 2017, 51.

Pocztowski A., *Wokół paradygmatu zarządzania zasobami ludzkimi* [in:] M. Budzanowska-Drzewiecka, K. Czernek, *Kierunki ewolucji nauk o zarządzaniu*, Wydawnictwo Uniwersytetu Jagiellońskiego, Kraków 2018.

Pocztowski A., *Zarządzanie zasobami ludzkimi*, Państwowe Wydawnictwo Ekonomiczne, Warszawa 2018.

Systemy wysoce efektywnej pracy, ed. by S. Borkowska, IPSiS, Warszawa 2007.

Ulrich D., *Human Resource Champions. The Next Agenda for Adding Value and Delivering Results*, Harvard Business School Press, Boston (Mass.) 1997.

Ziębicki B., *Efektywność organizacyjna podmiotów sektora publicznego*, Wydawnictwo Uniwersytetu Ekonomicznego w Krakowie, Kraków 2014.

Variety Management and Diversity Management as a Response to Complexity

Monika Jedynak, Ph.D.   https://orcid.org/0000-0002-0167-5013

Jagiellonian University

Abstract

The present paper compares variety management and diversity management as management approaches responding to the complexity of an organisation's functioning. Applying the systematic literature review method, the authors analysed 32 texts on this subject. An analysis of the key words constituted a basis for determining the framework of selected texts reflecting the scope of specificity of the studied approaches to management, including their entanglement in the entirety of management processes. Subsequently, an analysis of the abstracts and an analysis of the content of the selected texts were carried out to establish their typology and orientation towards a particular sector or region, as well as research methods followed by their authors. Thanks to this, it was possible to make a more comprehensive comparison between variety management and diversity management. The conducted analyses showed a far-reaching divergence of subjects in the examined approaches. Despite both of them being oriented towards management in complexity, they focus on completely different issues. Consequently, the authors formulated a proposal to integrate these approaches in order to achieve synergy of complexity management processes.

Keywords: variety management, diversity management, complexity management

Introduction

Complexity is currently regarded as a ubiquitous term employed to describe numerous phenomena of a highly heterogeneous nature. It reflects difficulties in solving problems with characterising a specified occurrence or with identifying laws which a given phenomenon is subject to. Predicaments with understanding complexity illustrate the universal dilemma related to the question about the main barriers to comprehending complexity: whether these are cognitive limitations of man, or whether they are rooted in the nature of complexity itself, which, in its essence, implies the mentioned limitations. In the literature on the subject, different types of complexity are mentioned.

Among those of greater importance, it is possible to distinguish[1] complexity marked by description length, algorithmic complexity, complexity as logical depth, complexity as a degree of variation of a physical object, and effective complexity. For the purposes of interpreting the phenomena studied in research on management, the last two conceptualisations are particularly helpful.

The complexity theory forms theoretical groundwork for subsequent considerations of complex issues of organisation management. The adaptation of the complexity concept to management research takes place in two fundamental methodological approaches.[2] The first approach stems from the traditional scientific paradigm applying restrictive computer simulations and mathematical investigations. The other approach rejects the mentioned restrictions and accepts the assumption that understanding complex systems requires the application of non-positivist methods such as long-term ethnographic methods and metaphorical analogies introducing an inductive approach.

However, the descriptive assets of the complexity theory do not translate directly into directives for efficient management specifying required behaviors of managers. This type of behaviors is present in some management concepts and models addressing the challenges that complexity poses to management systems. The present paper analyses two approaches of this type: variety management and diversity management. The authors understand variety management as an approach to management characterised by the acceptance of the need to develop multi-variant organisational solutions concerning products, processes, functions, and methods constituting a prerequisite for an organisation's success and competitive advantage. Although diversity management is also an approach to management, it is characterised by accepting and appreciating diversity in the internal dimension and in relations with the environment in particular.

The purpose of the paper is to compare these two approaches based on an analysis of research carried out in the scope they outline.

Research methodology

In the discussed studies, the modified method of systematic literature review was applied. Systematic literature reviews are a means of providing an objective theoretical evaluation of a particular topic.[3] The research procedure scheme was adjusted to the

---

[1]   M. Dombrowski, *Złożona natura złożoności*, "Diametros" 2013, 36.

[2]   L. Holmdahl, *Complexity Theory and Strategy. A Basis for Product Development*, 2005, http://www.complexityforum.com/articles/complexity-strategy.pdf (access: 12 September 2018); D. L. Levy, *Applications and Limitations of Complexity Theory in Organization Theory and Strategy* [in:] *Handbook of Strategic Management, Second Edition*, ed. by J. Rabin, G. J. Miller, W. Bartley Hildreth, Marcel Dekker Inc., New York–Basel 2000; S. Walby, *Complexity Theory, Globalization and Diversity*, British Sociological Association, York 2003.

[3]   K. Hopayian, *The Need for Caution in Interpreting High Quality Systematic Reviews*, "Education and Debate" 2001, 323.

main research objective, i.e., the identification and comparison of properties typical of research on variety management and diversity management. The first step in the research procedure was to select scientific papers discussing the problem areas based on an analysis of the Elsevier and Ebsco databases. Next, their key words were analysed in order to determine the scope of studied issues. Simultaneously, the abstracts and content of the selected publications were examined, which made it possible to identify the scientific character (type) of these publications

Variety management as a subject of research

The analysis of texts dedicated to variety management covered in total 15 papers published in the years 2003–2018. Their authors indicated 45 key words altogether. Their lists and references to the texts in which they occur are presented in Table 1.

Table 1. Analysis of the key words used in papers on variety management

Keywords	Publications[4]														
	1	2	3	4	5	6	7	8	9	10	11	12	13	14	15
Business processes	v														
Supply chain	v														
Information technology	v														
Mitigation strategies	v														
Metrics	v													v	

---

[4]   1: A. Da Cunha Reis, L. F. Scavarda, B. M. Pancieri, *Product Variety Management: A Synthesis of Existing Research*, "African Journal of Business Management" 2013, 7, 1; 2: T. Takenaka, H. Koshiba, Y. Motomura, K. Ueda, *Product/Service Variety Strategy Considering Mixed Distribution of Human Lifestyles*, "CIRP Annals—Manufacturing Technology" 2013, 62; 3: F. Salvador, C. Forza, *IT Support to Product Variety Management*, IE Working Paper No. WP04-21, 2014; 4: A. C. Lyons, *Lessons from Empirical Studies in Product and Service Variety Management*, "International Journal of Production Management and Engineering" 2013, 1, 1; 5: X. de Groote, E. Yuceson, *The Impact of Product Variety on Logistic Performance*, Proceedings of the 2011 Winter Simulation Conference; 6: P. E. C. Johansson, S. Mattsson, L. Moestam, A. Fast-Berglund, *Multi-Variant Production—Product Variety and Its Impact on Production Quality in Manual Assembly*, "Procedia CIRP" 2016, 54; 7: Y. A. Kim, *The Impact on Customers' Perception of Product Variety*, "Korea Review of International Studies" 2010; 8: T. Blecker, N. Abdelkafi, B. Kaluza, G. Friedrich, *Variety Steering Concept for Mass Customization*, "Discussion Papers of the Institute of Business Administration at the University of Klagenfurt" 2003; 9: H. ElMaraghy, G. Schuh, W. ElMaraghy, E. Piller, P. Schonsleben, M. Tseng, A. Bernard, *Product Variety Management*, "CIRP Annals—Manufacturing Technology" 2013; 10: A. Moseley, L. Hvan, Z. Lee Hansen, *Operational Impact of Product Variety in the Process Industry*, Proceedings of the 7th International Conference on Mass Customization and Personalization in Central Europe, 2018; 11: A. M. Deif, A. ElMaraghy, *Variety and Volume Dynamic Management for Value Creation in Changeable Manufacturing Systems*, "International Journal of

Keywords	Publications[4]														
	1	2	3	4	5	6	7	8	9	10	11	12	13	14	15
Service		v													
Emergent synthesis		v													
Customisation		v													
Customer relationship			v												
Product configuration			v												
Data management			v												
Variety management				v							v				
SKU proliferation				v											
Mass customisation				v			v								
Product variety					v	v	v	x							
Logistics					v										
Performance					v										
Cycle Time						v									
Operations management						v									
Multi-serial production												v			
Production quality						v									
Perceived production complexity						v									
Consumer behavior							v								
Variety									v			v			
Design									v						
Manufacturing									v				v		
Complexity										v				v	
Production performance										v					
Process industry										v					
Dynamic analysis											v				
Value creation											v				
Capacity scalability											v				

Production Research" 2017, 55, 5; 12: A. Rao, W. R. Hartmann, *Quality vs. Variety: Trading Larger Screens for More Shows in the Era of Digital Cinema*, 2015, https://www.google.com/search?q=Rao+A.%2C+Hartmann+W.R.%2C+2015%2C+Quality+vs.+Variety&ie=utf-8&oe=utf-8&client=firefox-b (access: 15 April 2019); 13: F. K. Pil, M. Holweg, *Linking Product Variety to Order-Fulfilment Strategies*, "Interfaces" 2004, 35, 5; 14: S. Bednar, J. Modrak, *Product Variety Management as a Tool for Successful Mass Customized Product Structure*, "Polish Journal of Management Studies" 2015, 12, 1; 15: P. Helo, Q. Xu, Y. Kristianto, R. Jiao, *Decision Support for Product Variety Management*, "Journal of Engineering and Technology Management" 2013.

Keywords	Publications[4]														
	1	2	3	4	5	6	7	8	9	10	11	12	13	14	15
Advanced technology											V				
Quality												V			
Production													V		
Polices													V		
Ordering													V		
Strategy													V		
Design optimisation														V	
Configuration														V	
Demand														V	
Product line heterogeneity														V	
Product variant analysis															V
Product portfolio															V
Decision support system															V

Source: prepared by the author.

The research findings presented in Table 1 allow one to conclude that variety management is a management approach of multifaceted character, even though its orientation is aimed rather at "hard" management aspects. In the course of the synthesis of this approach, the following properties can be identified:
- Variety management concerns selected functions of company operations (e.g., production, logistics, design and development), thus determining an approach to their implementation that is not linear.
- Variety management means a modification of a set of management instruments (e.g., in terms of business processes, supply chains, decision support systems).
- Variety management is closely related to consumers' behaviour and changing preferences; consequently, it constitutes an organisation's response to such changes.
- Similarly to other management approaches, what is also measured in the case of variety management is the efficiency of its application.

It is also worth noting that despite the shared subject of studies broadly understood as variety management, the analysed scientific papers are characterised by a significant diversification of content demonstrated also in a low repetitiveness of the key words.

Table 2, in turn, includes such analysis results as the features of the publications relating to their character (theoretical, empirical, or both), the occurrence of the sectoral or regional orientation, universality, as well as the research methods used by the authors.

Table 2. The types of the analysed papers on variety management and the research methods used in them

	Type of study	Publications														
		1	2	3	4	5	6	7	8	9	10	11	12	13	14	15
Type	Theoretical	v		v					v			v				v
	Empirical															
	Both		v		v	v	v	v		v	v		v	v	v	
Orientation	Sectoral		v		v				v				v	v		
	Regional		v		v								v			
	Universal	v		v		v		v	v		v	v			v	v
Methods	Systematic literature review	v														
	Classical literature review		v	v	v	v	v	v	v	v	v	v	v	v	v	v
	Analysis of variance		v													
	Heuristic modelling			v												
	Simulation study					v										
	Participatory observations					v										
	Sensitivity analysis					v										
	Standardised survey							v	v							
	Participatory observations							v								
	Descriptive statistical methods								v		v			v		
	Exemplification									v						
	Case study										v				v	
	Semi-structured interview										v					
	Regression analysis										v		v			
	Simulations models											v				

Source: prepared by the author.

The studied texts were mostly of a theoretical and empirical nature. Some of them were exclusively theoretical. Purely empirical texts were not identified. Nine of the analysed texts had a general character, without focusing on a specific character of any sector or region. The specificity of these variables was taken into consideration in the other papers. It was only in one case that the author employed the systematic literature review method. In the remaining ones, literature analyses had a classical character. The empirical parts were completed based on uncomplicated quantitative and qualitative methods. In some cases, the triangulation approach was used by combining several research methods.

Diversity management as a subject of research

The analysis of texts on diversity management covered in total 17 papers published in the years 2002–2018. Their authors indicated 59 key words altogether.

Their lists and references to the texts in which they occur are presented in Table 3.

Table 3. An analysis of the key words used in the papers on diversity management

Keywords	Publications[5]																
	1	2	3	4	5	6	7	8	9	10	11	12	13	14	15	16	17
Diversity management	v		v	v	v	v	v	v	v	v	v	v	v	v	v	v	v
Workforce	v																
Diversity effect	v																

5   1: C. W. Von Bergen, B. Soper, T. Foster, *Unintended Negative Effect of Diversity Management*, "Public Personnel Management" 2002, 31, 2; 2: A. Sharma, *Managing Diversity and Equality in the Workplace*, "Cogent Business & Management" 2016, 3; 3: N. S. Gwele, *Diversity Management in the Workplace: Beyond Compliance*, "Curationis Congress Paper" 2009; 4: J. E. Olsen, L. L. Martins, *Understanding Organizational Diversity Management Programs: A Theoretical Framework and Directions for Future Research*, "Journal of Organizational Behavior" 2012, 33, 8; 5: E. Matuska, A. Sałek-Imińska, *Diversity Management as Employer Branding Strategy: Theory and Practice*, "Human Resources Management & Ergonomics" 2014, 8, 2; 6: P. A. Edewor, Y. A. Aluko, *Diversity Management, Challenges and Opportunities in Multicultural Organizations*, "The International Journal Diversity in Organizations, Communities & Nations" 2007, 6, 6; 7: B. Y. Kim, *Managing Workforce Diversity: Developing a Learning Organization*, "Journal of Human Resources in Hospitality & Tourism" 2006, 5, 2; 8: H. K. Kim, U. H. Lee, Y. H. Kim, *The Effect of Workplace Diversity Management in a Highly Male-Dominated Culture*, "Career Development International" 2015, 20, 3; 9: M. O. Abaker, P. A. Al-Titi, N. S. Al-Nasr, *Organizational Policies and Diversity Management in Saudi Arabia*, "Employee Relations" 2018; 10: S. Groeneveld, *Diversity and Employee Turnover in the Dutch Public Sector*, "International Journal of Public Sector Management" 2011, 24, 6; 11: M. Jin, J. Lee, M. Lee, *Does Leadership Matter in Diversity Management? Assessing the Relative Impact of Diversity Policy and Inclusive Leadership in the Public Sector*, "Leadership & Organization Development Journal" 2017, 33, 2; 12: S. Hennekam, J. Peterson, L. Tahssain-Gay, J. P. Dumazert, *Managing Religious Diversity in Secular Organizations in France*, "Employee Relations" 2018, 40, 5; 13: G. A. Maxwell, *Minority Report. Taking the Initiative in Managing Diversity at BBC Scotland*, "Employee Relations" 2003, 26, 2; 14: N. R. Goodman, *Taking Diversity and Inclusion Initiatives Global*, "Industrial and Commercial Training" 2013, 45, 3; 15: C. Wildermuth, M. O. Wildermuth, *Seeking Common Ground: An Alternative Diversity Training Paradigm*, "Industrial and Commercial Training" 2011, 43, 5; 16: J. Lauring, J. Selmer, *Positive Dissimilarity Attitudes in Multicultural Organizations. The Role of Language Diversity and Communication frequency*, "Corporate Communication: An International Journal" 2012, 17, 2; 17: V. E. McCuiston, B. R. Wooldridge, *Leading the Diverse Workforce. Profit, Prospects and Progress*, "The Leadership & Organization Development Journal" 2004, 25, 1.

Keywords	Publications[5]																
	1	2	3	4	5	6	7	8	9	10	11	12	13	14	15	16	17
Gender issues		v															
Environment		v															
Gender management		v															
Career and gender		v															
Strategic HR		v															
Cultural diversity			v			v											
Workplace diversity			v														
Relationship				v													
Diversity approaches				v													
Employer branding					v												
Management strategies					v												
Globalisation						v								v			
Multicultural organisations						v										v	
Organisational behavior						v											
Learning organisation							v										
Hospitality industry							v										
Performance								v									
Organisational commitment								v									
Male-dominated culture								v									
Middle East									v								
Saudi Arabia									v								
Foreign employees									v								
Gulf Countries									v								
Saudisation									v								
Employee turnover										v							
Gender										v							
Ethnicity										v							
Public sector										v							
Person-environment fit										v							
The Netherlands										v							
Inclusive leadership											v						
Diversity											v						
Public management											v						

Keywords	Publications[5]																
	1	2	3	4	5	6	7	8	9	10	11	12	13	14	15	16	17
Religious diversity												v					
Secularism												v					
France												v					
Equal opportunities													v				
Television													v				
Scotland													v				
Global diversity														v			
Diversity and inclusion														v			
Cultural Intelligence														v			
Social inclusion														v			
Diversity training															v		
Human resources															v		
Intercultural relations															v		
Prejudice															v		
Discrimination															v		
Team effectiveness															v		
Human resources management															v		v
International teams																v	
Dissimilarity attitudes																v	
Openness to diversity																v	
Communication																v	
Language																v	
Leadership																	v

Source: prepared by the author.

Similarly to variety management, diversity management is multifaceted and multi-threaded. However, problem orientation in the case of diversity management is completely different. Its distinguishing features are as follows:
- Diversity management concerns the "soft" aspects of management. It refers, inter alia, to workplace, organisational culture, diversity of people in organisations, and relations.
- Diversity management emerges as a synergistic approach to activities such as organisation learning, human resource management, and employer branding.
- Hence, diversity management is oriented entirely towards people, both employees and stakeholders.

Even though, as it was stated above, diversity management concerns people-related issues, the key words analysis in Table 3 proves the broad range of the authors' interests. This, in turn, translates into enriching the works on the subject.

Table 4 presents analysis results, including the features of the publications relating to their character (theoretical, empirical, or both), the occurrence of the sectoral or regional orientation, and universality.

Table 4. The types of the analysed papers on diversity management and the research methods used in them

	Type of study	Publications[6]																
		1	2	3	4	5	6	7	8	9	10	11	12	13	14	15	16	17
Type	Theoretical	v	v	v	v	v	v	v							v	v		
	Empirical																	
	Both								v	v	v	v	v	v			v	v
Orientation	Sectoral							v	v	v	v	v	v	v			v	
	Regional			v		v			v	v	v	v	v	v			v	v
	Universal	v	v		v		v								v	v		
	Classical literature review	v	v	v	v	v	v	v	v	v	v	v	v	v	v	v	v	v
	Participatory observations													v				
	Standardised survey									v	v	v					v	v
	Descriptive statistical methods					v			v	v		v					v	
	Exemplification													v				
	Case study													v				
	Semi-structured interview												v	v				
	Regression analysis								v									

Source: prepared by the author.

6   1: C. W. Von Bergen, B. Soper, T. Foster, op. cit.; 2: A. Sharma, op. cit.; 3: N. S. Gwele, op. cit.; 4: J. E. Olsen, L. L. Martins, op. cit.; 5: E. Matuska, A. Sałek-Imińska, op. cit.; 6: P. A. Edewor, Y. A. Aluko, op. cit.; 7: B. Y. Kim, op. cit.; 8: H. K. Kim, U. H. Lee, Y. H. Kim, op. cit.; 9: M. O. Abaker, P. A. Al-Titi, N. S. Al-Nasr, op. cit.; 10: S. Groeneveld, op. cit.; 11: M. Jin, J. Lee, M. Lee, op. cit.; 12: S. Hennekam, J. Peterson, L. Tahssain-Gay, J. P. Dumazert, op. cit.; 13: G. A. Maxwell, op. cit.; 14: N. R. Goodman, op. cit.; 15: C. Wildermuth, M. O. Wildermuth, op. cit.; 16: J. Lauring, J. Selmer, op. cit.; 17: V. E. McCuiston, B. R. Wooldridge, op. cit.

The texts on diversity management were mostly of a theoretical or mixed nature. Their character was universal or they dealt with issues concerning specific regions or sectors. With respect to all texts, the classical literature review method was applied, accompanied occasionally by uncomplicated quantitative or qualitative methods.

Conclusion

The paper presents an analysis of variety management and diversity management based on the assumption that these two management approaches result from searching for indispensable management activities imposed by the complexity of an organisation's operations.

The conducted study allows the authors to conclude the following:

- Although both approaches are inspired by complexity, it is necessary to emphasise that their respective problem orientations are substantially different. This means that these two approaches achieve similar objectives related to an organisation's response to complexity in completely different areas and by means of different tools.
- Variety management is a much broader approach. Nevertheless, diversity management, which focuses almost exclusively on people, demonstrates a greater internal diversification.
- Both approaches to management are entangled in the broader context of organisational management comprising various constructs such as strategies, management areas, management functions, or management results, which indicates their partial participation in holistic management.
- Management of complexity requires a synergy of actions taken. Based on this assumption, it is recommended that in the future these two approaches be integrated as co-existing rather than competing tendencies. Measuring conditions necessary for, and the effects of, such integration undoubtedly constitute an interesting research challenge.

Bibliography

Abaker M. O., Al-Titi P. A., Al-Nasr N. S., *Organizational Policies and Diversity Management in Saudi Arabia*, "Employee Relations" 2018.

Bednar S., Modrak J., *Product Variety Management as a Tool for Successful Mass Customized Product Structure*, "Polish Journal of Management Studies" 2015, 12, 1.

Blecker T., Abdelkafi N., *Complexity and Variety in Mass Customization Systems: Analysis and Recommendations*, "Management Decision" 2006, 44, 7.

Blecker T., Abdelkafi N., Kaluza B., Friedrich G., *Variety Steering Concept for Mass Customization*, "Discussion Papers of the Institute of Business Administration at the University of Klagenfurt" 2003.

Da Cunha Reis A., Scavarda L. F., Pancieri B. M., *Product Variety Management: A Synthesis of Existing Research*, "African Journal of Business Management" 2013, 7, 1.

Deif A. M., ElMaraghy A., *Variety and Volume Dynamic Management for Value Creation in Changeable Manufacturing Systems*, "International Journal of Production Research" 2017, 55, 5.

Dombrowski M., *Złożona natura złożoności*, "Diametros" 2013, 36.

Edewor P. A., Aluko Y. A., *Diversity Management, Challenges and Opportunities in Multicultural Organizations*, "The International Journal Diversity in Organizations, Communities & Nations" 2007, 6, 6.

ElMaraghy H., Schuh G., ElMaraghy W., Piller E., Schonsleben P., Tseng M., Bernard A., *Product Variety Management*, "CIRP Annals—Manufacturing Technology" 2013.

Goodman N. R., *Taking Diversity and Inclusion Initiatives Global*, "Industrial and Commercial Training" 2013, 45, 3.

Groeneveld S., *Diversity and Employee Turnover in the Dutch Public Sector*, "International Journal of Public Sector Management" 2011, 24, 6.

Groote X. de, Yuceson E., *The Impact of Product Variety on Logistic Performance*, Proceedings of the 2011 Winter Simulation Conference.

Gwele N. S., *Diversity Management in the Workplace: Beyond Compliance*, "Curationis Congress Paper" 2009.

Helo P., Xu Q., Kristianto Y., Jiao R., *Decision Support for Product Variety Management*, "Journal of Engineering and Technology Management" 2013.

Hennekam S., Peterson J., Tahssain-Gay L., Dumazert J. P., *Managing Religious Diversity in Secular Organizations in France*, "Employee Relations" 2018, 40, 5.

Holmdahl L., *Complexity Theory and Strategy. A Basis for Product Development*, 2005, http://www.complexityforum.com/articles/complexity-strategy.pdf (access: 12 September 2018).

Hopayian K., *The Need for Caution in Interpreting High Quality Systematic Reviews*, "Education and Debate" 2001, 323.

Jin M., Lee J., Lee M., *Does Leadership Matter in Diversity Management? Assessing the Relative Impact of Diversity Policy and Inclusive Leadership in the Public Sector*, "Leadership & Organization Development Journal" 2017, 33, 2.

Johansson P. E. C., Mattsson S., Moestam L., Fast-Berglund A., *Multi-Variant Production—Product Variety and Its Impact on Production Quality in Manual Assembly*, "Procedia CIRP" 2016, 54.

Kim H. K., Lee U. H., Kim Y. H., *The Effect of Workplace Diversity Management in a Highly Male-Dominated Culture*, "Career Development International" 2015, 20, 3.

Kim Y. A., *The Impact on Customers' Perception of Product Variety*, "Korea Review of International Studies" 2010.

Kim B. Y., *Managing Workforce Diversity: Developing a Learning Organization*, "Journal of Human Resources in Hospitality & Tourism" 2006, 5, 2.

Lauring J., Selmer J., *Positive Dissimilarity Attitudes in Multicultural Organizations. The Role of Language Diversity and Communication frequency*, "Corporate Communication: An International Journal" 2012, 17, 2.

Levy D. L., *Applications and Limitations of Complexity Theory in Organization Theory and Strategy* [in:] *Handbook of Strategic Management, Second Edition*, ed. by J. Rabin, G. J. Miller, W. Bartley Hildreth, Marcel Dekker Inc., New York – Basel 2000.

Lyons A. C., *Lessons from Empirical Studies in Product and Service Variety Management*, "International Journal of Production Management and Engineering" 2013, 1, 1.

Maxwell G. A., *Minority Report. Taking the Initiative in Managing Diversity at BBC Scotland*, "Employee Relations" 2003, 26, 2.

Matuska E., Sałek-Imińska A., *Diversity Management as Employer Branding Strategy: Theory and Practice*, "Human Resources Management & Ergonomics" 2014, 8, 2.

McCuiston V. E., Wooldridge B. R., *Leading the Diverse Workforce. Profit, Prospects and Progress*, "The Leadership & Organization Development Journal" 2004, 25, 1.

Moseley A., Hvan L., Lee Hansen Z., *Operational Impact of Product Variety in the Process Industry*, Proceedings of the 7th International Conference on Mass Customization and Personalization in Central Europe, 2018.

Olsen J. E., Martins L. L., *Understanding Organizational Diversity Management Programs: A Theoretical Framework and Directions for Future Research*, "Journal of Organizational Behavior" 2012, 33, 8.

Pil F. K., Holweg M., *Linking Product Variety to Order-Fulfilment Strategies*, "Interfaces" 2004, 35, 5.

Rao A., Hartmann W. R., *Quality vs. Variety: Trading Larger Screens for More Shows in the Era of Digital Cinema*, 2015, https://www.google.com/search?q=Rao+A.%2C+Hartmann+W.R.%2C+2015%2C+Quality+vs.+Variety&ie=utf-8&oe=utf-8&client=firefox-b (access: 15 April 2019).

Salvador F., Forza C., *IT Support to Product Variety Management*, IE Working Paper No. WP04-21, 2014.

Sharma A., *Managing Diversity and Equality in the Workplace*, "Cogent Business & Management" 2016, 3.

Takenaka T., Koshiba H., Motomura Y., Ueda K., *Product/Service Variety Strategy Considering Mixed Distribution of Human Lifestyles*, "CIRP Annals—Manufacturing Technology" 2013, 62.

Von Bergen C. W., Soper B., Foster T., *Unintended Negative Effect of Diversity Management*, "Public Personnel Management" 2002, 31, 2.

Walby S., *Complexity Theory, Globalization and Diversity*, British Sociological Association, York 2003.

Wildermuth C., Wildermuth M. O., *Seeking Common Ground: An Alternative Diversity Training Paradigm*, "Industrial and Commercial Training" 2011, 43, 5.

Editor
Zofia Sajdek

Proofreading
Katarzyna Zajdel, Nativic
Joanna Bilmin-Odrowąż

Typesetting
Marta Jaszczuk

Jagiellonian University Press
Editorial Offices: ul. Michałowskiego 9/2, 31-126 Krakow
Phone: +48 12 663 23 80, +48 12 663 23 82, Fax: +48 12 663 23 83